THE ISLAMIC WORLDVIEW

THE ISLAMIC WORLDVIEW

Islamic Jurisprudence: An American Muslim Perspective
Volume One

AZIZAH AL-HIBRI, PH.D., J.D.

Cover and interior design by Monica Alejo /ABA Publishing.

Printed in the United States of America.

18 17 16 15 14   5 4 3 2 1

Library of Congress Cataloging-in-Publication Data

al-Hibri, Azizah, 1943- author.
Islamic worldview : Islamic jurisprudence : an American Muslim perspective / Azizah al-Hibri, Ph. D., J.D.
pages cm
Includes bibliographical references and index.
ISBN 978-1-62722-284-6 (alk. paper)
1. Islamic law. 2. Ijtihad (Islamic law) I. Title.
KBP440.3.A449 2014
340.5'9138--dc23
2014042882

Discounts are available for books ordered in bulk. Special consideration is given to state bars, CLE programs, and other bar-related organizations. Inquire at Book Publishing, ABA Publishing, American Bar Association, 321 N. Clark Street, Chicago, Illinois 60654-7598.

www.ShopABA.org

DEDICATION

To my Brother Ibrahim
My knight in shining armor . . .
May he rest in peace.

CONTENTS

Preface

This book is part of a larger project about Islamic law that has been in the making for more than thirty years. It includes studies in family law, constitutional law, women's rights, law and ethics, as well as other areas relevant to our world today. During these years, I published some of my evolving views in legal and philosophy journals and edited collections. I lectured widely about them at universities, think tanks, cultural centers, and places of worship. I established KARAMAH, a non-profit organization that teaches many Muslim women in the United States and around the world our understanding of Islam. We have organized seminars for policy makers, judges, lawyers, and the community. But during all that time I did not venture to publish whole books on the subject until the Islamic worldview as a whole became clearer to my mind. In recent years, I was able to reach this point of clarity, and hence decided to share what I learned about Islam with the public. My decision was accelerated by the increased use of violence around the world by groups that act under the color of religion, the mainstreaming of intolerant interpretations of Islam internationally, the growth of a young generation of American Muslims that is not quite familiar with its faith, and the sporadic rise of anti-Muslim sentiment in this country as exemplified by the anti-*sharīʿah* movement.

In this book, I do not assume any knowledge of Islam on the part of the reader. In my teaching I had realized that many students, including Muslim ones, who believed they were informed about the religion turned out to be informed instead about cultural practices in certain Muslim countries. This is an unfortunate confusion, especially for Muslims who live and practice in the United States. Discovering and correcting this misinformation was time-consuming. For this reason, this book begins at the beginning, assuming no knowledge of Islam on the part of the reader. It begins by defining the sources of the revelation and explaining the fundamental concepts and foundational principles (i.e., the building blocks) of Islam. It then describes the Islamic worldview resulting from them. The importance of this approach is that it empowers the reader to extend her/his knowledge beyond known rulings to new situations that could arise at a later date.

Because this book is foundational, it constitutes a critical introduction to all my subsequent writings. It also provides the underpinnings for various topics and areas of law. In developing my analysis and arguments in it and elsewhere, I relied on my philosophical as well as my legal training in the United States, combined with the lessons I learned from the women's rights movement in the 1960s of which I was a part. I also relied on my excellent knowledge of Arabic, the language of the Qur'an.

Most importantly, I was guided in my understanding of Islam by the example and knowledge of my grandfather, Sheikh Muhammad Toufic El-Hibri al-Idrissi al-Hassani, who was a major scholar, businessman, and philanthropist at the turn of the last century. He was the founder of the Islamic scout movement around the world and paid special attention to two areas: education and orphans. His life was dedicated to service, and his faith was alive in the lives of others whom he helped. Attending his scholarly discussions helped me understand that Islam is a religion of reason and compassion. Despite the fact that he was raised and lived in a time quite different from ours, he had the insight to encourage me to think about religion and started me down that road. I know he did not do the same with his male grandchildren.

My grandfather belonged to a line of scholars who hesitated to put their writing on paper lest they be wrong and mislead others. I belong to that same school of thought. However, today we live in a world where ridiculous *fatwās* and Facebook pronouncements filled with anger and ignorance are creating a great deal of chaos and pain. These developments have changed my evaluation of the situation. Today, it is wrong not to write. It is wrong to remain silent when thousands of young Muslim men are being led to self-destruction in the name of Islam. Even if a view I hold is wrong, it cannot be as wrong as those views that fly directly in the face of everything Islam stands for and cost the lives of many innocent people. So, here is my best effort at explaining my faith. But knowing the human condition, which is far from perfect, I offer these views with the traditional scholarly proviso: *wallāhu a'lam* (and God knows best).

Over the course of my life, I had great opportunities to develop my thinking and advance my research. For the academic opportunities, I must thank some distinguished American institutions. Parts of this project were supported by a Fulbright grant to Qatar in summer 2001 where I was able to meet some distinguished scholars at the *sharī'ah* school there and discuss some of my views with them. Another part was supported by the National Humanities Center during that same year. Harvard Divinity School and the Legal Division of the Library of Congress were kind enough to have me as a visiting scholar for a semester in 1985 and 2000, respectively. The University of Richmond, where I taught for twenty years, supported me through summer research grants and research assistants whose help was invaluable. For help with editing references and transliteration in this book, I would like to thank my research assistant, Ms. Hind Essayegh, a member of the KARAMAH family, for her hard work. For help with copy editing of Arabic words, many thanks go to Jay Willoughby who volunteered valuable time to accelerate this process.

During the 1990s, I was working very hard on producing this book, but the ideas had not matured yet. In the process, I accepted various invitations from USIA (the United States Information Agency) to travel to Muslim countries and speak about my work. By then my writing on Islam and democracy had appeared and was very well received in the American Muslim community. It was perhaps one of the earliest contributions of its kind, if not the earliest one, by an American Muslim, and USIA wanted to show me off. I wanted to meet all these Muslims from far away countries and colorful cultures that I had only heard about as a child from my family. As I discovered later, visiting these countries under USIA auspices initially raised for my audience a credibility gap. But it was soon bridged by my work, and I learned from these travels an immense amount about Muslims around the world, their concerns and aspirations, and their knowledge of Islam. After the events of September 11th, my world and that of many other American Muslims changed, and I reduced my travels drastically, focusing on Muslim women in Europe who sought KARAMAH's guidance.

I cannot end this preface without recognizing two important men in my life. My brother, Ibrahim El-Hibri, my lifetime hero who fought the battles of having me go to college at the American University of Beirut, where I studied with Dr. Seyyed Hossein Nasr. My brother also fought to have me continue my education abroad at a time when Muslim women in my circle did not leave home except to get married. In addition to all this, he financed every bit of this education, not once but twice to help me get a Ph.D. in Philosophy and J.D. Even after his death, his philanthropy continues to support KARAMAH. I think of him every time I read about a brother committing the crime of "honor killing" against his sister. I have been quite blessed to have this exceptional human being as my brother and ally. Although we did not always see eye to eye on many matters, he always had my back and respected my views. The warmth of his love, his quiet wisdom, and his deep kindness remain with me years after his passing.

The second man in my life is a silent sufferer. He is my husband, who lived through all the ups and downs of my life with grace and affection. As a student of Professor Fazlur Rahman at the University of Chicago, he is quite knowledgeable in Islamic Studies. He has been a great sounding board for my ideas and sometime helper in researching my footnotes. We have sacrificed a large portion of our family time together for this project, but he is as excited about it as I am.

These are the people and forces in my life that got me to this point. So, I guess there is a lot of truth to the saying, "it takes a village . . ." I have led quite a privileged life, and it is time to give back. Here is the first installment. While I thank everyone for their support, I point out that I alone am responsible for the shortcomings. I only hope that the reader finds some value in this book.

1

Islamic Jurisprudence in the United States*

I. Introduction

A quick historical overview of Islam in America will help place this book within its proper context. For a long time, Islam has been viewed in this country as a foreign religion. Yet, its presence here predates the slavery period.[1] During that period, enslaved African Muslims were not permitted to freely practice their religion, so many practiced it secretly.[2] They were not yet beneficiaries of our constitutional First Amendment protections.

This situation improved slowly at the turn of the 20th century. It accelerated with the rise of the civil rights movement, and the arrival of several waves of immigrants from Muslim countries. Unfortunately, this trend experienced a major setback when the

*An earlier version of the historical part of this chapter was published in "Islamic and American Constitutional Law: Borrowing Possibilities or a History of Borrowing?," *University of Pennsylvania Journal of Constitutional Law,* vol. 1, no.3 (1999), 492. An earlier version of the second part of this chapter appeared as "Developing Islamic Jurisprudence in the Diaspora: Balancing Authenticity, Diversity, and Modernity" in *Journal of Social Philosophy* 45, no. 1 (2014), 7–24.

catastrophic events of September 11th, 2001, were linked to Muslim extremists. Immediately, American Muslims came again under suspicion and were subject to hostility in public spaces. Muslim women who wore head scarves became obvious targets. To rectify this situation and allay the nation's fears, President George W. Bush visited the Islamic Center in Washington, D.C., less than one week after the attack. Addressing the nation from there, he emphasized that "the face of terror is not the true face of Islam . . ." and that "Islam is peace." Denouncing the hostility towards American Muslims, he said: "That's not the America I know. That's not the America I value . . ." and noted that "our fellow Americans must treat each other with respect."[3] Still, the consequences of that attack were devastating to Muslim civil rights in this country.* Furthermore, the attack led the United States to wage long wars in Muslim countries.

These escalating events provided the backdrop for the anti-*sharī'ah* movement that swept the United States in the past few years. Its major thesis was that Islam, a foreign religion antithetical to Western values, is invading this country and threatening to take it over. Not only did this movement threaten the religious freedom of American Muslims, but it also stoked the fears of the average American who was still reeling from the tragic events of September 11th and the subsequent wars. The American Muslim became suspect again, even when resorting to court to seek divorce or child custody.

In many ways, this is not a new situation. Suspicion of Muslims is deeply rooted in America and has had historical manifestations as early as the 18th century.[4] During that period, several American novels featured either fictional Muslim spies in America or oppressed Muslim women in the seraglio.[5] Many 18th-century authors, from Voltaire to Prideaux and Volney, wrote important works about Islam that were eagerly read in the United States.[6] Unfortunately, some authors were not quite concerned about accuracy.[7]

Various books about Islam that appeared in the 18th century created an atmosphere of disdain, hostility, and distrust of Muslims.

*See the text of speech at http://georgewbush-whitehouse.archives.gov/news/releases/2001/09/20010917-11.html. It was delivered on September 17, 2001.

Amongst them was a book entitled *The Nature of the Imposture*, whose title refers to the Prophet.[8] The message of the book, based on the author's view of the Muslim state, was that false religion and military power could combine to subdue people.[9] It was used by Matthew Lyon, a staunch critic of federalists, to attack President Adams.[10]

Another book, entitled *Cato's Letters*, an English work that became highly influential in this country, pronounced the Prophet Muhammad a tyrant and argued that tyrants like him destroyed their people with the people's own consent.[11] In support of their view, authors cited the example of the Turkish Empire and other Muslim states that they claimed forbade printing and thus restricted free speech.[12] Other authors corroborated these views directly or indirectly.[13] Even Volney, who was a great admirer of old civilizations, could not but comment on the state of apathy and indolence that had permeated many Muslim countries.[14]

Volney and many other writers were concerned about the reason for the decline of Islamic civilization. They wanted later civilizations, especially the American one, to avoid a similar fate. Their conclusions varied. Some blamed what they perceived to be the Islamic attitude of fatalism.[15] Others blamed what they believed to be the discouragement of free thinking within Islamic civilizations.[16] There was, however, general agreement that tyranny fostered by religion, and the Muslim people's acceptance of it, were at the heart of the problem.[17] Subsequent discussion centered on how the American system of governance could avoid such a fate.[18]

The West, looking from the outside, viewed Muslim regimes as embodiments of Islamic principles.[19] As the discussion in this book will show, nothing could have been further from the truth. The Western outlook made it more difficult for most authors to understand or present Islam as it was revealed in the Qur'an.[20] This problem has persisted in various degrees in this country for the last couple of centuries. Despite some serious interfaith efforts, Islam has continued to be misunderstood by non-Muslim Americans from the point of view of the "Other." It is time that this situation is changed and the American people, especially those entrusted with our constitutional protections, understand Islam not as an "Other," but rather as a serious participant in the building of this country since its inception. The history of enslaved Muslims needs to be restated in our own American Muslim voice, and our past and present contributions to this country need to be reexamined and recognized. Furthermore, it is time to understand Islam for what it really is. As a growing world religion, with a significant presence within the United States, Islam deserves to be understood from a privileged insider point of view.

II. THE CHALLENGE

WHILE THIS BOOK IS AN ATTEMPT TO DO THAT, ITS PRIMARY task is different, yet co-extensive with the above-mentioned objective.* Its primary task is to address a very basic question, namely:

> *Is practicing Islam in the American diaspora identical to its practice in other countries, or must a new Islamic jurisprudence be developed that takes into account the culture, customs and laws of this country?*

The urgency of this question arises from the fact that a significant number of American Muslims today have been born in the United States. Many of them are not only far removed from the social and cultural/religious context of their parents or ancestors, but are also deeply entrenched in the American experience. This poses a serious challenge, but not a new one. As case law shows, Catholics, Jews, and other people of faith have gone through a similar metamorphosis before finding a comfortable fit between their faith and their new country. In many ways, African American Muslims have already led the way for other American Muslims, but there is still a lot more work to be done, especially in the area of jurisprudence.

The question posed above can be answered from two perspectives: that of Muslims in the West and that of traditional Islamic jurispru-

*An earlier version of this section was published in the *Journal of Social Philosophy* 45 (2014), 7–24.

dence (TIJ). As this book will hopefully show, we actually need a combination of the two to produce a useful answer. Hence, only an American Muslim can and should venture to face this challenge.

From our perspective as American Muslims in a country that is technologically living the future of the majority of other countries, we find that questions such as "Is artificial insemination permissible?" and "Is donating a kidney acceptable?" require urgent answers for Muslim doctors as well as patients. The same is true of culturally and socially specific questions such as "May a Muslim woman run for political office?" and "May a Muslim obtain a mortgage to buy a house?" From the perspective of TIJ jurists of present and past, these questions have already been answered. While that is probably correct, it is important to recognize that they addressed it from within their own context, which may be very different from ours. For this reason, it is hard, for example, to rely on a financial *fatwā* (jurisprudential opinion) that is several centuries old to resolve a situation involving today's financial markets without further detailed examination. More needs to be done.

American Muslims need much more than recycled answers. They need a comprehensive Islamic worldview that addresses their various concerns thoughtfully and empowers them in the modern world and in their society as active and productive members. This requires a systematic approach to Islamic jurisprudence that understands how our American society functions, and hence can take into account the specificity of our American experience, while respecting the fundamentals of our religion. In other words, to be successful, this approach must take our American context seriously, while at the same time remaining authentic to the faith.

In developing this jurisprudence, it is important to remember that modernity is no longer cabined in the West. The world is now a global village that is being heavily affected by the Internet, and its recent social media innovations, such as Twitter and Facebook, have had a global impact. Among some youth outside the United States, the Internet has created aspirations to live the American dream, while for others, it has rung the alarm bells about controversial Western social values and hegemonic ambitions.

Some of the recent questions KARAMAH received from abroad included: May a Muslim woman travel alone?* Does she really need a *wali* (guardian) to have a valid marriage? Does she have the right to political leadership? These questions are occasioned by the pressures of changes taking place, sometimes regressively, in various countries. Witness the temporary decline in the status of women in Tunisia and Egypt after the first wave of what came to be known in the West as "the Arab Spring." Similarly, witness the stress faced by the new generation of European Muslim women whose private lives are still subject to traditional cultural rules confused with Islam itself.

Many of these rules are no longer satisfactory, as demonstrated by Malala Yousafzai, whose insistence on her right to an education almost cost her her life.[21] So, the need for a modern Islamic jurisprudence is urgent, and it is not limited to our own American community in the diaspora. By addressing these urgent issues, we too should benefit from the Internet, among other modes of communication. We should lay the foundations for the globalization of our Islamic jurisprudence for the American diaspora (IJAD).

Benefiting from the Internet is not a luxury but a necessity for us, given that extremists have learned how to wield its power to reach gullible youth. These extremists exploit religious words and symbols to spread their devastation and mischief. They use quasi-religious arguments to deny both, Muslims and non-Muslims alike, rights guaranteed by the Qur'an and the Prophet himself.[22] They are steeped in divisive sectarianism, outrageous patriarchal/authoritarian behavior, crimes against civilian populations, and totally senseless violence.

The misogyny of these extremist groups towards women has reached unprecedented levels in Islamic history. While Muslim jurists of the past were guilty, like those of other cultures, of being the product of their societies and local patriarchal biases and customs, they never approached nor condoned such patriarchal extremes as we see in many instances today. Historically, Muslim women were in the fore-

*KARAMAH: Muslim Women Lawyers for Human Rights is a nonprofit organization I founded with others in 1993 with the purpose of advancing human rights, especially those of Muslim women, through gender-equitable Islamic jurisprudence. It has a website at www.karamah.org.

front of Islamic thought and leadership, and their demise due to patriarchal ideologies happened gradually over centuries. Today, however, Muslim women are being shot for the simple reason that they desire an education, despite the fact that seeking knowledge is the duty of every Muslim, male and female.[23] Muslim women in areas of conflict are being exploited and raped. Helpless children, including orphans, are being attacked. Clearly, this criminal behavior is not about religion. It is, demonstrably, diametrically and utterly opposed to the values of TIJ, yet extremists continue to claim to be its defenders.

The extremist approach of hiding under religious cover has had a very confusing effect on our uninformed Muslim youth. Consequently, these extremist groups must be challenged religiously, intellectually, and politically to reinstate peace and harmony in society, as well as stop the corruption of fundamental Islamic values and principles, the destruction of civil society, and the horrific bloodshed. We, American Muslims, have a special duty to stand up to these extremist movements and make our voices heard.

This is not a rash choice, nor is it about a claimed "American exceptionalism" on our part. Rather, it is about a combination of factors, including opportunity. First, given the extensive misery and devastation left in the wake of these groups, it is our *farḍ* (duty) to respond, and the best way we know how to respond is through education. The religious and intellectual challenge to extremist ideas is not a luxury, nor should it be viewed as secondary to political efforts. Rather, it is a primary necessity that can effectively immunize the faithful Muslim masses against a corrupt, intolerant, and often violent ideology that masquerades as Islamic while it is antithetical to Islam. By exposing the ideologies of extremist groups for what they are, the faithful masses would be freed from confusion, guilt, and serious error.

Second, our endeavor is facilitated by the fact that American Muslims have at this time what many other Muslims do not have in their countries: political stability fostering the ability to write and think freely without fear of repression or retaliation either by the government or, more recently, by extremist elements. This is not to say that we are oblivious of the various attempts to chill American Muslims' ability to engage in religious free speech and exercise, especially since the events of September 11th. Rather, we are quite confident that all these attacks on Islam and Muslims will wither, in the end, under the umbrella of our constitutional protections.

Given these opportunities, and despite the challenges, we are committed to reviving and developing for American Muslims an understanding of Islam that is just, gender equitable, and humanistic. We hope that Muslims around the world, especially the youth, will also benefit from it, and that it will be suitable for them, understandably, in varying degrees, depending on their social conditions.

So, how do we get started developing such jurisprudence?

First, it must be clear to everyone that if IJAD is to be gender equitable, women must be involved in developing it. This is the lesson of the 1960s in the United States, when Christian and Jewish feminists challenged religious institutional patriarchy. Muslim women have also great precedents in the work of such women as the Egyptian Bint al-Shāṭi', the Syrian Widād Sakākīnī and the Lebanese Nazīrah Zayn al-Dīn, all of whom lived and wrote at the turn of the last century.

Second, we must realize that in pursuing our jurisprudential project, we face tough challenges both at home and abroad. At home, Muslims have to deal with severe prejudice against them. Some elected politicians have called Islam a "cult," insulted our prophet, and demonized our community. These politicians have and are still passing laws in the name of security that significantly impact liberties guaranteed under the U.S. Constitution to American Muslims. This unrelenting campaign at "re-Othering" Muslims has resulted in, among other things, burnt mosques, bullied Muslim children, and lost jobs and lives. At the same time, American Muslim authors and leaders have become suspect abroad as tools of American hegemonic policies. Such dual pressures may induce some authors to compromise on certain principles in order to please the majority at home or design a less controversial message for Muslim societies abroad. Neither approach brings about the necessary global change. What is needed is the courage to think freely in the face of bigots, extremists, and the misinformed to save the world from fracturing further.

In short, the development of an informed, thoughtful, and authentic IJAD, that is uncontaminated by fear or false compromise, is essential for social peace and justice in the lives of Muslims, at home and abroad. Its benefits will also flow to the rest of our society and the world at large. Put into the Western context they live in and understand, Westerners will be able to view Muslims not as a dreaded, radically different or evil "Other," but as yet another permutation in the mosaic of this diversity that we have learned to celebrate. At the same time, IJAD will offer a modern insight into Islam for generations of Muslims at home and abroad whose lives are full of questions and contradictions. Most importantly, in this free market of ideas, IJAD will expose extremism and bigotry for what they are: abhorrent social diseases.

So, how do we do that? How do we get there? This is a project too large for one human being to execute, but a committed group, working over a period of time, can go a long way towards achieving it. This book is only the beginning, and a long trek starts with the first step. We are now ready to answer an important question.

> *Is being in the diaspora relevant to the development of Islamic jurisprudence, or is Islamic jurisprudence neutral with respect to the culture, customs, and laws of the country in which it is developed?*

This question is especially important because we just noted the fact that our world today is a global village. So, should differences count?

Even though the world has become a global village, there are still important cultural differences between, say, a community in Alabama and another in Paris, Beirut, or even San Francisco. It was such differences that led the U.S. Supreme Court to issue its careful opinion on what counts as pornography, tying the definition to community perceptions and values. So, despite globalization, cultural differences still arise and the question posed in this section remains significant.

In developing Islamic jurisprudence, scholars have relied on certain basic principles. One of those states that "Laws change with change in time and/or place."[24] By that they have meant that secondary laws and regulations, as opposed to basic ones, change with the passage of time and change of society or culture. I will give two stark illustrations of this principle that also show how entrenched it is in Islamic jurisprudence.

In the days of *Khalīfah* 'Umar, the second *Khalīfah* (caliph) after the death of the Prophet Muhammad, a famine hit the land. So, he suspended the punishment for stealing until the famine ended. The underlying reasoning was that it was unfair to punish hungry people who may steal a loaf of bread in order to survive.[25] After all, preservation of life is one of the five basic values in Islam.[26] Furthermore, it is a well-known principle that the Law Giver (God) promulgated laws in the public interest (*maṣlaḥah 'āmmah*).[27] So, if the application of the law in certain circumstances contravenes the *maṣlaḥah* of the community, judges must act to prevent such injustice. There is a whole body of writings that articulates this jurisprudence of *maṣāliḥ* (pl. of *maṣlaḥah*), and the balancing of these against other factors, such as personal privacy, urgency, and/or due process.

Another example comes from the famous scholar Imām al-Shāfi'ī (d. 820) who established his famous school of jurisprudence in Baghdad. As a result of political pressures, he moved to Cairo. There, he found a society significantly different from that of Baghdad. So, he revised his original thoughts to make them more suitable to the customs and society of Egypt. This resulted in the second school of jurisprudence of Imām al-Shāfi'ī.[28]

Both these examples illustrate the flexibility of Islamic law to address new situations and circumstances in ways that maximize public interest, as intended by the Law Giver.

From these two examples, without more, we can conclude that Islamic jurisprudence is not neutral with respect to either modernity or cultural and geographic variance. In other words, if Iraqi and Egyptian societies were sufficiently different in medieval times to justify different jurisprudence, certainly the West, and particularly the United States, is sufficiently different from societies in the East to warrant its own jurisprudence, which takes into account the conditions, circumstances, and even technological innovations in this highly developed society.

Furthermore, this is a society steeped in democracy and First Amendment freedoms. It is also highly diverse. Its characteristics pose new questions in Islamic law that have not been considered before, except perhaps in Andalusia (Muslim Spain). They necessitate revisiting old answers to issues that were once viewed as settled. So, we American Muslim jurists have a lot of work ahead of us.

In our jurisprudential task, we face two obstacles: First, there is a significant level of Arabic language illiteracy in the Muslim *ummah* (world community). This is a serious deficiency because Arabic is the language of the Qur'an. Linguistic illiteracy leads Muslims to rely extensively (often exclusively) on the teachings of their religious leaders and local *imāms* who tend to present Islam from their own cultural perspectives. As a result, most Muslims come to know Islam culturally, and not juristically, through the perspective of others.

Second, those who teach the Qur'an often teach it through rote memorization. This method does not develop the students' analytic thinking nor help them recognize the Qur'an's deeper meanings and values. As a result, students become more vulnerable to the views of extremists who claim to defend Islam. For this reason, it is our obligation as Muslim jurists who believe in the richness of Qur'anic meanings, and in a just, secure, and happy society, to confront these modes of teaching and thinking and provide alternatives that better serve the *maṣlaḥah* of the Muslim masses and humanity at large.

While this task is daunting, it is not impossible. I have already published in law journals many articles introducing parts of IJAD that take into account the American specificity. These articles can be found today at http://www.karamah.org/articles. I have shared these articles with Muslim men and women abroad and they were generally well received. I imagine, however, that some aspects of IJAD would have to be revised by other communities to fit their local customs. This is quite expected and acceptable in Islamic law. One would hope that local women would be an integral part of that revision process. Furthermore, although the actual road and rate of progress to achieve change will differ from one society to the other, what is important is that they all embrace the same ultimate goal. That goal is the institution of a jurisprudence for Muslims around the world that promotes just, secure, and happy societies. Our IJAD offers that possibility.

We, Muslims in the United States, are in a special historic moment where we could redefine Islamic jurisprudence in ways that would give true effect to both the Qur'anic principles and the prophetic precedents. Muslim women in the United States could combine efforts with Muslim women abroad to make their voices heard and usher a new age of an authentic yet modern Islamic jurisprudence. However, our situation as American Muslim women is not that simple. We have other serious challenges to face here at home, as part of the Muslim community. Just like Muslim men, Muslim women in the United States are experiencing serious civil rights issues in schools, the workplace, at airports, and even in their private lives. As mentioned earlier, the prejudice we see against Muslims today cannot be solely explained by the tragic events of 9/11. It is deeply rooted in the Orientalist literature that found its way to America as early as the 18th century, and in the political rhetoric that dehumanizes Muslims.[29]

The pressures for compromising one's religion in exchange for social peace, a job, or even safety are not slight. The best illustration is the rising tide of anti-*sharī'ah* bills around the country. Early bills were either redundant or unconstitutional. They were redundant when they turned simply on affirming the supremacy of American law in American courts. They were unconstitutional when they demanded that courts treat the adherents of one religion differently from all others. Despite these facts, these types of bills continued spreading around the country and are now being drafted more skillfully to avoid constitutional challenges. This wave of bills is having a serious intimidating effect on Muslims, many of whom lived formerly under tyranny and are not very familiar with our constitutional protections.

One story broke my heart. A Muslim woman in the Midwest, whose neighboring state was about to pass such an anti-*sharī'ah* bill, was worried about her head cover. What if her state passed a similar bill? What would she do if the police stopped her and asked her about her head cover? Should she say that she was wearing it because she adhered to *sharī'ah*? Would she not be violating the anti-*sharī'ah* bill, then? She might end up in jail, she reasoned! The woman was so scared of that possibility that she had already prepared an answer. She told me in a soft voice that if the police were to stop her, she would say that she was wearing a head cover because of a skin disease. Yes, in America, Muslim women are being frightened about simple choices such as wearing a head cover. In America, Muslim women's bodies have become, like elsewhere, the battlefield of patriarchal conflicts. In America, we have a constitution and we must see to it that it protects us vigorously, or else America will weaken its moral compass, and our constitutional protections will evaporate before we realize it.

So, in the midst of all these pressures, how do we go about developing an authentic Islamic jurisprudence, not intimidated by current political and social pressures at home and abroad? What is authentic Islamic jurisprudence? To answer these questions, we turn to the next section.

What is required in order to engage in authentic Islamic jurisprudential activity in the diaspora?

This is a critical question because not only the religious leadership but also the Muslim grass roots are suspicious of Islamic jurisprudence originating in the West. The Muslim audience may not be that knowledgeable about its religion, but it tends to be politically jaded.

Muslim women leaders at KARAMAH fully appreciate the situation. So, we do not address an issue publicly unless we have studied traditional sources carefully and can defend our position in a scholarly fashion. This means that our work is very slow, but thorough. Where we have not researched the topic, we generally decline to answer. We are cognizant of cultural differences between us and jurists abroad (modern and ancient), and we use the same scholarly approach in addressing our Muslim and non-Muslim audience. In other words, we try to do it right, at least procedurally. Whether our conclusions are also right substantively is a matter subject to discussion and challenge through scholarly dialogue.

So, we need first to distinguish between three requirements for authentic Islamic jurisprudence in general: (a) procedural, (b) substantive, and (c) ethical. Procedural requirements consist of basic scholarly ones, such as knowledge of the Arabic language, its complicated grammar, subtleties of meaning, the foundation of Islamic jurisprudence (*Uṣūl al-Fiqh*), and logic. Substantive requirements include knowledge of sacred and traditional texts, reasons for the revelation (*asbāb al-nuzūl*), and the prophetic precedents. (More about all this in later chapters.) The third requirement demands that a scholar conduct her scholarship honestly and fairly, and without shaping the analysis to fit a predetermined outcome that serves non-scholarly interests. This requirement does not mean that the scholar is required to have a "neutral" point of view. There is no such thing. We all have points of view that spill into our work, despite our efforts. That is why, for example, women's voices are needed in the jurisprudential arena. What is required is that we do not permit this point of view to distort our analysis intentionally in order to achieve a desired result.

Let me provide an example of this point, which simultaneously illustrates other earlier points. Some of the modern jurists (Arab and non-Arab) have tried to interpret away a Qur'anic verse that has traditionally been understood to permit men to hit their wives (4:34).[30] Some (but not all) of these jurists were concerned about "exonerating" Islam in the eyes of the West or local modernists. In their rush to do so, these interpreters selected a meaning of the Arabic verb "to hit" which replaces the plain meaning of the word with a benign meaning, thus eliminating the problem. They did this by consulting ancient dictionaries that provide the root of the verb and the various permutations in its form and meaning. This effort would have been commendable had it been done correctly. It was not. These are the apologists that cannot advance a modern Islamic jurisprudence because they appear to be more concerned about what "others" think about Islam than about what Islam actually says. Our community generally does not appreciate this facile approach to sacred text.

A proper explanation of the verse referred to above is not achieved by providing a facile but incorrect solution about the meaning of a word. Rather, it is achieved by being thoughtful about the word at issue, in that *āyah* (verse) in the Qur'an, in the context of its Islamic worldview. Approached that way, the problem resolves itself. But this is a discussion and an analysis for another time.

Regardless of the intention of the jurist, facile jurisprudence reflects on the credibility of the jurist proposing it, especially if she is from the West. For this reason, American Muslim jurists ought to be very careful in interpreting Islamic law without bending to the pressures of the outside world as to what is acceptable or fashionable. In other words, while being very attuned to and accommodating of the needs of the modern world, jurists should not succumb to external legal hegemony. Rather, they should search for credible internal solutions, and there are many, that could properly justify their conclusions.

III. THE METHOD

In this book, I argue that the centerpiece of the Islamic worldview is *'adālah*, or divine justice.[31] Believing in that, I know that certain passages do not mean what they have been interpreted to mean over the ages, simply because Islam is thoroughly just. I therefore, dedicate myself to discovering the correct meaning by listening carefully to the ancient juristic views, explanations, and observations, and separating them from their cultural patriarchal assumptions. In the end, the answer is usually very simple and clear, once patriarchal and cultural layers have been peeled off.

In short, the task of engaging in jurisprudence is a very delicate and important one. But the effectiveness of a jurist, especially one in the diaspora, can be easily impeached if such jurist rushes to judgment or attempts to appease her society by bending the plain meaning of Qur'anic words or *āyahs*. On the other hand, if one's task is approached professionally, honestly, and seriously, a diaspora jurist would be no less authoritative than one from the Muslim countries, and hence would have as much a chance of influencing the Muslim world and gaining the respect of its local scholars.

Having made this point, we should not over-interpret it. We should not conclude that a "good" American Muslim jurist is one who rejects all influences of her society and works in a bubble. As stated earlier, proper jurisprudence takes into account the circumstances and culture in which it is being developed. Ignoring that will only produce an irrelevant jurisprudence. The issue here is not the need to resist all influences from one's milieu, although of course we can be selective about what influences we admit into our lives. Interacting with one's milieu is natural, human, and encouraged in Islamic jurisprudence. The issue is whether the jurisprudence of the scholar freely reflects such interaction, or rather reflects outside pressures to conform to certain views.

This is an old problem in a new guise. Historically, a class of interested and discredited jurists developed in the Muslim world. They were referred to as the "Scholars of the Authority" (*fuqahā' al-sulṭah*).[32] They were ready with *fatwās* and statements that appeased the rulers. Some of them persist to this day, but they will fade as tyranny and despotism fade in the Muslim world. We certainly do not want to transport this disease to the shores of the New World. However, it is happening more subtly. Such scholars are being rewarded for their views by appointments, grants, and other methods of inclusion and reward in our American academic system. Since many of these institutions are not in a position to evaluate the quality of work produced by these scholars, the rewards tend to be based on what views these institutions like to propagate or what stereotypes about Islam they espouse. Consequently, few American Muslim scholars in academia have been able to play a visible role in developing well-founded Islamic jurisprudence suitable for the modern age and acceptable to Muslims.

As a result, the quality of Islamic learning in American institutions has generally been less than satisfactory for the Muslim minority. To rectify this situation, the community has sought to develop its own circles of knowledge through its organizations and Islamic schools. The problem with these circles is that they do not always distinguish ancient cultural influences from authentic religious principles in jurisprudence. They are caught in a time warp. More often than not, they tend to replicate old patriarchal views, even as they try to modernize. This is especially true with respect to women's rights. What does Islam really say about that? Many community educators do not have a correct or full answer to this question. Furthermore, they may not be interested in teaching their audience about it—let alone practicing it. In the meantime, a new generation of Muslims (male and female) is ready, able, and willing to catch up with the 21st century and gender equity, but available jurisprudence in many of their communities lags behind. What we need is an intensive national educational campaign to spread IJAD in Muslim communities.[33] This task is seriously complicated by the wave of anti-*sharīʿah* bills that are sweeping the country and suggesting that Muslims are planning to overthrow our Constitution.

Having sounded these precautionary notes, let us consider now an example of legal issues indigenous to American Muslims. For example, in our society it is expected that every woman will get an education and work at one point in her life. To ignore these two facts is not helpful. They are of central importance to various stages of an American woman's life. How can a American Muslim woman, interested in a career path, ensure that after marriage her husband will not pressure her to become a stay-at-home mom even if he had promised her otherwise earlier? Of course, American law extends to her the possibility of divorce, but divorce is a radical solution. So, the question remains: From a faith perspective, is divorce an Islamic option in such a situation, or is she required under Islamic law to stay with the man who violated his promise? Furthermore, are there precautionary measures that can help her avoid this situation from the start?

Yes, there are. Despite the resistance of *imāms* arriving from various parts of the Muslim world to the United States, the fact of the matter is that there is serious (*Ḥanbalī*) jurisprudence in the Islamic tradition that permits the prospective wife to validly include stipulations in her marriage contract, and to seek annulment (*faskh*) if a stipulation is breached.[34] This part of that jurisprudence is more suitable for the needs of our minority community than one, for example, that requires the wife to continue her marriage after receiving a minor monetary compensation for the husband's breach of his promise. Of course, even under this jurisprudence, the wife could refuse to stay within the marriage and initiate *khulʿ* (divorce initiated by the woman), but there, too, we have an interpretation problem. Some *imāms* continue to hold on to the old patriarchal jurisprudence of *khulʿ*, which requires the husband's consent, instead of the revised jurisprudence adopted a few years ago by al-Azhar, a leading center of Islamic learning in the Muslim world. This revised jurisprudence dispenses with the consent of the husband as unnecessary and unsupported by prophetic precedent.[35]

American Muslim jurists need to be activists about developing jurisprudence suitable for this day and age in the United States. But different jurists may see things differently and produce schools of thought that are in disagreement on various issues. This is not regarded as a problem by traditional jurists, so long as these schools of thought are rooted in the basics of Islam and are consistent with its fundamentals. Indeed, ancient jurists considered differences among jurists to be a sign of God's mercy.[36] By this they meant that some schools of thought may not be suitable for addressing the needs of a particular Muslim. Through God's mercy, other schools may be better suited for these needs, and that a Muslim is free to espouse them. In other words, each American Muslim is free to choose the Islamic jurisprudence best suited to his or her circumstances.

A Californian Muslim may be much more comfortable with a certain school of thought than a Muslim from Tennessee. Their circumstances, including their communities, may be significantly different on some issues. They have the right to choose the school of thought that suits them best. Additionally, they have the right to choose (*takhayyur*) the jurisprudence that suits them best on any specific matter from any other school, even if it is not the school of thought they subscribe to. They can do this so long as (a) the choices they make are mutually consistent, (b) the resulting overall system is coherent, and (c) the choice is motivated by serious concerns and not opportunism. An additional external requirement is that (d) the resulting system be consistent with federal and relevant state laws.

KARAMAH has been engaged for over two decades now in the project of developing an enlightened egalitarian and gender-equitable jurisprudence suitable for the United States. This jurisprudence takes into account the *maṣlaḥah* of the community as a whole, and especially that of women, by building on the central notion of *'adālah* (justice) in Islam. This jurisprudence, while cognizant of women's issues and rights, also seeks to establish a balanced community in which there is *'adālah* for all. So, with an educational campaign about a credible American Muslim jurisprudential system like ours, I am inclined to think that many Muslim men, as well as women, would welcome this development. In fact, we keep getting questions at KARAMAH that reflect impatience about the pace at which the development of this jurisprudence is proceeding.

To push our point further on women's issues, we need to develop an Islamic jurisprudence that takes into account the fullness of a Muslim working woman's financial rights. This is not as novel a situation in the Muslim world as many seem to think. To the contrary, Muslim women have worked throughout Islamic history, but that jurisprudence has been suppressed in favor of a jurisprudence that treats women as traditional housewives confined to the home and not permitted to participate actively in public life. Thus, on this important subject, we do not need to reinvent the wheel; we only need to find it. When we do, our arguments will carry greater force because they will be rooted in Islamic history, practice, and jurisprudence.

Let us look even deeper into the development of an authentic Islamic jurisprudence in the diaspora by focusing on two major elements that could pose a challenge: (1) modernity and (2) the legal system.

As to modernity, the challenges facing American Muslims are no different than those facing Catholics, Orthodox Jews, Baptists, and other religious groups that are themselves continuously struggling to determine which aspects of modernity are acceptable to them and which aspects must be rejected. American Muslims need to go through the social issues posed by our modern society and decide which of these they can embrace, are willing to tolerate, or must reject. Some of this work has been done, but not in a systematic fashion. It is time to engage in this difficult task and build alliances with those Americans who share our vision.

It is worth noting that science and technology, which are playing a huge role in our new world, do not typically pose a challenge to Muslims. This is due to the Qur'anic encouragement of knowledge. However, with the new developments in the areas of reproduction and genetic engineering, ethical issues have been posed to all religions that need to be assessed and addressed. The inclination among Muslims is to take a positive view of these developments whenever possible. Underlying this attitude is the belief, based on the Qur'an, that everything in this world is a miracle of God, and that science and technology help us recognize that fact and benefit from it.

So, an effective and responsive jurisprudence in the diaspora is not only desirable, but also necessary. It must thoughtfully take into account the circumstances and culture in which it is being developed, without succumbing to pressures of appeasement or fear of criticism or retaliation.

However, to develop authentic Islamic jurisprudence suitable for our modern age and society, we need to have well-educated, home-grown Muslim jurists with a critical consciousness, a good foundation in scholarly prerequisites, and a strong moral compass that will prevent them from forming facile conclusions or bending to social pressure or appeasement.

As to the legal system, Muslims are no different in this regard from other people of faith in this country. Our constitution provides significant protections for freedom of belief and exercise, and where certain belief and our legal system conflict, there are constitutional processes and established methods for resolving these differences. This is why legal literacy in the Muslim community is important, especially when it involves immigrants from societies with distinctly different legal systems.

IV. FINAL THOUGHTS

RECOGNIZING THE URGENCY OF DEVELOPING *IJAD,* OUR WELL-meaning compatriots and government may feel the urge to help birth it. There are important ways in which non-governmental organizations (NGOs) can partner with and help Muslim NGOs (MNGOs) achieve their goals. These efforts must be governed by respect towards MNGOs' leadership, as well as their mission, vision, and struggle. Trying to replace these with others that seem "better" to the NGOs (as I have seen happen in some cases) raises concerns of cultural domination, at worst, and being tone deaf, at best.

Governmental support for domestic educational, counseling, and service programs is important, but governmental support is highly limited by the constitutional separation between faith and state.

Hence, MNGOs must look to other sources to educate their community about IJAD, which presents a significant limitation on this effort.

Additionally, educating the community across the country about IJAD is likely to trouble Islamophobes who have already claimed that Muslims are plotting to impose *sharī'ah* law on U.S. courts. To the contrary, these efforts should allay the concerns of these individuals. At present, Muslims with divorce, child custody, and other cases involving Islamic law end up in American courts. Unlike Catholics and Jews, they have no other conflict-resolution or arbitration body to turn to. As the Muslim community develops in the United States, it should consider establishing Islamic *beth dins*, similar to the Jewish ones, where various issues are arbitrated and judgments are legally enforceable.[37]

The challenge in establishing these *beth dins* for Muslims is that of qualifications. Ideally, an arbitrator on a Muslim *beth din* panel should not only be versed in Islamic law, but also in American law. This way, we can ensure that resulting judgments are in line with public policy, and are hence enforceable. Additionally, since many of the cases before American courts today involve divorce and child custody cases, members of a *beth din* arbitration panel must receive an education in gender-equitable jurisprudence. These requirements are very far from being achieved in the foreseeable future in our communities. But we are making an effort to get there.

Governmental support, while helpful within the United States, is lethal outside it. Association with the U.S. government abroad locks doors, ears, and hearts to our message. For a while now, Muslims around the world have been quite disenchanted with our government and suspicious of its foreign policies as undermining the national sovereignty, security, and well-being of Muslim countries. This attitude has not been helped with pictures on the Internet depicting the humiliation of Muslim detainees in Abu Ghraib or reports about their torture in Guantanamo.[38] Our shining image as a country of laws has been tarnished, and so, even our intellectual product as MNGOs will be tarnished. This is what our experience at KARAMAH over the last decade has shown. It has also shown that with some patience, once the population listens to our message, they are able to abandon their biases and evaluate it on the merits. Thus, the best course of action for our government is to leave MNGOs to go their own way. They will then have the opportunity to float or sink based on the quality of their contributions, as assessed by Muslims themselves. What is striking about this challenge is the fact that Islamic jurisprudence is no longer a highly theoretical or esoteric material for study. It is alive and active on the ground in a project that will ultimately engulf more than one billion lives. In this book, we take the first step towards meeting our challenge.

NOTES

****Please note that all dates in this book indicating the year a writer passed away are approximate due to various factors. They are also based on the Gregorian calendar.***

1. See ʿAbdullāh Ḥakīm, *Deeper Roots: Muslims in the Americas before Columbus*, 2nd ed. (Ta-Ha Publishers, 1996); see also Sulayman Nyang, *Islam in the United States of America* (Chicago: ABC International Group, 1999), 11–13.

2. See, e.g., discussion of this point by Sylviane A. Diouf, *Servants of Allah* (New York University Press, 1998), ch. 2.

3. See "Symposium: American Muslims and Civil Rights: Testimonies and Critiques," *Journal of Law and Religion*, vol. 19, no. 1 (2003–2004), 59–151; see also KARAMAH's video entitled *Civil Rights of Muslims in America*, focusing in particular on the law enforcement raids against homes, businesses, and institutions in Virginia in March 2002 and their impact on the community.

4. See Robert J. Allison, *The Crescent Obscured: The United States & the Muslim World, 1776–1815* (Oxford University Press, 1995), xv–xvii, 20, 35, and 59. A number of books on the Muslim world were published in the United States in the 1790s. Ibid., xv–xvii, 20. These novels, histories, captivity narratives, and biographies on Prophet Muhammad conveyed a picture of impoverishment caused by despotic

rulers, honest commerce perverted into piracy, and debased women. Ibid. In essence, to the Americans striving to forge a new country, these writings conveyed a lesson of what must be avoided.

5. See Timothy Worthington Marr, "Imagining Ismael: Studies of Islamic Orientalism in America from the Puritans to Melville" (unpublished Ph.D. dissertation, Yale University, 1997), 103, on file with the Yale University Library; see also Allison, *The Crescent Obscured*, 61–85 (on the orientalist view of Muslim women).

6. See, e.g., Humphrey Prideaux, *The True Nature of the Imposture Fully Displayed in the Life of Mahomet* (1697); Abbe Constantin Francois de Chassebouf Volney, *The Ruins; or, A Survey of the Revolutions of Empires* (1796); Abbe Constantin Francois de Chassebouf Volney, *Travels through Egypt and Syria in the Years 1783, 1784 & 1785* (1798) (henceforth *Travels*); Francois Marie Arouet de Voltaire, *Mahomet, the Imposter: A Tragedy in Five Acts* (1777).

7. See Allison, *The Crescent Obscured*, 59. Muslims were consistently depicted as submissive and accepting of religious and political despotism. See ibid. The claim that Islam is the source of political tyranny was often a central theme. Prideaux, for instance, depicted Prophet Muhammad as a religious heretic who had exploited religious indifference to create religious and ultimately political tyranny. See ibid., 38.

8. Prideaux, *The True Nature of the Imposture*.

9. See ibid., 23, 25, 27, 32, 68–69, 89–90, 127, 128, 135–36.

10. See Allison, *The Crescent Obscured*, 41. Lyon was jailed for charging Adams with using the "sacred name of religion" as a "State engine to make mankind hate and persecute one another." Ibid. Lyon was convicted, because of this statement and others he had made in Congress, and in letters to his constituents, of being a "notorious and seditious person, and of a depraved mind, and wicked and diabolical disposition." Ibid.

11. John Trenchard and Thomas Gordon, *Cato's Letters; or, Essays on Liberty, Civil and Religious, and Other Important Subjects* (1723), vol. 2, 131.

12. See ibid., vol. 3, 33: "In Turkey, printing is forbid [*sic*]. . . . Nor is printing in other Arbitrary Countries of much use but to rivet their chains." See also Allison, *The Crescent Obscured*, 47–48 (claiming that in the West, books and pamphlets allowed all issues to be discussed

freely and expressed in print, while in Turkey, only one book had been printed in the 18th century), citing John Foss, *A Journal of the Captivity and Sufferings of John Foss, Several Years a Prisoner at Algiers: Together with Some Account of the Treatment of Christian Slaves When Sick—and Observations on the Manners and Customs of the Algerines* (1798), 75–76.

13. See Allison, *The Crescent Obscured*, 51–54. For example, many American writers concluded that a wicked religion had fostered bad government, and a bad government thwarted social progress. See ibid., 53–54. Jean Charles Leonard Simonde de Sismondi concluded that the poison that had destroyed the Muslim world came from within it. See ibid., 51.

14. See *Travels*, 7–8; see also Allison, *The Crescent Obscured*, 48 (noting that the fatalistic attitude of Muslim people as leading to "indolence").

15. Allison, *The Crescent Obscured*, 48. Allison argues that Volney in particular considered the Islamic idea of predestination and the Muslim's willingness to accept everything and anything as the will of God lead to indolence. See ibid. The Turks, he argued, had no reason to change because their despotism, since it existed, was mandated by God. For another discussion of the notion of "fatalism" as Islamic, see Thomas Lippman, *Understanding Islam: An Introduction to the Muslim World*, rev. ed. (1995), 75–78.

16. See Allison, *The Crescent Obscured*, 50–51 (discussing how religious intolerance had stifled free inquiry and prevented men from rising out of their misery in Egypt and Syria).

17. The perception of tyranny in Muslim countries generally available to Westerners is illustrated in *Cato's Letters*:

> *It is even Capital, and certain death [in Turkey], only to reason freely upon their Alcoran A sure sign of Imposture [i.e., Islam, viewed as a false religion] But by Imposture . . . , Stupidity and Janazaries [military or police force] his Throne is supported; and his vast but thin Dominions, know no inhabitants but barbarous, ignorant, and miserable Slaves.*

Trenchard and Gordon, *Cato's Letters,* vol. 3, 32–33 (bracketed statement added by editor); see also ibid., vol. 1, 131 (noting the acceptance of Muslims of Mahomet, an "enem[y] of Liberty, Truth and Peace"); ibid., 300–301 (discussing the tyranny of Egypt, Persia, and Turkey); ibid., vol. 1, 187–89 (discussing the submissiveness of Muslims to tyranny); Allison, *The Crescent Obscured,* 51–53, 59 (discussing the Western use of Muslim culture as an illustrative example of the different consequences of religious and political beliefs); notes 8, 12–15 and accompanying text.

18. See Patrick Henry (Virginia Convention, June 16, 1788), in Bernard Bailyn, ed., *Debate on the Constitution* (1993), vol. 2, 696 (examining the issue that there is no provision in the Constitution against a standing army in times of peace); see generally Allison, *The Crescent Obscured,* at 57–59, citing the frequent reference to Muslim cultures during the constitutional debates of 1787–88.

19. See text relating to notes 13–16, in light of subsequent discussion in the article.

20. See generally, e.g., George Sale, *The Koran: Commonly Called the Alcoran of Mohammed,* 2nd ed. (1764), vol. 1. In a gesture reflecting public opinion, Sale referred to the Prophet as "infidel" and "imposter." However, elsewhere in his book, he noted the Prophet's piety, veracity, justice, liberty, clemency, humility, charm, excellent judgment, happy memory, cheerful temper, and inoffensive behavior toward his friends. Ibid., 54–55. Sale also praised the Prophet for his virtue as a leader, ibid., x, and commended the Prophet's ability to disseminate knowledge of the "true God" to the "pagan Arabs," ibid., 51. He also rejected the theory that Islam was spread by the sword. Ibid., vii. As to particular Islamic principles, Sale discussed the treatment of women, acknowledging that the Prophet enjoined Muslims to treat women with respect and recognize their right to inherit from their parents, husbands, and other family relations. Ibid., 183. Sale also noted that Islam put an end to the pagan custom of female infanticide. Ibid., 174.

21. For an early stand on the educational policies in Afghanistan, as reported to us then, see my op-ed entitled "How Islamic Are the Taliban,"

Philadelphia Inquirer, Mar. 11, 2001, http://articles.philly.com/2001-03-11/news/25325527_1_islamic-american-muslims-prophet.

22. For a quick summary of my thoughts on this subject, *see* my op-ed in *Huffington Post* entitled "Christian Minorities: Our Trust Betrayed," published September 25, 2013, http://www.huffingtonpost.com/azizah-alhibri/pakistan-church-attack_b_3987664.html.

23. See my "Islam, Law and Custom: Redefining Muslim Women's Rights," *American University Journal of International Law*, vol. 12, no. 1(1992), 34–44 (explaining the view of Islam of education, and the role of patriarchy).

24. For more on this, see my "Islamic Constitutionalism and the Concept of Democracy," *Case Western Reserve Journal of International Law* 24 (1992), 7–9, also at www.karamah.org/articles.

25. See, e.g., 'Alī Muḥammad al-Ṣallābī, *Sīrat Amīr al-Mu'minīn 'Umar Ibn al-Khaṭṭāb* [Biography of the Commander of the Faithful 'Umar Ibn al-Khaṭṭāb] (Beirut: Dār al-Ma'rifah, 2004), 230–31.

26. See the discussion in chapter 3, section V, para. C.i of this book on this topic.

27. See, e.g., Aḥmad al-Raysūnī, *Naẓariyyat al-Maqāṣid 'ind al-Imām al-Shāṭibī* [Theory of Objectives of *sharī'ah* [as viewed] by Imām al-Shāṭibī] (Herndon, VA: International Institute of Islamic Thought, 2007), 139.

28. Aḥmad al-Sharbāsī, *Al-A'immah al-Arba'ah* [The Four Imāms] (Beirut: Dār al-Jīl, n.d.), 130–31.

29. For more on this, see Edward Said, *Orientalism* (New York: Pantheon Books, 1978).

30. See, e.g., Muḥammad Shaḥrūr, *Naḥwa Uṣūl Jadīdah li'l Fiqh al-Islāmī* [Towards New Foundations of Islamic Jurisprudence] (Damascus: al-Ahālī, 2000), 323–24.

31. For more on this, see my article "Divine Justice and the Human Order: An Islamic Perspective," in *Humanity before God* (Minneapolis: Fortress Press, 2000), 238, 247–54.

32. Zayd bin 'Alī al-Wazīr, *Al-Fardiyyah: Baḥth fī Azmat al-Fiqh al-Fardī al-Siyāsī 'ind al-Muslimīn* [Individualism: Research on the Crisis of Political Individualist Jurisprudence of the Muslims] (McLean, Virginia: Yemen Heritage and Research Center, 2000), 360.

33. Our first full-fledged effort in educating the community and the rest of America about Islam, as we understand it, appeared in the form of a special issue of the *Journal of Law and Religion* on Islamic jurisprudence and law, vol. 15, nos. 1 and 2 (2000–2001). It appeared in late September 2001. This issue was well received and referenced in several nonacademic popular publications.

34. Wahbah al-Zuḥaylī, *Al-Fiqh al-Islāmī wa Adillatuhu* [Islamic Jurisprudence and Its Evidence] (Damascus: Dār al-Fikr, 1984), vol. 4, 3060.

35. See Egyptian Code, Act No. 1 of 2000 (Regarding Personal Status Law), bk. 3, ch.1, art. 20.

36. Muḥammad Abū Zahrah, *Tārīkh al-Madhāhib al-Islāmiyyah* . [History of Islamic Schools of Thought] (Cairo: Dār al-Fikr al-'Arabī, n.d.), vol. 2, 27–28.

37. See, e.g., www.bethdin.org, which describes the process.

38. See http://detaineetaskforce.org.

2

Basics of Islamic Law and Jurisprudence: The Qur'an and *Sunnah*

In this chapter and the next one, we introduce the basic sources of Islamic law and jurisprudence. Of these, the Qur'an has a unique divine stature for Muslims and hence is of paramount importance. No Islamic principle, interpretation, or law may contradict any part of it. However, to fully understand the meaning of the Qur'an, we have to study the *ḥadīth** (the words of the Prophet) and the *sunnah* (precedents set by his words, actions, and ratifications) that shed light on that meaning. A tertiary source of knowledge is the body of work written by scholars and jurists about the Qur'an and *sunnah* and related topics. Of those scholarly works, the older ones tend to be held in higher esteem because of their proximity to the time of revelation.

Ḥadīth is a collective noun. It can refer to a single *ḥadīth* or a group of *ḥadīths*, depending on the context.

I. BASIC SOURCES OF ISLAMIC LAW: THE QUR'AN

A. INTRODUCTION

The Qur'an is the basis of all Islamic law and morality. Muslims believe it is the Word of God revealed to the Prophet Muhammad (d. 633) through the Angel Gabriel over a period of approximately twenty-three years.[1] As the word of God, the Qur'an is immutable. It consists of 114 *sūrahs* (equivalent to chapters) collectively comprised of over 6,000 *āyahs* (equivalent to verses). Literally, *āyah* means a sign, miracle, or magnificent creation. The *sūrahs* vary in length, with the longer ones occurring at the beginning. We shall see later that this arrangement does not reflect the chronological order of the revelation.

The Qur'an was revealed orally, a few *āyahs* at a time, to an illiterate Prophet. He memorized them as they were revealed, and so did the *ṣaḥābah*.* The Prophet even taught these *āyahs* himself to *ṣaḥābīs* to ascertain that they memorized them and understood their meaning correctly.[2] In the end, it was possible for many *ṣaḥābīs* to memorize the whole Qur'an because it was revealed gradually in a culture used to relying on memory.[3] At the same time, some literate *ṣaḥābīs* recorded the *āyahs* as they were being recited by the Prophet. As a result, there were many partial records of the revelation. Ḥafṣah, wife of the Prophet, held the most complete one. Before his death, the Prophet instructed the *ṣaḥābah* on the proper organizational structure of the *sūrahs* and *āyahs* in the Qur'an, as dictated to him by the Angel Gabriel.[4]

Thus, to ensure accurate and complete transmission of the revelation, a contemporaneous dual system of the Qur'anic revelation was developed: oral and written. Those who memorized the whole Qur'an were called *ḥafaẓah*. As they began dying off, some *ṣaḥābīs* became con-

---

**Ṣaḥābah* is a collective term that refers to the group of *ṣaḥābīs* (singular masculine: *ṣaḥābī*, feminine: *ṣaḥābiyyah*), or companions of the Prophet. Usually it refers to those who spent some time with the Prophet and attended his gatherings, where he talked and taught with the people.

cerned about this situation. So, they asked 'Uthmān, the third Rightly Guided *Khalīfah*, to collect the whole Qur'an in one written document.* In a coordinated effort between the *ḥafaẓah* and the remaining *ṣaḥābīs* who had contemporaneously transcribed the revelation, the two systems of Qur'anic transmission were merged into one in an exacting process. All Qur'anic records of the *ṣaḥābah* were collected, authenticated, and compared with the oral memory of the *ḥafaẓah*. This yielded a single written copy of the Qur'an that reflected the whole revelation in one volume organized in accordance with the Prophet's instructions. All other written records, except for that of Ḥafṣah (out of respect for her), were destroyed. Several copies of the Qur'an were then made and sent to various parts of the Muslim lands.

Ḥafṣah's compilation of the revelation was destroyed after she passed away. The fact that her contribution to the preservation of the revelation was very significant may come as a surprise to the reader. But as we shall see later, women played a very important role in early Islam, preserving and interpreting the Qur'an as well as the *ḥadīth*. Over time, they were ousted from their established leadership positions and relegated to the private sphere. It is not accidental that this decline in the status of women went hand in hand with the decline of *shuratic* (consultative) democracy, a democratic form of government articulated in the Qur'an itself. This important concept was introduced and briefly practiced in the Arab Peninsula over 1,400 years ago at the height of the power of its authoritarian neighbors, the Byzantine and Persian empires.

B. UNDERSTANDING THE QUR'AN

As mentioned earlier, the Qur'an was revealed over a period of more than two decades. Some of its *āyahs* recounted stories about the genesis of the world, the fall of Adam, the life of Abraham, the miraculous birth of Jesus, and many other stories similar, but not identical, to those

*"The Rightly Guided *Khalīfah* " was a title (and description) given to the first four caliphs that succeeded the Prophet in leading the Muslim state.

in the Bible. As we shall see later in this book, these stories are not only educational parables; they also lay moral and legal foundations for principles that were further emphasized in other *āyahs* of the Qur'an. Together, they present the Qur'anic worldview by using multiple vehicles to reach various levels of human understanding. In Chapter 4, we shall provide an example of this interactive support between parable and principle in Qur'anic *āyahs*.

Some other *āyahs* established ethical principles, while yet others shed light on a specific incident, responded to a question, or established a certain principle or rule related to a matter at hand. These circumstances were referred to as *asbāb al-nuzūl*, or "occasions of the revelation," which were often recounted as stories. They provided the "proximate cause" for the revelation and helped followers to understand it. However, some *āyahs* had more than one proximate cause, and some proximate causes resulted in more than one *āyah*.

While some *āyahs* have a plain and definitive meaning, others require exegesis (*tafsīr*) or interpretation (*ijtihād*). In some cases, without knowledge of the related incident or proximate cause, the meaning of an *āyah* could be misconstrued. This is why the famous jurist 'Alī bin Aḥmad al-Wāḥidī (d. 1076) argued that it was not possible to know the correct interpretation of an *āyah* without knowing its story and the cause for its revelation.[5] An example of the need to know *asbāb al-nuzūl* is provided by *āyah* 2:115, which states:

> To God belongs the East and the West,
> So wherever you turn, there is the Presence of God . . .

Based on this *āyah*, a reader could conclude that Muslims need not pray facing the *qiblah* in Makkah.* Instead, they could pray in any direction they please. However, *sabab al-nuzūl* (singl. of *asbāb al-nuzūl*) cited by al-Wāḥidī for this *āyah* describes the following situation:[6] A group of Muslims prayed with the Prophet in a dark night.

**Qiblah* means the direction to which Muslims turn for prayer facing the *Ka'bah*, an ancient cubic structure built by Abraham and Ismā'īl (Ishma'el) in Makkah as the first house of God on earth.

They could not ascertain where the *qiblah* was. So each person prayed in the direction he thought was the correct one. Through this *āyah*, God assured them that all their prayers were accepted because His presence was everywhere. So, this revelation came as a response to a specific prayer predicament, and not as an articulation of a general rule about all prayers.

Nevertheless, the statement in the *āyah* was worded in general terms (*'āmm*). For this reason, jurists concluded that it was therefore applicable to all situations involving similar praying predicaments. This broader interpretation was based on the established juristic principle succinctly stated by the famous al-Rāzī (d. 1207) as: "The lesson is in the general wording, not in the specific *sabab*."[7] In other words, the wording of the statement is more indicative of the scope of its application than its historical proximate cause. Had jurists not adopted this principle, and instead strictly limited every statement in the Qur'an to its specific *sabab al-nuzūl* (the *khāṣṣ* meaning), the Qur'an would have been reduced to a historical document and not a beacon for Muslims at all times.

This juristic rule, however, does not detract from the importance of *asbāb al-nuzūl*. After all, *asbāb al-nuzūl* help determine the similar situations to which the statement may be applicable. For this reason, it was important for jurists to examine *asbāb al-nuzūl* carefully and authenticate the narrations about them. The process included an investigation of the narrator's reliability as well as the historical accuracy of the narration. Generally, the statement of a *ṣaḥābī* about *asbāb al-nuzūl* of an *āyah* was readily accepted if that *ṣaḥābī* witnessed the *āyah*'s revelation and had knowledge about the incident or cause that occasioned it. Narrations by others or by those who were not eyewitnesses of the event received greater scrutiny.

Historical knowledge was an important factor in evaluating the validity of narrations and the reliability of narrators. It included knowledge of which *āyahs* were revealed in Makkah (*Makkī*) and which ones were revealed later in Madinah (*Madanī*). Such demarcation provided a wealth of information about the context, the people involved, and other data important for authenticating *asbāb al-nuzūl* and determining the proper meaning of the *āyah*. The Makkan and Madinan societies differed in terms of their cultures. For example, the Madinan culture was less patriarchal than the Makkan one.[8] Further, the Prophet established the first Muslim state in Madinah. So, while Qur'anic revelations in the Makkan era tended to establish the overarching principles of Islam, in the Madinan era they tended to address constitutional, social, and other needs of the nascent state.

Historical knowledge also included knowledge of the context of the *āyah*. As mentioned earlier, the Qur'anic organization of *āyahs* and chapters was not arbitrary. According to tradition, it was decreed by the Angel Gabriel. This means that the order of the *āyahs* themselves is significant in understanding the thought or meaning expressed in an *āyah*. A jurist must look at the *āyah* or *āyahs* that occur before and after the one being studied and ask: "What is the wisdom of placing this *āyah* before (or after) this other one? What is the context?" Failing to answer this question properly could lead to erroneous interpretations.

Jurists must also carefully examine various aspects of the grammatical structure of the *āyah* in order to determine its meaning and scope. As we discussed earlier, such an examination is at times critical in determining whether the scope of a rule or thought contained in an *āyah* is limited by its *asbāb al-nuzūl*, or whether it is generalizable, and if so, to what extent. Other grammatical issues may arise as well. For example, in *āyah* 35:28, it is necessary to correctly determine the subject and object of the *āyah* in order to determine its proper meaning. The correct grammatical treatment of *āyah* 35:28 results in the following partial meaning: "Those who have knowledge fear God." A minor grammatical error in treating this *āyah* transposes its subject and object, reversing its meaning into: "God fears those who have knowledge." Not only is the latter meaning inconsistent with the attributes of God, but it is also inconsistent with the context of the *āyahs* before and after it which speak of God's miracles in nature and His omnipotence and omniscience.

Another important expertise a jurist must have is a good command of classical Arabic, the language of the Qur'an. Qur'anic words must be understood in terms of their meaning at the time of the revelation, not modern times. Furthermore, classical Arabic words are rich with scores of alternative meanings. The skilled jurist is the one who is able to determine the proper meaning of the word in the *āyah* according to *asbāb al-nuzūl*, the context of the *āyah*, and various other considerations, without introducing a personal bias for a specific meaning. For example, let us take a look at *āyah* 22:27, which states:

> And proclaim the Pilgrimage among men (*nās*); they will come to you on foot (*rijālan*) and (mounted) on every kind of camel . . .

The first part of the *āyah* refers to *nās*. *Nās* is derived from the word *insān*, which means "human being."[9] Despite this fact, the translator translated *nās* as referring to "men" only. Another troubling translation is that of *āyah* 2:125, which states: "Remember, we made the House [*Ka'bah*] a place of assembly for *men* and a place of safety." Like *āyah* 22:27, this *āyah* is also talking about pilgrimage to *Ka'bah* required of *both* men and women, and a safety that engulfs them both. A narrow translation, limiting it to men, distorts its meaning and leads non-Arabic-speaking Muslims to view the *Ka'bah* as a male domain. The above translation in 22:27 only compounds this problem and distorts Muslim women's rights to worship at *Ka'bah*. Unfortunately, some of the current practices in the surroundings of the *Ka'bah* lean in this direction. This patriarchal trend is not part of Islam, but part of gender-restrictive translations and cultural practices. It is similar to the now outmoded trend in the English language of referring to "humankind" as "mankind."

Incidentally, this patriarchal bias is not new, as illustrated by the story about Umm Salamah, the wise wife of the Prophet, to whom he turned for advice.[10] It is narrated that one day she heard the Prophet call out "*Yā ayyuha-n nās*,"—that is, "Oh *nās*." She immediately dropped what she was doing and stood up to join him. A woman who was with her pointed out to Umm Salamah that the Prophet only called the *nās*. Umm Salamah answered: "Indeed, I am included in the *nās*."[11] Al-Nawawī (d. 1277) noted in his commentary that this story is evidence that women were included in the address to *nās*.[12]

Given that women, like men, perform the pilgrimage, a more appropriate translation of this verse would be:

> And proclaim the Pilgrimage among people (*nās*); they will come to you on foot (*rijālan*) and (mounted) on every kind of camel . . .

Now, some who are familiar with the Arabic language may object to this reading on the basis that the second half of the verse specifically mentions *rijālan*, which means "men." This is not so. Here the translator got it right. *Rijālan*, which *usually* means "men," has a secondary meaning that is derived from *rijl* or "foot."[13] Given the context, the *āyah* is calling upon people to come to pilgrimage mounted and on foot. Nothing in the verses before or after this one suggests that the address excludes women. Indeed, the opposite seems to be true since women have the same pilgrimage duties as men.

Last but not least, a jurist must have a good command of logic. Confused logic can lead to confused conclusions or worse. For this reason, jurists developed extensive rules of logic, included as part of *uṣūl al-fiqh* (the foundations of Islamic jurisprudence) and utilized them masterfully in Qur'anic *tafsīr* and other branches of Islamic thought.

Thus, a jurist who engages in *tafsīr* and interpretation of Qur'anic text is required to have a combination of areas of expertise that includes knowledge of *asbāb al-nuzūl*, context of the *āyah*, logic, and command of classical Arabic and its grammar. As we shall see in Section II.B of Chapter 3, the jurist must also have other areas of expertise, such as knowledge of the *ḥadīth* and *sunnah*, which shed light on the meaning of the *āyahs*. Finally, the jurist must be able to interpret the meaning of the *āyah* objectively, without regard to personal preference or benefit. The latter requirement would bar, for example, patriarchal interpretations (and perhaps some feminist ones as well) in preference for the Qur'anic ideal of *'adālah* (justice and fairness). Given the above demanding combination of skills and knowledge, few modern jurists satisfy them, whether in the East or West. As a result, many modern commentaries or even translations of the meanings of the Qur'an are not reliable.

C. Qur'anic Philosophy

To understand the Qur'anic message properly, one must understand its overarching philosophy. However, this topic is very rich and a proper discussion is beyond the scope of this book. We shall therefore focus on those aspects of Qur'anic philosophy that directly impact our current project. The following three are fundamental to our later discussions and thus demand our attention.

1. Equality of All Human Beings

According to the Qur'an, all human beings were created from a single *nafs* (soul), and the most honored among them in the sight of God is the one who is most righteous.[14] The Prophet explained this further by saying: "Oh People, your God is One, your father [Adam] is one, so, no Arab is better than a non-Arab nor is a red person better than a black one, nor is a black person better than a red one, except with regard to piety."[15] Despite the generally held view that in Islam men are viewed as superior to women, later chapters in this book will argue otherwise. Unfortunately, patriarchal interpretations that afflicted Judaism and Christianity also afflicted Islam as a result of the time and culture in which jurists lived.

2. Diversity

The Qur'an encourages racial, ethnic, cultural, and other types of diversity as blessings from God.[16] It tells us that they were created so that humanity enjoys these differences through interaction, communication, and "getting to know" each other (*lita'ārafū*). As Islam spread across continents, ancient Muslim jurists realized that what may suit one culture may not be quite suitable for another. So, they encouraged each community to introduce its own customs into its laws, so long as these customs did not contradict basic Islamic principles.[17] As a result, Islamic laws of Muslim countries till this day differ significantly among each other on various matters. Witness, for example, the difference in constitutional and family laws between Egypt and Saudi Arabia (both Muslim countries). By leaving room for custom, the Law Giver (God) emphasized the importance of cultural diversity and the ability of each society to make its own choices within the framework of fundamental Islamic principles.

3. Gradualism

The third fundamental feature of Qur'anic philosophy is that of gradualism.[18] It applies to many aspects of Islam, including those of divine revelation and education. But it does not apply to Islam's first principles, such as the principle that there is only one God and Muhammad is His prophet, nor to prohibition of capital crimes, such as female infanticide.[19] These matters are fundamental. Understanding the importance of change through education and comprehension, the Qur'an was not revealed all at one time. Instead, the Qur'an was revealed gradually in accordance with the needs and capabilities of the people. For example, Arabs consumed substantial amounts of alcohol in pre-Islamic times. So, the Qur'anic prohibition on drinking alcohol was imposed gradually. First, the prohibition was only advisory; then, it was made binding but only at the time of prayer. Later, the prohibition became absolute.[20]

Again, the Qur'an did not prohibit slavery outright in a world in which slavery was widely practiced. Instead, it provided rules and principles that, if followed by Muslims, would have totally eliminated slavery in a generation or two. The Prophet himself taught that all Muslims, whether free or slaves, were equal.[21] He also chose a former slave as his *mu'adhdhin* (the one who calls for prayers) and helped female slaves around town in their chores. But the community and the world were not ready for this change.

Addressing the Prophet's frustration at the slow pace of change, the Qur'an points out that he was not there to control the affairs of the people, but only to remind them of what they ought to do.[22] For, God granted humans dignity, and an important part of that dignity is free will. If there is to be responsibility at Judgment Day, individuals must reach their own conclusions and freely make their own choices.

It is now fifteen centuries since the revelation informed us that "All people are created from the same soul";[23] since Prophet Muhammad declared that "Women are the full siblings [or split halves] of men";[24] and since *Khalīfah* 'Umar asked his famous rhetorical question,

"When did you enslave people whose mothers gave them birth as free?"[25] (suggesting that every human being is born free). Racism and patriarchy are still rampant around the world, but, finally, the world is making progress on these fronts. It is just saddening that these fundamental principles laid down by the Qur'an such a long time ago were not instituted by Muslim societies sooner.

Similarly, in the area of ethics, the Qur'an describes various actions and words as "good" and others as "better."[26] This approach recognizes that humans differ in their capacity to understand and change their behavior. For example, in the area of criminal law, some Muslims may insist on the rule of "an eye for an eye" in determining punishment. The Qur'an does indeed mention this standard of justice.[27] However, it says at the same time that it is better to forgive than to punish, adding: Do you not wish that God forgive you in the afterlife?[28] The Prophet echoes this thought in his *ḥadīth*: "The one who does not show mercy [on earth], will not be shown mercy [in Heaven]."[29]

By providing a spectrum of good and better behavior, the Qur'an allowed for the varying abilities of individuals to forgive. But while it provided a broad horizon for forgiving behavior, it limited retributive behavior by the Principle of Proportionality. The "eye for an eye" standard prohibits disproportionate retribution and revenge. But the forgiveness standard advances society towards harmony. The Qur'an urges Muslims to adopt the higher standard, for which they will be rewarded in the afterlife.

The same approach applies to the introduction of Islamic democratic principles. Given the pervasive authoritarian ideology in the ancient world, it was clear that human consciousness would need time to recognize the evils of authoritarianism and reject it in favor of democracy. So, the Qur'an provided basic principles for a constitutional democracy without providing the details for a specific system. Prophet Muhammad provided a model of a democratic state in Madinah that was actually based on a charter. Muslims in later times were free to interpret these basic principles in light of their customs and the demands of their historical consciousness, as informed by the era in which they lived.[30] Ideally, this meant that Muslim constitutional models would initially rely on a few basic democratic elements, but remain flexible in order to progress over time. Unfortunately, despite all efforts, the force of authoritarianism in 7th century Arabia and the world around it was hard to defeat. As a result, despotism replaced the democratic model of Madinah and thwarted its development.

The decline of democratic governance and the rise of unshackled authoritarianism in many Muslim countries prompted Muslim jurists to consider the proper means for introducing change. Many discouraged an abrupt change in the system of government, even for a good cause, if it resulted in chaos, conflict among Muslims, or bloodshed.[31] This position may reflect a preference by such jurists for maintaining the status quo, but the better view is that this position is the direct result of the established juristic principle of avoiding *nizā'* (conflict). This principle permeates all of Islamic law, including commercial and family law. The preferred Islamic approach is one that builds consensus to achieve a desired change, rather than advocate it by the use of divisive force. On the other hand, the use of force may be excused if it is shown to be either unavoidable or the lesser of two evils.[32]

D. ISLAMIC *SHARĪ'AH*[33]

Properly understanding the Qur'an is especially important for the Muslim legal community because the Qur'an is the primary source of Islamic *sharī'ah*—that is, the system of Islamic legal rulings (*aḥkām*). The Qur'an is supplemented by prophetic *ḥadīth* and scholarly contributions that constitute secondary and tertiary sources of *sharī'ah*. Together, the three sources form the foundation of the Islamic *sharī'ah* legal system in various Muslim countries.

Prophetic *ḥadīths* are of two kinds: divinely inspired and prophetic. Divinely inspired *ḥadīths* are viewed as part of the primary source of *sharī'ah*. There are differing views, however, about the status of other prophetic *ḥadīths*. The difference depends on whether the Prophet is viewed as incapable of error in any circumstances, or subject to human error and correction by the Divine.[34]

Additionally, it is important not to confuse (a) divine *sharī'ah* revealed in the Qur'an or to the Prophet with (b) the product of scholarly human effort (*ijtihād*) which is part of positive law. The first is binding; the second is not. The first is immutable; the second is ever-changing because it reflects the culture of its community and addresses its needs. The second also reflects, whether consciously or otherwise, the personal preferences or biases of the jurist. Violating the first has dual repercussions, worldly and in the afterlife, while violating the second has repercussions only on earth.

Because *ijtihād* often reflects the cultural and personal values of the scholar, it stands to reason that different *ijtihāds* result in different, sometimes diametrically opposed, interpretations. These differences have been traditionally accepted in Islamic jurisprudence. Indeed, they were celebrated based on the *ḥadīth*: "Difference among scholars is [divine] mercy to Muslims."[35] Muslims are free to choose from the different interpretations those that best fit their circumstances and culture.[36] After all, the Prophet repeatedly enjoined Muslims to "facilitate and not complicate."[37] We shall discuss *ijtihād* further in Chapter 3.

Qur'anic *āyahs* containing legal rules are relatively few. They number a few hundred *āyahs* out of a total of 6,000.[38] They provide the foundation of the Islamic legal system and deal with two basic categories: matters of worship (*'ibādāt*) and course of dealing among people (*mu'āmalāt*). Rules relating to matters of worship are articulated in great detail in the *sunnah*. For example, while the Qur'an enjoins Muslims to pray, the Prophet showed them how to pray. He said: "Do as I do,"[39] and Muslims from then on prayed as he did. Since matters of worship were rooted in the Qur'an and detailed in the *sunnah* by the Prophet himself, a clear and broad scholarly consensus developed around them, with minor disagreements on tertiary matters.[40]

This level of detail in the rules is also evident in some areas, such as family law, inheritance, and criminal law.[41] For example, the laws of marriage and divorce, as well as those of inheritance, are carefully detailed in the Qur'an itself. Indeed, inheritance laws are quite specific and require at times advanced mathematical skill.[42]

General rules, however, are more prevalent in the Qur'an. They address all areas of the law, including, for example, constitutional and environmental law. In the absence of applicable specific rules, general rules provide a conceptual umbrella that can accommodate different approaches consistent with that general rule. For example, a major constitutionalist principle in Islam is that governance be based on *shūrā* (consultation).[43] However, the principle itself does not specify the form of government required. Since it is possible to have, for example, a parliamentary system or a presidential one based on *shūrā*, barring other considerations, both forms of governance would satisfy the general rule. This approach provides much-needed flexibility for various societies to choose those forms of consultative governments that best suit their cultures and needs.

Underlying this approach is a very important principle—namely, that Islam is suitable for every time and place. So, just as it was suitable for those in the desert society of the Arabian Peninsula almost 1,500 years ago, it is also suitable for more complex civilizations in other places and other centuries. Witness, for example, the changes and social and administrative complexities arising from the days of the Umayyad Caliphate, the Abbasside Caliphate, to that of the Ottoman Caliphate. Furthermore, Islam is not an Eastern religion. It is a world religion. As its history illustrates, it is hospitable to various cultures and sufficiently flexible to accommodate various developments in a constantly changing new world. However, such accommodation can only be achieved by purging from Islamic jurisprudence the remnants of antiquated cultural influences and oppressive patriarchal bias.

Muslims do believe that the Revealed Truth in the Qur'an is absolute and eternal. But that is not to say that our human understanding of it is static. Indeed, the Revealed Truth is at once both absolute and dialectical. It is absolute because God is Omniscient, Omnipotent and Beneficent, and the Qur'anic Truth reflects these divine attributes. It is dialectical because our developing human understanding can only grasp this Absolute Truth in a dialectical manner commensurate with our state of consciousness, knowledge, and social development. However, our understanding grows and changes as our consciousness and societies develop. This fact was understood by traditional scholars who expected continuous revitalization and renewal (*tajdīd*) of Islamic jurisprudence at least once every century. Modernity, fueled by rapid developments in technology and its effect on the lives of individuals and society as a whole, poses an imminent danger to those Muslims afraid of change. But it provides an enticing invitation to Muslims who are looking for it. After all, history is replete with examples of exceptional contributions by Muslims in areas such as science, mathematics, physics, astronomy, and medicine, among others. These contributions were based on the belief, derived from the Qur'an, that nature is an embodiment of God's miracles (*āyahs*),[44] not a challenge to His existence.

Other basic Qur'anic principles relate to such important issues as freedom of belief, interfaith relations, and the dialogue of civilizations, all of which will be discussed when these issues are later addressed. Incidentally, Qur'anic principles are all interrelated because Muslims believe that the Qur'an is a seamless web of ideas. One cannot understand one part of it in isolation from the rest. Hence, it must be read as an organic whole in which each part is important for understanding the other parts and the overall architecture of Islamic philosophy.

II. BASIC SOURCES OF ISLAMIC LAW: THE *SUNNAH*

A. INTRODUCTION

Literally, from a legalistic point of view, the word *sunnah* means "the law, the way." For example, it is the *sunnah* of our world that people grow old and die. It is a *sunnah* of nature that the solar system moves along set orbits. But in this discussion, we are using the word to refer exclusively to the *sunnah* of Prophet Muhammad, which is a major source of Islamic *sharī'ah*. It comprises his words (*ḥadīth*), actions, example, and even silences and indications that have significance in explaining the religion, regulating aspects of it (such as prayer), or promulgating religiously significant rules, ranging from those for ablution (*wuḍū'*) and standards of cleanliness to those relating to the equality of humans, gender and family issues, and human and animal rights. This *sunnah* is not viewed by Muslims as a historical body of information of little relevance to the modern world. Rather, it is the result of divine injunctions. In *āyah* 16:44, for example, the Qur'an states:

> And We have sent down the Message
> So that you may explain clearly to people what has been
> revealed to them,
> And that they may give thought.

In another *āyah* (59:7), the Qur'an states:

> So take what the Prophet gave you [as part of the Message]
> And what he forbade, do not engage in.

The Prophet emphasized these divine injunctions. He stated: "pray as you see me pray,"[45] and "take [learn] from me your [pilgrimage] rituals."[46] He also explained through his words and actions the meanings of Qur'anic verses that may have seemed complex, ambiguous, or unclear to some Muslims. (Examples of this will be given in several places in this book.) His explanations were very important for a full understanding of many matters, even the most sensitive ones. For example, women asked him about matters relating to menstruation and prayer, intercourse and fasting, and pregnancy and divorce.[47] He also addressed matters ranging from constitutional and social issues to human dignity, war ethics, and even animal rights. As a result of the Prophet's enlightening explanations of and elaboration upon *sharī'ah* matters, jurists held that any attempted interpretation of a Qur'anic verse must be tested for accuracy, not only against other Qur'anic *āyahs*, but also against the *sunnah*. Thus, the *sunnah* became the second foundation of all Islamic jurisprudence, and *ḥadīth* is at its core.

The Prophet exhorted Muslims to follow his *sunnah*. He frowned upon those who were willing to ignore it and praised those who followed it. On one occasion, he said, "Those who observe my *sunnah* like me, and those who like me will be with me in paradise.'"[48] Another *ḥadīth* stated, "Those who are disinclined towards my *sunnah* are not of me."[49] For this reason, Muslims take the *sunnah* of the Prophet very seriously; they view him not only as the exemplary Muslim, but also as divinely inspired. The Qur'an itself emphasizes that the Prophet does not speak of his own inclination, but from revelation or divine inspiration.[50] Given the importance of the *sunnah*, the question arises whether the Prophet was *ma'ṣūm* (infallible).

It is agreed among Muslim jurists that the Prophet was *ma'ṣūm* in matters of religion, in particular the Qur'anic revelation. But what about words of the Prophet regarding non-religious matters? To understand the answer, we need to delve deeper into *ḥadīth* studies. A unique category within *ḥadīth* is that of the *al-ḥadīth al-qudsī* (sacred *ḥadīth*). *Ḥadīth* within this category is reported by the Prophet himself to be divinely inspired, sometimes through a dream. It differs from the Qur'an in that the inspiration but not the words are God's.[51] This category is different from that of *al-ḥadīth al-nabawī* (*ḥadīth* of the Prophet) that reflects both the words and thoughts of the Prophet on religious matters. Jurists agree that the Prophet is *ma'ṣūm* in all sacred *ḥadīths*. As to the Prophetic *ḥadīths*, they note that he had a unique position. If he erred in matters of religion, he was readily corrected by God.[52] Witness the *sūrah* entitled "*al-Mujādilah*" ("The Arguing Woman," 58:1). It informs us that

> God has indeed heard the statement
> Of the woman who pleads with you concerning her husband
> And carries her complaint in prayer to God:
> And God always hears the arguments between both
> Sides among you

In this case, the Prophet was divinely instructed to change his ruling on a matter of concern to the woman who argued with him about it. We will come across a couple of other such examples during the rest of this book. In one case, the Prophet stated that he wanted something, but God wanted another, and so he changed his ruling.[53]

These incidents led the jurists to conclude that the Prophetic *ḥadīth* on matters of religion was, in the end, also free from error because had it been in error, it would have been divinely corrected.

This leaves the third category of statements by the Prophet, namely those that are non-religious. One example belonging to this category is the story about the Prophet passing by men who were pollinating palm trees. He inquired about their work and noted that the trees would bear fruit whether they pollinated them or not. The men stopped their work. The Prophet passed by the same trees a year later and noticed that they did not bear fruit. He inquired about the situation and the men told him that they followed his advice. He responded: "You are more knowledgeable about your worldly affairs."[54] Understanding that the Prophet does not have special knowledge of worldly matters, his companions often asked him whether a certain decision was based on divine inspiration or was a worldly one. If it was a worldly one, they evaluated it and sometimes offered the Prophet alternative advice.

For this reason, not every prophetic *ḥadīth* is binding. Those specifying how to pray or how to perform pilgrimage are binding because they relate to matters of worship and religion. On the other hand, those *ḥadīths* that do not transmit, explain, or clarify the message of Islam are not. That is the case precisely because the Prophet emphasized that he was a human being. In one instance, he said, "I am human. If I order you in a matter of your religion, then follow it, but if I order you in a [worldly] matter of my own opinion, I am human."[55] Nevertheless, many Muslims follow the example of the Prophet in his personal life on the basis that he was an exemplary Muslim.

Concerned that the religious knowledge he is transmitting might get lost in time, the Prophet exhorted Muslims to "take my *sunnah* and . . . hold on to it with your molars!"[56] That was a prescient advice, given later developments in the transmission of his *ḥadīth*. For, in the early days of the revelation, the Prophet had prohibited the recording of his *ḥadīth* so that Muslims would not confuse it with the Qur'an, which is the only source of divine law. Therefore, a significant part of the *ḥadīth* was not recorded until the second and third centuries A.H. (After *Hijrah*—i.e., 9th and 10th century A.D.) during the Abbasid rule.[57] To protect the authenticity and reliability of *ḥadīth* at that time, it became necessary for Muslim scholars to develop a sophisticated science of authentication in order to minimize error.[58]

B. *Ḥadīth* Studies

Many prophetic *ḥadīths* were transmitted to Muslims through multiple channels or ways. Let us understand what this statement means, as well as introduce terms that will become relevant to discussions in later chapters.

A *ḥadīth* may be narrated by one or more people at the point of origin, which is usually the time of the Prophet or soon thereafter. The primary narrator(s) is (are) then quoted (paraphrased) by subsequent narrators, who in turn are quoted (paraphrased) by even later narrators. The effect is to create a "tree" structure where the primary narrators can be viewed as constituting the trunk of a tree. Then each branch of that tree would originate from one primary narrator quoted (paraphrased) by a secondary narrator, quoted (paraphrased) in turn by other narrators in a linear chain of subsequent narrators. These narration branches also sprout their own sub-branches with multiple secondary, tertiary, and later narrators quoting/paraphrasing the earlier narrators, and so on. The effect is sometimes a large number of ways by which a *ḥadīth* is transmitted through a large number of chains or branches. Since *ḥadīths* are sometimes transmitted by meaning and not verbatim, the effect is to have many chains or branches that may have different wording. This is an added complication in cases where the variance in meaning has jurisprudential significance.

1. Methodology for Assessing the Authenticity of *Ḥadīths*

A *ḥadīth* is examined in light of two major factors that determine its authenticity:

a. The soundness of its *isnād* (chain of narration). This examination includes the identity and reliability of the narrators in the narration chain, mode of narration, strength of the narration chain (i.e., does it have a missing link, an unreliable link in the chain? etc.), existence of different chains of narration for the same *ḥadīth*, and other factors, which will be discussed in greater detail later.

b. The soundness of its *matn* (its substance or content). In examining the *matn* of a *ḥadīth*, the paramount consideration is whether its content is consistent with the Qur'an, or even with other equally or more reliable *ḥadīths*. Inconsistency with the Qur'an is a fatal *matn* defect because the Qur'an is the sacred book of Islam. So, if a *ḥadīth* is inconsistent with the Qur'an, it is discounted. However, depending on the strength of its *isnād*, it may be possible at times to re-interpret a *ḥadīth* so as to eliminate the inconsistency. Other considerations in assessing the soundness of the *matn* of a *ḥadīth* include, for example, whether a *ḥadīth* makes sense to a logical person, and whether its words are ones that are consistent with the Prophet's manners and use of language.

If either one of the two factors (i) or (ii) reveals a serious defect, the *ḥadīth* is rejected as false (*mawḍūʿ*) or weak (*ḍaʿīf*).

Studying the *isnād* of a *ḥadīth* was of critical importance for many reasons. Some narrators were old and subject to forgetfulness and error. Others were hard of hearing. Yet others were known liars or interested parties fabricating narrations to appease their rulers. Jurists had to parse through these and many other possibilities with respect to each person in the chain of narration. They also checked the chain of attribution for historical accuracy and ascertained that it made chronological sense. Additionally, they sought to determine how many individuals narrated the *ḥadīth*. A *ḥadīth* narrated by a single person was, with certain exceptions, subjected to greater scrutiny. Jurists also differed among themselves in identifying defects in the *isnād* or *matn* of a *ḥadīth*.

However, determining the soundness of the *isnād* of a *ḥadīth* is quite complicated. For example, since a chain of *isnād* is as strong as its weakest link, the determination requires looking for a weak link in a *ḥadīth*. This process usually entails checking every link in the narration chain. Once a weak link is identified, it casts doubt upon the whole chain. As a result, the chain suffers and the *ḥadīth* through that chain is usually rejected. Note that the *ḥadīth* itself may nevertheless still be deemed authentic if it comes to us through another chain of *isnād* that is determined to be sound. Clearly, this investigative task requires a thorough knowledge of various areas, including the biographies of the narrators and historical and cultural information about the relevant epochs and communities. Additionally, where a *ḥadīth* has been narrated through various troubled chains, we may have to check *every* chain anyway because these chains may be used to support each other and, in certain cases, collectively cure minor defects in individual chains.

Determining the soundness of *matn* was as important but somewhat less onerous of a task. If a *ḥadīth* appeared to conflict with the Qur'an, then the *ḥadīth* had been misunderstood, inaccurately narrated, or simply fabricated. An example of mistaken narration was pointed out by no other than 'Ā'ishah herself, the young wife the Prophet married after the death of Khadījah. Upon hearing the *ṣaḥābī* Abū Hurayrah narrate that the Prophet said that bad omens reside in women, homes, and horses, she became quite upset. She corrected the narrator, saying, "What the Prophet used to say was: 'In the times of *Jāhiliyyah* [pre-Islamic], people found bad omens in women, homes and animals.'"[59] It appears that the narrator Abū Hurayrah had not heard the beginning of the Prophet's sentence and narrated only the last part. Had 'Ā'ishah not been around to correct him, we would be struggling till this day with this *ḥadīth* and its negative view of women.

Clearly, it is much simpler to forgo the examination of the soundness of *isnād* and move directly to examining the soundness of the *matn* of the *ḥadīth*. While this approach has its merits, it can give rise to analytical risks (such as circular arguments), which we shall discuss later. In this book, when we assess the authenticity of a *ḥadīth*, we shall examine both factors.

The project of authenticating *ḥadīths* was taken extremely seriously by jurists and scholars. Many travelled for weeks to meet someone who claimed to have heard a *ḥadīth* by the Prophet. They would investigate the narration, its substance, and its chain of attribution.

They would try to find out whether the narrator was transmitting the exact words of the Prophet or transmitting the meaning of the statement. Often, what was transmitted was the meaning and not the exact words, a situation which raised questions about the level of comprehension of the narrator, especially in light of the richness of classical Arabic words and grammar.[60]

If the scholars were satisfied, they included the *ḥadīth* in their collection, indicated whether it was a verbatim quote, and informed others about it. At that time, word did not travel fast, so scholars in Madinah, for example, did not have all the *ḥadīths* collected in Egypt or Iraq, or vice versa. This was due to the fact that after the death of the Prophet, the *ṣaḥābīs* spread out to various Muslim regions and shared their knowledge. Their knowledge with respect to *ḥadīth* was not always identical. It depended, for example, on how much time they spent with the Prophet, or what narrations were transmitted to them. This situation changed once the *ḥadīth* was finally recorded.

2. Ranks of *Ḥadīth*

Ḥadīths were ranked according to their degree of reliability. The highest rank was *ṣaḥīḥ* (authentic), the intermediary rank was designated as *ḥasan* (good), and the lowest one was labeled *ḍaʿīf* (weak).[61] These ranks were also refined further in accordance with additional criteria.

In short, a *ṣaḥīḥ ḥadīth* has full jurisprudential force and effect. A *ḥasan ḥadīth* provides a strong argument in favor of the ruling, while a *ḍaʿīf ḥadīth* does not usually have much effect.[62] Some *ḥadīths* were deemed *mawḍūʿ* (fabricated), and these were, of course, rejected.

According to Sheikh Muḥammad Jamāl al-Dīn al-Qāsimī, a 20th century scholar and author of *Qawāʿid al-Taḥdīth*, there are very few *ḥadīths* that actually achieve in themselves the rank of *ṣaḥīḥ* (authentic) status.[63] For this reason, scholars relaxed their standards to include the *ḥasan* classification as a lower grade of *ṣaḥīḥ*.[64] But how are these two ranks defined?

A *ṣaḥīḥ ḥadīth* is one in which:

a. Each link in the narration chain transmits with precision and fairness the narration of the preceding link in the chain;

b. The transmitted narration does not contradict other, more reliable, narrations (i.e., is free of *shudhūdh*); and
c. The transmitted narration is free of any defects (*'ilal*).[65]

On the other hand, a *ḥasan* (good) *ḥadīth* is one

a. that is transmitted by narrators who were *close* to achieving the status of *thiqah* ("trustworthiness");
b. where the *ḥadīth* is recounted in a form different from that of the others; and
c. where the *ḥadīth* is free of defects or contradiction with other, more reliable, *ḥadīths*.[66]

So, a *ḥasan ḥadīth* is not quite reliable. Al-Qāsimī states that "it is called '*ḥasan*' (good), because we assume good will on the part of the narrator."[67] This is a very generous standard, but it is constricted by the requirement that the narrated version of the *ḥadīth* be free of known defects, such as a temporal or spatial lacuna between two adjacent links in the chain of narration. In other words, a *ḥasan ḥadīth* is one which appears to be true in light of knowledge about those narrating it, and the fact that there is no harm in admitting it because it does not contradict another reliable *ḥadīth*, nor does it have a *'illah* (defect) that would disqualify it. When another narration of the *ḥasan ḥadīth* is transmitted through a different chain, then, even if the versions do not quite coincide, they are viewed as supporting each other and the *ḥasan ḥadīth* becomes classified as *ṣaḥīḥ*.[68] However, it was reported about Abū Ḥātim al-Rāzī (d. 810), the distinguished narrator of *ḥadīth*, that he was asked by his son about a specific *ḥadīth*. The father said that its classification was *ḥasan*. The son then asked him if he could use it to support an argument. Abū Ḥātim answered: "No."[69]

The above discussion teaches us a few things. First, we need to look beyond the final ranking of the *ḥadīth* to determine how it was determined. Was it a *ṣaḥīḥ ḥadīth* in itself or, for example, a *ḥasan ḥadīth* that moved up the ranks? Also, were there other scholars who disagreed with the classification? If so, then their views could help us reassess that classification.

3. Methods of Transmittal

Not all narrations were transmitted the same way. One mode of transmittal is of special importance to our later discussions. It is called *'an'anah*. It is one where narrator A states that the narration was transmitted *'an* (i.e., comes from) narrator B. *'An* is a term of art indicating that A's narration relies on a narration by B. It does not necessarily indicate either that A met B or that he heard the *ḥadīth* from him. To indicate actual hearing, A would have to say *sami'tu* (i.e., "I heard").

Scholars of *ḥadīth* have generally accepted *'an'anah ḥadīths* so long as it was established that A and B, directly linked in the narration chain with *'an*, fulfill the following conditions:

a. They have met each other, and
b. A, who based his narration on B's narration, is not known for *tadlīs*.[70]

There are two types of *tadlīs*: *tadlīs al-isnād* and *tadlīs al-shuyūkh*.[71]

1. *Tadlīs al-isnād* is exemplified by the following scenario: A narrates a *ḥadīth 'an* B. A and B are contemporaries. They met, but A did not hear the *ḥadīth* directly from B, or A and B never met. Yet A leaves the audience with the impression that he had heard the narration directly from B.
2. *Tadlīs al-shuyūkh* is where the narrator describes other narrators in the chain of *isnād* in ways that aggrandizes them, or refers to them in ways that confuse the audience as to their true identity. For example, a narrator stated that he heard a *ḥadīth* from Muḥammad bin [son of] Sanad. But by using this name, the narrator attributed Muḥammad to his grandfather and not to his father, which is the name by which he is known, thus confusing the audience.

The first form of *tadlīs* is regarded as the more serious and morally repugnant one.

As we might expect, *tadlīs* was highly condemned by scholars.

C. Additional Observations

Sometimes, differences among jurists arose from their varied interpretations of the *ḥadīth* or a related Qur'anic *āyah*. Such differences were, however, acceptable, because jurists held that they were all fallible and only God knew the truth. Al-Shāfi'ī (d. 820) points out that if two individuals engaged in *ijtihād* and reached different conclusions on the same matter, it does not follow that one of them is right. They could both be wrong, despite the fact that each jurist based his reasoning on all the evidence available to him, because that evidence could be partial. That is, however, the extent of what jurists can do, and so their error would be excused.[72]

Differences among scholars were sometimes rooted in their evaluation of the narrators in a chain of *isnād* of the *ḥadīth*. For example, they may reach different conclusions as to the trustworthiness of a narrator or about the time of his narrating. Being spread over a large geographical area, some scholars may be in possession of relevant information not shared by others. For this reason, scholars preferred that any critique of a narrator be coupled by an explanation that allows others to evaluate it. Additionally, the time of the narration was regarded as an important factor in determining such matters as consistency with historical facts or reliability. This became increasingly important as the narrators advanced in age and some became known to have become confused or to have suffered memory loss.

There were also deeper differences that systematically affected Qur'anic interpretations and *ḥadīth* interpretations and classification. These included philosophical and political ones. For example, scholars differed about the nature of the Qur'an (was it created?), the meaning of its *āyahs* (was the meaning limited to the plain meaning of the text and its explanation, or were there deeper hidden meanings?), about human nature (were humans created free or is human action predetermined?), and about constitutionalism (were subsequent Muslim rulers legitimate or were they usurpers of power?).

Additionally, some of the *sunnah* of the Prophet dealt with specific situations relating to his historical era and his community and were applicable within that specific framework. Other parts of the *sunnah* were general and, thus, suitable for all times and places, as with many of the Qur'anic general rules. Obviously, failure to draw this distinction properly tended to result in unnecessary rigidity of interpretation.[73] In practice, it has also resulted in significant differences of opinion.

To summarize, because of all the above considerations, reliance on *sunnah* to support a ruling requires special care and training. It requires knowledge of various matters relating to a *ḥadīth*, such as its degree of authenticity, soundness of its *isnād* and *matn*, knowing the biographies and reputations of its narrators, its modes of transmission, context, and any critiques and interpretations relating to it, as well as familiarity with ancient classical Arabic.

Sometimes, it is useful to reexamine the *isnād* and *matn* of a *ḥadīth* with fresh eyes and compare the conclusions of earlier jurists with each other. It is also helpful to know whether the *ḥadīth* was quoted in the words of the Prophet, or whether the narrator provided what s/he considered to be the meaning of the *ḥadīth*. Furthermore, not all the utterances or actions of the Prophet constituted *sunnah*. Some were the utterances and actions of a mere human, so we need to be clear on which *ḥadīths* are of this last type. After all, the Prophet himself was clear about this distinction and pointed it out on more than one occasion.[74] In situations requiring nonreligious expertise, he readily deferred to experts.

Most, but not all, scholars viewed all *ḥadīths* in *Ṣaḥīḥ al-Bukhārī* that are also narrated in *Ṣaḥīḥ Muslim*, two major collections of *ḥadīth*, as belonging to the highest rank of the *ṣaḥīḥ* category. So does *Muwaṭṭa' Mālik*, another famous work. Those that only occurred in *Ṣaḥīḥ al-Bukhārī* held a lower rank, but were still viewed as more reliable than those *ḥadīths* in *Ṣaḥīḥ Muslim*. Other collections of *ḥadīth* were ranked below them.[75]

D. IMPORTANCE OF *SUNNAH*

The *Sunnah* is quite important as a source of religion, second only to the Qur'an. Indeed, it complements and sheds light on it. The *Sunnah* is also very important for what it reveals about the Prophet as a person, and as a role model for all Muslims. For example, the Prophet offered a modern example of gender relations in his own household. His first wife, Khadījah, was initially his employer. Admiring his moral qualities, she proposed to him in marriage. She was many years his senior, but he accepted the offer and they lived happily until her death years later.[76] Despite this example, many Muslims still find the idea of a woman engaging in business and that of a young man marrying an older woman objectionable. This attitude, which is based on patriarchal custom, is contrary to the *sunnah* of the Prophet. The Prophet's personal behavior in the home has also been ignored. According to reliable biographers, the Prophet did household chores: He cut meat, played with the children, sewed his shoes, and never asked another person to wait on him.[77] The Prophet also had numerous female *ṣaḥābīs* who attended his meetings. We know that because they also asked the Prophet for additional special meetings where they could address their own concerns. These and many other examples have been pushed to the background of the consciousness of Muslim societies, leaving in the fore narrated *ḥadīths* and examples that were more suited to the jurists' social and cultural assumptions.

This problem does not exist in the area of gender relations only. It was in fact more prevalent in constitutional matters. The Prophet himself was the elected head of the city-state of Madinah, the first Muslim state. He acquired this position through *bay'ah* (a form of election) and conducted his affairs through *shūrā* (consultation).[78] Thus, he set the perfect example for those who followed on how to understand and practice these two concepts. Unfortunately, very few Muslim leaders followed these principles in their practice. This historic failure in following the example of the Prophet, despite claims to the contrary, shows the hold culture has over minds and the difficulty of embracing one's faith fully when it conflicts with custom. One result of this tension has been self-serving interpretations of both Qur'anic text and *ḥadīth* to gloss over that conflict.

NOTES

1. Good sources in the English language for an introductory but substantive overview of Islam include the following: Seyyed Hossein Nasr, *Islam: Religion, History, and Civilization* (2003); Nasr, *The Heart of Islam: Enduring Values for Humanity* (2002); Fazlur Rahman, *Islam*, 2nd ed. (1979).

2. See, e.g., Abū 'Abdillāh al-Qurṭubī (d. 1272), *Al-Jāmi' li Aḥkām al-Qur'ān* [Compilation of Qur'anic Rulings] (repr., Beirut: Dār Iḥyā' al-Turāth al-'Arabī, 1985), vol. 1, 39, who wrote in some detail about the Prophet and the Qur'an in this famous authoritative work. See also Muḥammad al-A'ẓamī, *Dirāsāt fi'l Ḥadīth al-Nabawī* [Studies in the Prophetic *Ḥadīth*] (Riyadh: Al-Maktab al-Islāmī, 1992), vol. 1, 48–50 (describing the efforts of the Prophet to teach Muslims himself, as well as sending others to teach those further away).

3. The pre-Islamic *Jāhiliyyah* culture of the Arabian Peninsula was known for its love of poetry. Poetry was memorized because very few individuals were literate. For more on literacy in pre-Islamic times, see A'ẓamī, *Dirāsāt*, vol. 1, 43–44, 47 (mentioning that there were only 17 literate men in the Quraysh tribe when Islam was revealed, and that there was a number of women in the Makkan Muslim society who could read and write).

4. Al-Qurṭubī, *Al-Jāmi'*, vol. 1, 60.

5. Abū al-Ḥasan al-Wāḥidī al-Nīsābūrī, *Asbāb al-Nuzūl* [Occasions of the Revelation] (Damascus: Dār Ibn Kathīr, 1988), 7.

6. Ibid., 31–33; see also al-Qurṭubī, *Al-Jāmi'*, vol. 2, 79–80, quoting the *ḥadīth* scholar al-Tirmidhī and noting that there is some disagreement about the explanation of *sabab al-nuzūl* for this *āyah*.

7. Muḥammad Fakhr al-Dīn al-Rāzī (d. 1209), *Tafsīr al-Fakhr al-Rāzī* [The Exegesis of al-Rāzī] (better known as the Grand Exegesis) (Beirut: Dār al-Fikr, 1981), vol. 26, 107–8 (describing this principle as "an established principle" in the foundations of jurisprudence); see also on this point Bassām al-Jamal, *Asbāb al-Nuzūl* [Reasons for the Revelations] (Casablanca: Al Markaz al-Thaqāfī al-'Arabī, 2005), 354–60. For a commentary on this rule and its importance for understanding the

application of *āyahs* in modern times, see 'Abd al-Ḥamīd Mutawallī, *Al-Islām wa Mabādi' al-Ḥukm fi'l Māriksiyyah wa'l Dīmuqrāṭiyyah al-Gharbiyyah*, [Islam and the Principles of Governance in Marxism and Western Democracy] (Alexandria: Al-Ma'ārif, 1990), 42–48.

8. This was evident from a comment by 'Umar, who was from Quraysh, a Makkan tribe. He said, "We the men of Quraysh used to 'possess' our women; and then we came to Madinah and found its women 'possessing' their men." By "possess" he meant "to be in charge of" or "to have control over." Al-Rāzī, *Al-Tafsīr*, vol. 10, 93.

9. See, e.g., the definition provided in the ancient lexicon *Lisān al-'Arab* [The Tongue of Arabs] by Muḥammad Ibn Manẓūr (repr., Beirut: Dār Iḥyā' al-Turāth al-'Arabī, 1992), vol. 1, 231–33. While noting that the word *nās* commonly has a masculine gender, Ibn Manẓūr does not attribute to it a masculine meaning. He also notes that the word *insān* from which it is derived has a masculine gender and includes women.

10. Here is the famous incident about Umm Salamah. The Prophet executed a peace treaty with the Makkan tribes on terms that made the Muslims who came with him unhappy. They wanted to perform pilgrimage in Makkah that year, and the treaty did not permit them to do so. The Prophet told Umm Salamah about the situation, and she advised him on what to do. He followed her advice and a serious crisis was averted. 'Abd al-Ḥalīm Abū Shuqqah, *Taḥrīr al-Mar'ah fī 'Aṣr al-Risālah* [The Liberation of Women in the Age of Message]. (Cairo: Dār al-Qalam li'l Nashr wa'l Tawzī', 2002), vol 3, p. 231.

11. This story is narrated by Ibn al-Ḥajjāj Muslim al-Nīsābūrī (d. 874) in *Ṣaḥīḥ Muslim* [The Authentic *Ḥadīths* [as compiled by] Muslim], in Muḥyī al-Dīn Abū Zakariyyā al-Nawawī's *Ṣaḥīḥ Muslim bi Sharḥ al-Nawawī* [The Authentic *Ḥadīths* of (i.e., collected by) Muslim, with Explanation by Muḥyī al-Dīn al-Nawawī] (repr., Beirut: Dār Iḥyā' al-Turāth al-'Arabī, n.d.), vol. 15, 56–57; see also 'Abd al-Ḥalīm Abū Shuqqah, *Taḥrīr al-Mar'ah fī 'Aṣr al-Risālah* [The Liberation of Women in the Age of the Message] (Cairo: Dār al-Qalam li'l Nashr wa'l Tawzī', 2002), vol. 2, 429.

12. Al-Nawawī, *Ṣaḥīḥ Muslim bi Sharḥ al-Nawawī*, vol. 15, 58.

13. Ibn Manẓūr, *Lisān al-'Arab*, vol. 5, 157.

14. Qur'an 4:1, 7:189, 49:13. I am using throughout this book the 'Abdullāh Yūsuf 'Alī translation of the Qur'an entitled *The Qur'an: Text, Translation and Commentary*, 4th ed. (1983) (henceforth *Qur'an Translation*). I have revised the translations of select passages for greater accuracy and modernization of the language.

15. Aḥmad Ibn Ḥanbal, *Musnad Aḥmad* [The Supported (*Ḥadīths* collected by) Aḥmad], in *Al-Fatḥ al-Rabbānī*, ed. Aḥmad al-Banna (Cairo: Dār al-Shihāb, n.d.), vol. 19, 228.

16. See note 14 (we were all created from the same *nafs* and were made into male and female and nations and tribes to enjoy each other's company, but the closest to God is the most righteous); Qur'an 30:22 (mentions differences in "tongues and color" as part of God's diversity miracles).

17. For an excellent discussion on this point, see Muhammad Hashim Kamali, chapter on *'Urf* [Custom], in *Principles of Islamic Jurisprudence* (Cambridge, UK: Islamic Texts Society: 2003); Ruqayyah Ṭaha Jābir al-'Alwānī, *Athar al-'Urf fī Fahm al-Nuṣūṣ* [The Effects of Custom in Understanding Text of Rulings] (Damascus: Dār al-Fikr, 2003); see also Subḥī Maḥmaṣānī, *Al-Awḍā' al-Tashrī'iyyah fi'l Duwal al-'Arabiyyah* [Legal Systems in the Arab World], 3rd ed. (Beirut: Dār al-'Ilm li'l Malāyīn, 1965), 438–39, 478–80.

18. See, e.g., Kamali, *Principles*, 19–20; Maḥmaṣānī, *Al-Awḍā'*, 92; Mutawallī, *Al-Islām wa Mabādi'*, 71–75; Muḥammad al-Ghazālī, *Kayfa Nata'āmal ma' al-Qur'ān.* [How Do We Deal with the Qur'an] (Herndon, VA: International Institute of Islamic Thought, 1991), 142–47.

19. Qur'an 2:163 (about the unicity of God), 81:8–9 (about female infanticide).

20. Qur'an 2:219, 4:43, 5:90.

21. See discussion in chapter 4.

22. Qur'an 88:21–22.

23. See, e.g., Qur'an 4:1, 6:98, 7:189.

24. Abū Dāwūd Sulaymān al-Sijistānī (ninth century), *Sunan* [Sunnahs] (repr., Beirut: Dār al-Jīl, 1988), vol. 1, 60, *ḥadīth* no. 236; see also Abū 'Īsā Muḥammad al-Tirmidhī (ninth century), *Sunan* [Sunnahs] (repr., Beirut: Dār al-Kutub al-'Ilmiyyah, 2000), vol. 1, 90, *ḥadīth* no. 113.

25. See Muḥammad al-Ṣallābī, *Sīrat Amīr al-Mu'minīn 'Umar Ibn al-Khaṭṭāb* [Biography of the Commander of the Faithful: 'Umar Ibn al-Khaṭṭāb] (Beirut: Dār al-Ma'rifah, 2004), 337; also quoted in Muḥammad al-Ghazālī, *Kayfa Nata'āmal*, 186.

26. See, e.g., Qur'an 7:145, 39:18, 39:55.

27. Qur'an 5:45.

28. Qur'an 24:22, 64:14. For a discussion of Islamic criminal law and the concept of forgiveness, see my "The Muslim Perspective on the Clergy-Penitent Privilege," *Loyola of Los Angeles Law Review* vol. 29, 1723–32, esp. 1728–29 (1996).

29. Muḥammad al-Bukhārī, *Ṣaḥīḥ al-Bukhārī* [The Authentic Prophetic *Ḥadīths*], in al-'Asqalānī's *Fatḥ al-Bārī: Sharḥ Ṣaḥīḥ al-Bukhārī* [Divine Enlightenment: Explanation of al-Bukhārī's *Ṣaḥīḥ*], collection of authentic prophetic *ḥadīths* by al-Bukhārī, with commentary by al-'Asqalānī (repr., Beirut: Dār al-Kutub al-'Ilmiyyah, 1989), vol. 10, 537, *ḥadīth* no. 6013.

30. See note 17.

31. See, e.g., Muḥammad Rashīd Riḍā, *Al-Khilāfah* [The Caliphate] (repr., Cairo: Al-Zahrā', 1988), 43–46; 'Abd al-Razzāq al-Sanhūrī, *Fiqh al-Khilāfah wa Taṭawwuruhā* [Jurisprudence of the Caliphate and Its development] (Cairo: Al-Hay'ah al-'Āmmah al-Miṣriyyah li'l Kitāb, 1989), 262–63 (arguing that under some circumstances Muslims may obey a Khalīfah deficient in qualifications in order to avoid chaos).

32. See, e.g., Riḍā, *Al-Khilāfah*, 140–41; Munīr Ḥāmid al-Bayātī, *Al-Niẓām al-Siyāsī al-Islāmī* [The Islamic Political System] (Amman, Jordan: Dār al-Bashīr, 1994), 260–61; Maḥmūd al-Khālidī, *Ma'ālim al-Khilāfah fi'l Fikr al-Siyāsī al-Islāmī* [Features of the Caliphate in Islamic Political Thought] (Beirut: Dār al-Jīl, 1984), 307–8.

33. Literally, the word means a way, path, or system (*manhaj*). Hence, it is proper to refer, for example, to Jewish and Christian *sharī'ah*.

34. For more on this subject, see Mutawallī, *Al-Islām wa Mabādi'*, 12–13; 'Abd al-Ghanī 'Abd al-Khāliq, *Hujjiyyat al-Sunnah* [Proof-Value of the *Sunnah*] (Beirut: Dār al-Qur'ān al-Karīm, 1986), 96ff.; Muḥammad al-Mir'ashlī, *Ikhtilāf al-Ijtihād wa Taghayyuruhu wa Athar dhālik fi'l-Futyā* [Differences and Change in *Ijtihād*, and Their Effect

on *Fatwā* Rulings] (Beirut: Al-Mu'assasah al-Jāmi'iyyah li'l Dirāsāt wa'l Nashr wa'l Tawzī', 2003), 74 (mentions disagreement on this matter and provides the view of the majority that the Prophet is subject to human error and correction by the Divine).

35. Abū Ḥāmid al-Ghazālī (d. 1111), *Iḥyā' 'Ulūm al-Dīn* [Reviving Islamic Studies] (repr., Egypt: Muṣṭafā al-Bābī al-Ḥalabī Press, 1939), vol. 1, 34, attributes to the Prophet a *ḥadīth* that states "Difference [of *ijtihād*] within my *ummah* [community] is mercy." See also Maḥmaṣānī, *Al-Awḍā'*, 481; Abū 'Abdillāh Muḥammad bin 'Abd al-Raḥmān Ibn al-Ḥusayn Ṣadr al-Dīn (d. 1378) (henceforth Ṣadr al-Dīn), *Raḥmat al-Ummah fī Ikhtilāf al-A'immah* [Mercy to the *Ummah* Lies in the Disagreement of the Imāms] (repr., Beirut: Mu'assasat al-Risālah, 1994), 7–15.

36. For a discussion of this point, see Maḥmaṣānī, *Al-Awḍā'*, 481; see also Abū Isḥāq al-Shāṭibī, *Al-Muwāfaqāt fī Uṣūl al-Sharī'ah* [Concordances in the Fundamentals of *Sharī'ah*] (repr., Beirut: Dār al-Ma'rifah, n.d.), vol. 4, 132–35 (arguing that individuals should not choose their school of thought based on their personal inclination but rather on the judgment that is most likely to be correct).

37. Al-Bukhārī, *Ṣaḥīḥ*, vol. 10, 643, *ḥadīth* no. 6125; Abū Zakariyyā al-Nawawī, *Riyāḍ al-Ṣāliḥīn* [Meadows of the Righteous], with commentary by Shu'ayb al-Arnā'ūṭ (repr., Beirut: Mu'assasat al-Risālah, 1992), 303.

38. Kamali, *Principles*, 25 (states that less than 10 percent of the Qur'an relates to law and jurisprudence); Mutawallī, *Al-Islām wa Mabādi'*, 17 (puts the number of verses containing legal rulings at 200 out of 6,000 *āyahs* in the whole Qur'an). Al-Jamal, *Asbāb al-Nuzūl*, 156, quoting al-Rāzī, puts it at fewer than 600 verses. Presumably, the difference arises from their working definitions.

39. Al-Bukhārī, *Ṣaḥīḥ*, vol. 2, 142, *ḥadīth* no. 631.

40. Muḥammad Abū Zahrah, *Uṣūl al-Fiqh* [Foundations of Jurisprudence] (Cairo: Dār al-Fikr al-'Arabī, n.d.), 86.

41. See, e.g., Qur'an 4:92 (rules regarding manslaughter), 4:19 (prohibiting inheriting women, like chattel, against their will), 4:11–12 (inheritance rules with respect to spouses and children).

42. See, e.g., Qur'an 2:229 (on limit on number of divorces for the same couple), 2:233 (on the obligations of the father and rights of the mother with respect to their children), 4:7 (decreeing that women must have a share in the inheritance). As to the complexity of these laws, see Imām Muḥammad Abū Zahrah, *Aḥkām al-Tarikah wa'l Mawārīth* [The Laws of Legacy and inheritance] (repr., Cairo: Dār al-Fikr al-'Arabī, 1987), 3, noting that this topic constitutes one-third to one half of all religious knowledge, and devoting his book to present the rules in a simplified and accessible form.

43. Qur'an 42:38, 3:159. For more on this concept see my "Islamic Constitutionalism and the Concept of Democracy," *Case Western Reserve Journal of International Law* vol. 24, no. 1, 21–24 (1992).

44. Chapter 55 of the Qur'an recounts all the miraculous aspects of God's creation in nature and the universe. See also, e.g., Qur'an 12:105, 16:11, and 17:12, where the word *āyah* is used to mean "miraculous sign." In 16:11, we are told that God sends *āyahs* to thoughtful people.

45. Al-Bukhārī, *Ṣaḥīḥ*, vol. 10, 537, *ḥadīth* no. 6008.

46. Al-Qurṭubī, *Al-Jāmi'*, vol. 1, 39.

47. For example, a woman called Umm Sulaym asked the Prophet a very intimate question about sexuality and ritual cleanliness. Both the Prophet and Umm Sulaym were shy. She prefaced her intimate question to him with the statement: "Oh Prophet of God, God is not embarrassed by Truth." She then proceeded to ask her question and he answered it without hesitation. Al-Nawawī, *Ṣaḥīḥ Muslim bi Sharḥ al-Nawawī*, vol. 3. 223 (*Bāb al-Ḥayḍ*) [section on menstruation]. As a result, it is a general understanding among scholars that one should not be shy in discussing matters of faith.

48. Al-Tirmidhī, *Sunan*, vol. 3, 475, *ḥadīth* no. 2678.

49. Al-Bukhārī, *Ṣaḥīḥ*, vol. 9, 129, *ḥadīth* no. 5063; ibid., 138.

50. Qur'an 53:3–4.

51. For more on divinely inspired *ḥadīth* (*ḥadīth qudsī*), see Muḥammad Jamāl al-Dīn al-Qāsimī, *Qawā'id al-Taḥdīth* [Rules Narrating *Ḥadīth*] (Beirut: Dār al-Nafā'is, 1987), 64–70.

52. 'Abd al-Ghanī 'Abd al-Khāliq, *Hujjiyyat al-Sunnah*, 153–58. For more on the type of *ijtihād* in which the Prophet engaged, see

al-Mir'ashlī, *Ikhtilāf al-Ijtihād* 70–73 (arguing that the Prophet engaged in *ijtihād* and distinguishing different types).

53. Al-Qurṭubī, *Al-Jāmi'*, vol. 5, 168; Abū Ja'far al-Ṭabarī, *Jāmi' al-Bayān fī Tafsīr al-Qur'ān* [Comprehensive Exegesis in Qur'anic Interpretation] (repr., Beirut: Dār al-Ma'rifah, 1978), vol. 5, 37.

54. See, e.g., al-Mir'ashlī, *Ikhtilāf al-Ijtihād*, 73; see also Wahbah al-Zuḥaylī, *Uṣūl al-Fiqh al-Islāmī* [Foundations of Islamic Jurisprudence] (Damascus: Dār al-Fikr, 1986), vol. 2, 1064; Muslim, *Ṣaḥīḥ*, vol. 15, 117.

55. Al-Qāsimī, *Qawā'id*, 278; Ibn Mājah, *Sunan Ibn Mājah* [*Sunnas* of Ibn Mājah], verified by Muḥammad 'Abd al-Bāqī (Reprint, Beirut: Dār al-Kutub al-'Ilmiyyah, n.d.), vol. 2, 825, *ḥadīth* no. 2471 (different wording but same meaning); Abū Dāwūd, *Sunan*, vol. 3, 300, *ḥadīth* nos. 3583, 3585 (repeating in different contexts that the Prophet is human who can make mistakes in matters other than revelation and religion). Al-Bukhārī, *Ṣaḥīḥ*, vol. 12, 419, *ḥadīth* no. 6967 (he can make mistakes in judicial decisions).

56. Al-Qāsimī, *Qawā'id,* 41; Ibn Mājah, *Sunan*, vol. 1, 16, *ḥadīth* no. 42.

57. The Prophet initially prohibited recordation of his statements to avoid confusing them with Qur'anic revelations. It appears, however, that the Prophet permitted recordation of *ḥadīth* toward the end of his life after the difference between the Qur'an and *ḥadīth* became clearer to Muslims. See Akram Ḍiyā' al-'Umarī, *Buḥūth fī Tārīkh al-Sunnah al-Nabawiyyah* [Research in the History of Prophetic *Sunnah*]. 4th print. N.p.: 1984, 6–7; Muḥammad Abū Shahbah, *Difā'un 'an al-Sunnah* [A Defense of the *Sunnah*] (Beirut: Dār al-Jīl, 1991), 6, 19–23.

58. See, e.g., Kamali, "The *Sunnah,*" *Principles*, ch. 3; see also al-Qāsimī, *Qawā'id*, 77ff.; Abū Shahbah, *Difā'un* [A Defense of the *Sunnah*], 13–34; A'ẓamī, *Dirāsāt*, vols. 1 and 2. This book offers a thorough study of the *ḥadīth* and its history.

59. Sa'īd Fāyiz al-Dakhīl, *Mawsū'at Fiqh 'Ā'ishah Umm al-Mu'minīn* [Encyclopedia of the Jurisprudence of 'Ā'ishah, Mother of the Believers] (Beirut: Dār al-Nafā'is, 1989), 608; Ibn Ḥanbal, *al-Musnad,* vol. 17, 198–200.

60. Al-Qāsimī, *Qawā'id,* 229–34.

61. See, e.g., Kamali, *Principles*, 110–11; al-Qāsimī, *Qawā'id*, 111–93; see also Ṣubḥī al-Ṣāliḥ, *'Ulūm al-Ḥadīth* [The Studies of *Ḥadīth*] (Beirut: Dār al-'Ilm li'l Malāyīn, 12th print, 1959), 141 (divides *ḥadīth* into two categories: *Maqbūl* [acceptable] and *Mardūd* [rejected]; the first refers to *ṣaḥīḥ ḥadīth*, the second to *ḍa'īf ḥadīth*).

62. See, e.g., Kamali, *Principles*, 110–11; al-Qāsimī, *Qawā'id*, 11–13 (noting also that a *ḍa'īf ḥadīth* may become acceptable under certain conditions).

63. Al-Qāsimī, *Qawā'id*, 109.

64. Ibid., 105.

65. Al-Qāsimī, *Qawā'id*, 81–82; see also Ṣubḥī al-Ṣāliḥ, *'Ulūm al-Ḥadīth*, 196 (carefully defining *shudhūdh*).

66. Al-Qāsimī, *Qawā'id*, 105; see also al-Ṣāliḥ, *'Ulūm al-Ḥadīth*, 156.

67. Al-Qāsimī, *Qawā'id*, 105; see also al-Ṣāliḥ, *'Ulūm al-Ḥadīth*, 156.

68. Ibid., 105.

69. Ibid., 109–10.

70. Ibn al-Ṣalāḥ, *'Ulūm al-Taḥdīth* [Studies of Narration of *Ḥadīth*] (Damascus: Dār al-Fikr, 1986), 61.

71. Ṣubḥī al-Ṣāliḥ, *'Ulūm al-Ḥadīth* 171.

72. Muḥammad Ibn Idrīs al-Shāfi'ī, *Al-Umm* [The Mother] (repr., n.p.: Dār al-Wafā', n.d.), vol. 1, 228.

73. Mutawallī, *Al-Islām wa Mabādi'*, 33–37. For examples of flexibility of interpretation, see notes 73–76 and section III later in the text.

74. See note 50.

75. Al-Qāsimī, *Qawā'id*, 84, 249. Note that this classification applies to *Sunni* scholars. *Shī'ī* scholars have more stringent requirements, and hence different classifications.

76. 'Umar Kahālah, *A'lām al-Nisā'* (Beirut: Mu'assasat al-Risālah, 1977), 326–31.

77. Al-Ghazālī, *Iḥyā'*, vol. 2, 354; see also Abū al-Ḥasan al-Nadawī, *Al-Sīrah al-Nabawiyyah* [The Prophetic Biography] (Jeddah: Dār al-Shurūq, 1977), 370; Al-'Umarī, *Buḥūth fī Tārīkh*, vol. 2, 644–45.

78. Qur'an 60:12, 48:10 (mentioning *bay'ahs* of Muslim men and women); Ibn Hishām (ninth century), *al-Sīrah al-Nabawiyyah* [The Biography of the Prophet] (repr. Beirut: Dār al-Fikr, n.d.), vol. 2, 441–42, 431, 434.

3

Basics of Islamic Law and Jurisprudence: *Ijtihād*

I. Introduction

The word *ijtihād* is derived from the triliteral root j.h.d., from which the following triliteral nouns are derived: *juhd*, which means "effort," and *jahd*, which means "discomfort" or "hardship."[1] The noun *ijtihād* is not unrelated to these two meanings. It means to exert effort or endure hardship in pursuit of a goal or matter. In the context of jurisprudence, it is defined as "exertion of effort by a jurist to reach a ruling." Under this definition, according to a prophetic *ḥadīth*, Solomon engaged in *ijtihād* when he decreed that a contested child should be split in half between two claimant mothers, thus setting the stage for discovering the real mother.[2] Another famous *ḥadīth* by the Prophet says that if a *ḥākim* [judge/jurist] engages in *ijtihād* and reaches the right ruling, he receives two rewards from God, but if he reaches the wrong ruling, he will still receive one reward.[3] The reason for the single reward in the latter case is presumably his *juhd*, exerted to reach the right conclusion.

Ijtihād is an important and fundamental source of Islamic law and jurisprudence, which ranks below the Qur'an and *sunnah* in its authoritativeness. It is a product of human reason and judgment that relies on them as its foundation. *Ijtihād* is necessary because it addresses, among other things, issues arising in our modern times. Among these are in vitro fertilization, surrogate motherhood, euthanasia, how to pray while flying, how to fast in countries with very long or short days, and whether modern-day interest is *ribā* (usury).

However, *ijtihād* is also necessary in interpreting the Qur'an and *ḥadīth* themselves. For example, even where the Qur'anic ruling was detailed, sometimes questions arose as to the meaning of a word in it. For example, jurists disagreed about the meaning of the word *qurū'* in verse 2:228. The verse specifies the length of the waiting period (called *'iddah*) required of a divorced woman before she can religiously marry another man. The period is measured by *qurū'*, a word which has multiple meanings in Arabic, referring to menstruation. Different meanings yield different waiting periods. Jurists exerted *ijtihād* to select and defend what they considered the proper meaning.

Ijtihād becomes even more necessary with respect to Qur'anic verses that state general rules. For example, the Qur'an mentions *bay'ah* (a form of voting in which allegiance is pledged to a candidate) and *shūrā* (consultation by decision makers) as requirements for legitimate government in Islam. The *sunnah* of the Prophet, through the example of the State of Madinah, further clarified these concepts. But today, the development of Western constitutional models and the continued advancement of modern technologies serving the election process have impacted these concepts in various ways. For example, with new technologies, it is now possible for millions of Muslims to participate instantaneously and meaningfully in a *bay'ah*. This state of affairs has not been quite possible since perhaps the days of the small society of Madinah. What is needed today are modern jurists who are ready to develop the concepts of *bay'ah* and *shūrā* in accordance with our times.

Other Qur'anic passages depended in their meaning on understanding the correct grammatical structure. The most obvious example is verse 35:28, which we discussed earlier. Those not sufficiently familiar with Arabic language and grammar could read the verse as stating that God fears scholars. Read properly, it states that of God's servants, those who truly fear him are the scholars. This is exactly the opposite but correct meaning. *Ijtihād* becomes necessary when grammatical issues are less obvious and more complicated than those in the above example.

Additionally, the Qur'an was silent in many areas. This was part of God's design not to regulate every part of Muslims' lives. A great deal of room was left for adopting different actions or policies in these areas, based on personal or cultural needs and desires, so long as these do not contradict basic Islamic principles. Jurists called these areas *'afw* (forgiving), insofar as they provided Muslims with a great deal of flexibility. Acts in these areas were neither prohibited nor enjoined. They fell into the broad spectrum of permissible acts that a person could engage in or ignore.[4] Jurists point out that, in Islam, nothing is forbidden unless it is expressly forbidden by the Qur'an and the Prophet, and nothing is enjoined unless it is expressly enjoined by the Qur'an and the Prophet. Everything else is *'afw*. This area of *'afw* was a fertile ground for *ijtihād*.[5]

The Prophet himself legitimated *ijtihād* in his lifetime and encouraged *ṣaḥābīs* to engage in it to indicate his approval.[6] On one occasion, the Prophet instructed travelling *ṣaḥābīs* to perform the afternoon prayer (*'aṣr*) with him when they rejoined him. (Note that prayers in Islam are mandated at specific intervals during the day. They cannot be performed before the related intervals and performing them afterwards makes them tardy.) The *ṣaḥābīs* were delayed in their travel, and were faced by a dilemma: Do they perform *'aṣr* prayer during the mandated interval but before reaching the Prophet, or do they postpone the prayer and perform it late with the Prophet? They split in their *ijtihād* on this matter. Some prayed *'aṣr* on time, while others waited to join the Prophet. When the two groups joined the Prophet, they asked him to tell them who was right. The Prophet's answer was, "you were both right."[7] The reason for this result is that both groups used their best judgment to reach their conclusions. This incident contributed to the climate of tolerance, friendship, and respect among jurists who understood that more than one *ijtihād* could be right, and all *ijtihāds* could be wrong, because in the end they were dealing with human, not divine, reason, regardless of all their efforts.

Early jurists viewed disagreements among them as a sign of God's mercy,[8] because these disagreements injected Islamic laws with the degree of flexibility necessary for a religion which proclaimed itself suitable for all times, all people, and all societies.[9] This view was articulated in the *ḥadīth*: "Difference among scholars is mercy to the community."[10] As one may expect, scholars from different societies, and even from the same society, disagreed in their *ijtihād*. No doubt that some of them were wrong at times. But so long as the *ijtihād* was based on (linguistic, historical, and religious) knowledge and was conducted piously and in good faith, it was taken seriously by other scholars.[11] Furthermore, individual Muslims who were not *mujtahids* (those who engage in *ijtihād*) were free to select the school of jurisprudence they found most convincing and follow its guidance.[12] Islam guaranteed for each individual the freedom of choice in such matters because ultimately, each Muslim will have to account personally to God for that individual's own choices.

Not only did *ijtihād* differ among scholars but, in some cases, the *ijtihād* of a single jurist changed over time and in different *milieus*. As stated earlier, the famous Imām al-Shāfi'ī provides a prime example of this fact. He established his first school of thought in Iraq. However, when he moved to Egypt he discovered that it was not suitable to the Egyptian culture. As a result, al-Shāfi'ī developed his second school of thought, which took his Egyptian experience into account.[13] It may seem strange that Islamic rules can change not only in terms of interpretation, but also in terms of application to context. To understand this important point, we need to understand a basic concept of Islamic jurisprudence, namely *maqāṣid al-sharī'ah* (The objectives of *sharī'ah*), which states that God, the Lawmaker, promulgated all laws for the *maṣlaḥah* (best interest) of the *'ibād* (the people). This law and related jurisprudence will be further discussed later in this chapter.

II. SCHOOLS OF *IJTIHĀD*

A VARIETY OF SCHOOLS OF *IJTIHĀD* DEVELOPED, EACH BEST SUITED to its own community and that community's culture, with its attendant customs and traditions.[14] What distinguished these schools was not only their proliferation, but also the "etiquette of disagreement" that developed among them.[15] Jurists respected their own diversity and avoided claiming the absolute truth of their own views, because they understood that only God has absolute knowledge and therefore does not err. As a result, scholars often ended their discussions with the phrase *wallāhu a'lam* (God knows best). This modesty and "etiquette of disagreement" did not discourage serious discussions among the scholars. The discussions were lively, but civil.

The fact that, in stating their opinions, Muslim scholars were not dogmatic left the final decision to the Muslim individual. A Muslim may rely on the *ijtihād* of a jurist, or may discuss the matter at length with other Muslims, but in the final analysis, a Muslim has to take personal responsibility for her or his own actions. It is for this reason that Islam has no clergy mediating the relationship between God and humans. Islam has only *mujtahids* and jurists. Furthermore, the field of *ijtihād*, which is based on serious scholarship, is open to all qualified Muslims.[16]

For a number of reasons, very few major schools of thought remain viable today. These include the four *Sunnī* schools of thought—*Ḥanafī*, *Mālikī*, *Shāfi'ī*, *Ḥanbalī*—and the *Shī'ī Ja'farī* School. Almost all Muslim countries have formally adopted the *ijtihād* of one of these schools as the primary basis of their family law. Syria, Egypt, and Jordan have adopted the *Ḥanafī* School of jurisprudence, while Morocco, Algeria, and Kuwait have adopted the *Mālikī* School. Saudi Arabia follows the *Ḥanbalī* School of jurisprudence, while Iran is *Ja'farī*. Among the *Sunnī* schools, the *Ḥanafī* School is a leading proponent of reliance on *ra'y* (opinion), while the others favor in various degrees reliance on the tradition of *ḥadīth*.[17] *Ḥanbalī* and *Shāfi'ī* schools of thought tend to be stricter than the other two *Sunnī* schools.

In their formulation of family law, many Muslim countries resorted to the doctrine of *takhayyur* (selection). This doctrine permits them to supersede some rulings of the school of thought they espouse by replacing them with more suitable ones from another Islamic school of thought. An example of the application of this doctrine occurred recently in Morocco when the state dropped the *Mālikī* provision that permitted the father to compel his underage daughter into marriage.[18] The *Ḥanafī* School gives the Muslim woman the greatest scope of rights in this area, a topic which will be discussed in a later work.

The fact that Muslim countries today have permitted themselves to adopt officially one school of thought as the governing school in their jurisdiction represents a serious departure from early Islamic practice and an infringement on the religious freedom of Muslims. It is the culmination of two trends in Islamic history: the rise of authoritarianism after the death of the Prophet and the four Rightly Guided *Khalīfahs* and the impact of Westernization on modern Islamic countries. The rise of authoritarianism was accomplished successfully with the end of *al-Khilāfah al-Rāshidah* (the Rightly Guided Caliphate). It was replaced through the use of force by the Umayyad dynasty, which retained the name of *Khilāfah,* but subverted Qur'anic democratic processes developed for choosing the *Khalīfah.* The newly revised processes insured dynastic succession.

The rise of the Umayyad dynasty ushered a period of illegitimate governance in the Muslim world, which has continued to this day. Its repercussions have affected, among other things, the very jurisprudence that will be discussed in this book. Authoritarian governments were dissatisfied with the freedom of *ijtihād* practiced by scholars. For obvious reasons, these authorities preferred that *ijtihād* serve their own narrow political interests, especially on such critical issues as Islamic constitutionalism. Consequently, they made the life of dissident *mujtahids*—and there were many—difficult. Many famous *mujtahids,* such as Imām Mālik Ibn Anas (d. 795), Imām al-Shāfi'ī, Imām Ibn Ḥanbal (d. 855), and Imām Abū Ḥanīfah (d. 767), suffered indignities and mistreatment at the hands of rulers for exercising their right of free thought and speech.[19] Given this political atmosphere and the fact that women had been gradually removed from public and jurisprudential life, women were in no position in those days to wage a successful fight for their rights or to make their *ijtihād* heard.

III. Qualifications of the *Mujtahid*

While jurists agreed about the basic qualifications required in a *mujtahid,* they disagreed on supplementary ones. In category (a) and (b) below are summaries of basic qualifications, both general and specific, required in a jurist. Category (c) is a collection of various juristic views on desirable supplemental requirements. As we move down these categories, we discover that qualifying as a jurist becomes increasingly difficult—almost impossible.

A. General Basic Prerequisites

i. A *mujtahid* must be a Muslim who believes in God, His angels, His Books,[20] His Prophets, the Day of Judgment, and that which is predestined by God, whether it is good or bad.[21]
ii. Rationality and maturity.[22]

Maleness is not a requirement because 'Ā'ishah, the wife of the Prophet, engaged in *ijtihād*. So, the right of women to *ijtihād* was preserved early on.

B. Specific Basic Prerequisites

This category requires knowledge of the following areas:

i. The Qur'an and related studies
ii. The *sunnah* and related studies
iii. Matters on which Muslims have reached consensus
iv. The Arabic language, its grammar, syntax, and rhetoric
v. Reasoning by analogy, which requires knowledge of the *ratio* (rationale, *raison d'être*) of a ruling[23]

C. SUPPLEMENTARY PREREQUISITES

A *mujtahid* must have knowledge of the following:

i. That the basic principle in *sharīʿah* is that a person's *dhimmah* (the legal and ethical personality) is *ab initio* unencumbered with duties so that nothing is a duty unless proof from *sharīʿah* is produced, and nothing is prohibited without such proof as well;
ii. Objective of *sharīʿah* in the ruling under consideration, including knowledge of its overarching goal of protecting the *maṣlaḥah* of the people (public interest);
iii. Basic juristic principles (some of which will be discussed below), and the fundamentals of jurisprudence;
iv. Areas of disagreement among jurists;
v. Customs;
vi. Logic.

The jurist must also exhibit justice and fairness.

The following characteristics are also required (desirable) in a jurist:

i. Good moral behavior;
ii. Chastity and piety;
iii. Asking God for guidance;
iv. Confidence and testimony by others that the person is qualified;
v. Correspondence between actions and words;
vi. Thoughtfulness and acute observation.[24]

This last category sums up the various supplementary requirements different jurists demanded in a *mujtahid*. Together, they erect a very high bar that ultimately discouraged people from engaging in *ijtihād*. To the extent that the requirements prevented unqualified people from engaging in *ijtihād*, the effect was desirable. Unfortunately, however, the effect was broader than intended, and had a chilling effect even on those reasonably qualified individuals. So, *ijtihād* suffered and became frozen in its tracks, despite significant changes in the world around it. The result was an intellectual lull. In learning about their religion, average Muslims relied increasingly on established practices in their societies. These had often incorporated outdated cultural influences that were several centuries old. It is important to note, however, that this discussion applies mostly to the *Sunnī* tradition in Islam, espoused by an overwhelming majority of Muslims around the world. The *Shī'ī* tradition, which has a different history, encouraged *ijtihād*. Consequently, *Shī'ī ijtihād* remains active to this day.

As time passed, Muslims suddenly found themselves juristically unprepared for the wave of modernization and technological developments. In particular, Muslim immigrants in the West were faced with an avalanche of new challenges rooted in rapid technological innovations, their obsolete social customs, and historical stereotypes of East-West relationships. At the same time, they were still acting on the basis of centuries-old jurisprudence developed by their forefathers for a different time and place. Frustrated by this situation, some individuals took it upon themselves to update Islamic jurisprudence to address modern times. Many of those who did so in the West were highly unqualified. Some who barely knew Arabic, the language of the Qur'an, produced Qur'anic translations and commentaries. Others went further and delved into jurisprudence. Relying on their "mom and pop" knowledge of the religion or other English-language sources, they introduced a great deal of error and confusion into the scene. This is a shocking violation of academic integrity in any field, let alone a sacred one. But there was a need, and these individuals met it as best as they could.

Jurists in the East tried to help, but they did not necessarily or sufficiently understand the complex reality, whether financial, social, or technological, in the West. For example, to address the issue of *ribā* (usury) in modern times, you need to know more than the Islamic principles governing this matter. You need to know, for example, the characteristics of various financial instruments being invented daily on Wall Street and how they work. You need also to have the logical prowess to understand how these facts (juristic principles and financial information) interact with each other to produce a proper modern ruling. This means that the jurist must also be knowledgeable about modern finance and skilled in logic in order to produce meaningful and helpful jurisprudence on modern financial instruments and banking practices. Unfortunately, there has been a knowledge gap between the jurists and the modernists, which must be bridged before Islamic jurisprudence can be renewed and revitalized.

For these reasons, claims about *ijtihād* and knowledge of jurisprudence should be evaluated very carefully, especially by U.S. courts. For example, today, the word "*imām*" no longer refers to a jurist as it did centuries ago. Now, it usually refers to someone hired by a mosque to lead prayers because he has some basic knowledge of the Qur'an and Islam. Very few American mosques are fortunate enough to have resident jurists. It is important that lawyers and judges be aware of this fact when an "Islamic expert witness" is presented in court.

IV. BASIC JURISTIC PRINCIPLES

THERE ARE IMPORTANT JURISTIC PRINCIPLES THAT WERE formulated over the centuries. Muslim jurists have generally relied on them. Here are some of these principles:

1. No *ijtihād* is acceptable in the presence of a *naṣṣ* (definitive text). The word "text" here refers to sacred text and *ḥadīth*. As mentioned earlier, *ijtihād* is necessary only when there is textual ambiguity, uncertainty, or even silence on a certain matter. But where the text is clear, definitive, and explicit, there is no room for *ijtihād*. So, when the Qur'an states that there is only one God, this principle is not open to *ijtihād*. The principle of God's oneness is clear, definitive, and explicit. Similarly, when the Prophet decrees that daily prayers are five, there is no room for *ijtihād* to change this number. This principle, however, does not end related discussion about, for example, the nature of God or the religious status of additional prayers.
2. A *dhimmah* (the legal and ethical personality of a person) is innocent *ab initio*. The Qur'an states that God forgave Adam for

his sin of disobedience. Consequently, there is no Original Sin in Islam. Based on this view, Islamic law presumes a person's *dhimmah* innocent of all crimes and liabilities until proven guilty. As the Ottoman civil code, named *al-Majallah,* puts it: "Every person's *dhimmah* is born innocent of any wrongdoing. As a result of this principle, whoever makes claims against a person must produce proof."[25]

3. The Law Giver (God) propagated the Law for the *maṣlaḥah* of his creatures (public interest). Therefore, Islamic laws must accord with people's *maṣlaḥah*. When they do not, they must be reexamined, reformulated, and perhaps even suspended.[26] This is what *Khalīfah* 'Umar did in *'Ām al-Ramādah* (the year of famine). He suspended the punishment for theft, although it is specified in the Qur'an. The *maṣlaḥah* protected by the principle of respecting private property became secondary to the *maṣlaḥah* of saving lives.
4. Avoidance of *nizā'* (conflict). Islamic law prohibits transactions whose very nature leaves room for conflict. For this reason, the Qur'an prohibits usurious and other transactions that give rise to a feeling of injustice and oppression, and hence can result in conflict. The ideal of the Muslim community is one of harmony, trust, and peace. This ideal is described in the Qur'an itself as characterizing marital relations, among other things. On the political level, the Qur'an also encourages Muslims to seek peace whenever the other party in conflict leans towards it.[27]
5. It is not permissible to cause harm or to retaliate against harm with harm. This rule has two parts. As to the first part, *al-Majallah* explains that harm is prohibited in Islam because it is a form of injustice. It provides the following examples (among others): It is prohibited to sell (without disclosure) defective merchandise because this act harms the buyer. It is also prohibited to hunt in certain areas if hunting there would scare the population and cause animals to migrate. As to the second part, *al-Majallah* notes that it is impermissible to retaliate against harm with another harm. Instead, the harmed person must resort to the judge for removal of the original harm.[28]

6. Change in Time, Place, and Circumstance. As already stated, a major principle of Islamic jurisprudence is that laws change with the passage of time and change of place or circumstances.[29] The laws subsumed under this principle are not basic Islamic laws, but rather laws that took customs into account in their formulation. Therefore, as times changed, they became inappropriate and perhaps obsolete. The Ottoman *al-Majallah* gives the following example, where the law changed because of a change in custom: For early jurists, it was sufficient for a purchaser of a house to inspect some of its rooms, because in accordance with their custom, all rooms of the house were identical. As this custom changed, and rooms began to have different designs, later jurists required that a purchaser be accorded the opportunity to inspect every room in the house.
7. What is established by custom is to be treated as if it were established by stipulation. In other words, if a term of an agreement is not specified, such as the currency in which wages are to be paid to a worker, wages will be paid in the currency customarily used in that country.[30] A more significant example derives from the marriage contract. Customs are incorporated in it as if they were stipulations. An example of this is housework. Jurists argued a long time ago that Muslim wives are not required to perform housework. Their reasoning for this conclusion is that the marriage contract is not a service contract. However, Muslim women are expected to perform housework because when a marriage contract is silent on this point, local custom supplements it. As a result, housework becomes the duty of the wife. In the United States, where this custom is weakening as a result of the women's movement, it could be argued that such automatic supplementation is no longer justified.

V. PROMINENT METHODS OF *IJTIHĀD*

THROUGHOUT HISTORY, CERTAIN TYPES OF *IJTIHĀD* BECAME prominent. Of these, we shall discuss the following: *ijmā'* (consensus), *qiyās* (reasoning by analogy), and *maqāṣid al-sharīʿah* (reasoning based on determining the purposes of *sharīʿah*). The first two are classical categories that are usually highlighted separately as basic sources of Islamic law. I chose not to do so in this introduction because such approach may distort the fact that they are both simply forms of human *ijtihād*. The first category is different from the other two in that its validity is based on a purely formal requirement. The other two present substantive approaches to *ijtihād*. I shall now briefly introduce these categories.

A. *Ijmāʿ* (Consensus)

As mentioned earlier, the consensus of Muslims (*ijmāʿ*) without more is, in itself, a source of law. This principle is based on the Prophetic statement that "my *ummah* (community of believers) would never agree upon an error."[31] In the view of some prominent jurists, this *ḥadīth* is supported by various Qur'anic verses, none of which are as explicit.

Consensus is usually considered the third ranking source of law in Islam. It is binding and basically asserts the infallibility of the *ummah* collectively, an interpretation not shared by all jurists. In fact, the famous Egyptian scholar, Muḥammad ʿAbduh (d. 1905), rejected this interpretation and did not accept the view that the above-mentioned *ḥadīth* addressed the principle of *ijmāʿ al-ṣaḥābah*.[32]

Surprisingly, despite the clear reference in the *ḥadīth* to the whole *ummah*, jurists tended to define consensus in more restrictive terms. For example, the majority of jurists defined it in terms of agreement within their own ranks. This raised the important question of "Who is a jurist?" or the related question of "Who defines who is a jurist?" These questions, given the cultures in which jurists lived (or live), suggest that minority opinions, reformists, and women scholars may often be overlooked or excluded from the count for consensus by definition. Additionally, there is the problem of silent jurists and how to interpret their silence.[33]

At times *ijmāʿ* is claimed even when it does not really exist. I faced such a situation when I was lecturing at a university in an Arab country a couple of decades ago. I was sharing the podium with a religious scholar who was a member of the faculty there. I was asked by the audience whether a woman had the right to execute her own marriage contract without a *wali* (in this context, understood to mean "guardian"). The questioner had heard me make that statement earlier, and wanted me to repeat it before the scholar so that he could refute it. I repeated my statement, citing the jurisprudence of the great Imām Abū Ḥanīfah on the matter. Abū Ḥanīfah's jurisprudence is followed in vast areas of the Muslim world today. Reasoning from the Qur'an and classical jurisprudence, Abū Ḥanīfah argued that a mature woman can execute her own marriage contract without a *wali*. (We shall examine this argument later.) Women in the audience were shocked by my answer and demanded that the sheikh correct me. The auditorium was silent with anticipation. Then the sheikh spoke. He said, "Scholars have reached *ijmā'* on the need for the woman to have a *wali* when she is getting married, but Abū Ḥanīfah deviated from them." So Abū Ḥanīfah's position was described as "deviating" from the consensus. But what consensus is this when the founder of one of the four major *Sunnī* schools does not join it? The *ijmā'* the sheikh referred to was a *mere* majority view.[34] However, had he said that clearly, there would have been a riot even among the women in the audience. That public had been saturated with the view that indeed there was an *ijmā'* on this matter, and whoever violates it sins.

While most jurists defined *ijmā'* in terms of the consensus of scholars, some prominent scholars defined it alternatively as: (i) the consensus of the *ṣaḥābah*, who sought it in running their affairs, (ii) that of the inhabitants of Madinah during the early period of Islam, since they were closest to the source of the message, or (iii) that of *ahl al-bayt* (Fāṭimah, daughter of the Prophet, her husband 'Alī, and their sons and the *imāms* in their progeny).[35] All these definitions present their own challenges. For example, jurists need to justify the claim that the consensus of the particular class of people selected is the only one that counts. That has not been a simple task.[36]

Further concerns relate to the feasibility of establishing that all jurists have reached consensus on a particular matter. While modern technology can drastically alleviate this concern, it does not remove all difficulties and challenges. For example, some jurists have wondered whether consensus must be explicit, and if not, how would one legitimately define "tacit" consent?[37] Other issues raised relate to the period during which consensus is binding. Some have argued that it binds only those living in the community at that time, others have argued that it binds those that follow them, and yet others have argued that it binds both.[38] Some prominent jurists, such as al-Shawkānī, argued that consensus is not binding, but only helpful in formulating one's own *ijtihād*.[39] Thus, while *ijmā'* is an important concept in Islamic jurisprudence, given the exponential growth of the community, its cultural diversity, and the thorny juristic issues involved in defining and determining *ijmā'*, this concept has become less functional in solving today's problems.

B. *Qiyās* (Reasoning by Analogy)

Under this approach, jurists reason by analogy in order to extend a ruling from one situation to another that is similar to it in some respects, but for which neither a clear *naṣṣ* (definitive text) exists in the Qur'an nor is it addressed by the *ḥadīth*. When resorting to *qiyās*, jurists focus on the *'illah* (cause, *ratio*) of the ruling. For example, the *'illah* in the ruling that a man may not propose to a women while she is engaged to another is, according to some jurists, avoidance of *nizā'*, or conflict, a principle discussed earlier.[40] But is this ruling applicable also to commercial contracts, or are they different precisely because marriage contracts in Islam are not analogized to sales, but rather viewed as part of *'ibādāt* (matters of worship)? Or is this difference irrelevant to the conclusion? I can make cogent arguments for and against the answer. So, how reliable is *qiyās*?

Qiyās, or reasoning by analogy, is not deductive, and in fact the form of an argument based on this reasoning is not logically valid because it is not necessarily true every time.[41] Reasoning by analogy is inductive, based on comparing various characteristics of an element or situation to another and finding them sufficiently similar to extend a conclusion about the first to the second. Depending on whether the jurist considered all the relevant similarities and evaluated all the possibly relevant dissimilarities, the conclusion may be true at times and false at others. This mode of reasoning is not foreign to Western jurists, and judges engage in it, despite its risks, on a daily basis. In fact, this concept is embedded in the very notion of "precedent," for it would not be possible to deem a ruling as precedent for a case unless we can determine that the case at hand sufficiently resembles it from a legal perspective. This is the Achilles heel of reasoning by analogy, yet it appears to be indispensable for conducting our affairs.

The shortcoming of *qiyās* was a serious concern for many Muslim jurists.[42] The possibility of error weighed heavily on them. This is why the Prophet encouraged them to engage in *ijtihād* in his famous statement that the jurist who engages in *ijtihād* and reaches the wrong conclusion would still receive a reward for the effort.[43]

Recognizing the pitfalls surrounding analogical reasoning, the famous jurist al-Ghazālī (1111) rejected it. He regarded such reasoning as one that builds speculation upon speculation, thus raising the concern of multiplying the possibility of error. On the other hand, the famous *Mālikī* jurist Ibn Rushd (Averroes, 1198), espoused the position that one *qiyās* could become the basis for another.[44]

There are many other issues and views surrounding the use or proper application of *qiyās* to a situation. One of them is whether a human can or even may attempt to fathom God's intent in promulgating a rule. This point will be discussed further later. The concern that *qiyās* may lead to unfair or unjust results at times, gave rise to yet another, more controversial mode of *ijtihād* through *istiḥsān*. *Istiḥsān*, which will be discussed later, enabled a jurist to abandon a well-established law in favor of another in order to advance public interest.

C. *MAQĀṢID AL-SHARĪʿAH* (THE INTENT OF *SHARĪʿAH*)

The principle that the Law Giver propagated the Law for the *maṣlaḥah* (interests) of the people plays an important role in Islamic jurisprudence. In fact, it gave rise to a whole approach based on determining *maqāṣid al-sharīʿah* (the intent, goals, or *telos* of *sharīʿah*). This approach is very important insofar as it attempts to understand divine wisdom in rulings and seek their proper application based on that understanding. A corollary of this approach is that if enforcing a rule in a certain situation would result in greater harm than good, it needs to be reviewed and perhaps suspended, as mentioned earlier. So, the theory provides flexibility to alleviate hardship in society at large and serve its interests. An important juristic principle that informs this approach is that of "warding off that which is corrupt and promoting that which is beneficial."[45]

The most prominent figure in this area was the *Mālikī* scholar Imām Abū Isḥāq al-Shāṭibī (d. 1388). He defined *maqāṣid al-sharī'ah* in term of three levels of *maṣlaḥah*:

i. Interests that are Necessities (*Ḍarūriyyāt*): These are defined as religious and worldly interests without which life would not be right. With them, there is safety and happiness; without them, there is corruption, chaos, and loss of life.[46] Necessary interests have been reduced to five, listed in order of importance: preservation of one's faith, self, mind, progeny, and property.[47]

ii. Interests that are Needs (*Ḥājiyyāt*): These are defined as interests that, if not observed, would lead to discomfort and hardship in life, but not to corruption or more extreme consequences. Examples of these matters are found in areas such as: prayers, customs, and practices. In the area of prayer, juristic license (*rukhṣah*) exists to alleviate hardship, as in the case of shortening prayers for travelers. In the area of custom, hardship is also reduced by not prohibiting what God has permitted. For example, a requirement that women cover their faces is a cultural one that imposes hardship on women. It is not required by religion.[48] In the area of practices, hardship could be alleviated in cases involving, for example, unnecessarily onerous commercial practices because they damage the economic interest of the community.[49]

iii. Interests that are Luxuries (*Taḥsīniyyāt*): The word *Taḥsīniyyāt* derives from the word *taḥsīn* and so has "beauti-

> fying purposes."[50] Luxuries include the best of local customs, practices, morality, and etiquette. Examples of practices included in *Taḥsīniyyāt* are humility, modesty, charity, and cleanliness (including ritual cleanliness).[51]

The first level of necessities is the foundation of the other two. *Ḥājiyyāt* are subordinate to *Ḍarūriyyāt* and support it. *Taḥsīniyyāt* are subordinate to and serve the two other levels.[52] Imbalance in the last two levels, if not severe, is not likely to have an adverse effect on the first. But imbalance in the first disrupts the other two.[53]

Jurists devoted a great deal of effort to understand various rules in light of this classification. They relied, among other things, on the example of *Khalīfah* 'Umar, who suspended punishment for theft in a year of famine. However, it is important to note that the famous jurists al-Rāzī (d. 1207) and Ibn Ḥazm (d. 1064) questioned this approach, raising important theological issues. Al-Rāzī was concerned that, in identifying a *maṣlaḥah* in divine law, some may erroneously conclude that God promulgated the law intending that *maṣlaḥah*. But, he notes, it is not our place to pretend to know what God intended, if anything, in these laws.[54] Ibn Ḥazm makes a stronger point, when he argues that humans should not be even asking questions about God's reasons for promulgating a rule.[55] In support of this position, Ibn Ḥazm quotes verse 21:23 in the Qur'an, which states: "He cannot be questioned about what He does . . ."[56] As a result, Ibn Ḥazm rejected *qiyās* (reasoning by analogy) because God the Omnipotent is not bound by any rules, including *qiyās*.[57]

D. *Istiḥṣān* (Literally, "To Prefer Something Because It Seems Good (*Ḥasan*)")

This method of *ijtihād* permits a jurist to abandon the rigid application of rules when fairness and equity become an issue. While *istiḥsān* remains bound by the higher principles of the Qur'an and *sunnah*, it permits setting aside established rulings in the interest of equity or public interest. Precedents from the history of early Islam are cited as supportive of this approach, including that of *Khalīfah* 'Umar setting aside the Qur'anic punishment for theft in the year of famine. Thus, through *istiḥsān,* a judge may discard an applicable ruling, and introduce instead another one, based on the judge's analysis of the equities in the situation. This approach is based not only on the *ḥadīth* cited in the previous section, but also on Qur'anic *āyahs,* such as the one that states, "God wants to facilitate things for you. He does not want to put you in hardship."[58] Of course, this approach goes even beyond *qiyās* in attempting to determine the *'illah* of a ruling and God's intentions. It relies even more heavily on human opinion—for example, in determining what creates hardship and how to facilitate. For this reason, *istiḥsān* is an even more controversial method of *ijtihād* than *qiyās* or the *Maqāṣidī* approach.[59]

E. *Al-Maṣāliḥ al-Mursalah* (Considerations of Public Interest)

Another method of *ijtihād* addresses matters of public interest, whose validity was not addressed either in the Qur'an or *sunnah.* Based on this method, jurists can develop rules that are consonant with broader Islamic principles, such as securing a benefit and warding off harm, in order to advance social welfare. Examples of such rules are those permitting the adoption of daylight saving time, choice of a parliamentary system of government, and implementation of traffic laws. This method affects only the realm of *mu'āmalāt* (practices, course of dealing among people) but not that of *'ibādāt* (matters of worship) because of the momentousness of the issues there combined with the fact that only God knows people's true intent.[60]

VI. Conclusion

This chapter, along with chapter 2, provides a brief introduction about Islamic law, with emphasis on its juristic aspect. The information provided is very important for understanding later chapters. It is based primarily and fundamentally on the Qur'an, which Muslims view as the eternal, unchangeable, and divine word of God. To be a Muslim is to believe in the Qur'an as a whole, and in the Prophet Muhammad and his *sunnah*. The Prophet's *sunnah* (including *ḥadīth*) sheds important light on the Qur'an and provides additional instructions. However, not all of the *ḥadīth* is authentic or reliable because of various historical factors. Authentic *ḥadīths* are binding. Other sources of Islamic law include contributions made by the *ṣaḥābah*; their followers; and jurists, both ancient and modern. Their contributions often incorporated their local customs and perspectives. This chapter provided some of the principles, rules, and theories they espoused. A basic Islamic juristic principle is that laws based on custom change with time and place. So, it is permissible, even encouraged, in Islam to revisit prior *ijtihād* in light of current customs that are consistent with the basic principles of the religion. We shall attempt to do just that in this book.

NOTES

1. Al-Mir'ashlī, *Ikhtilāf al-Ijtihād wa Taghayyuruhu wa Athar dhālik fi'l-Futyā* [Differences and Change in *Ijtihād*, and Their Effect on *Fatwā* Rulings] (Beirut: Al-Mu'assasah al-Jāmi'iyyah li'l Dirāsāt wa'l Nashr wa'l Tawzī', 2003), 57–58. By the way, these two words consist of only three letters in Arabic because the vowels that occur in them are not represented by letters in these instances.

2. Ibid., 71–72.

3. Ibid., 58; Ibn Ḥajar al-'Asqalānī, *Fatḥ al-Bārī: Sharḥ Ṣaḥīḥ al-Bukhārī* [Divine Enlightenment: Explanation of al-Bukhārī's *Ṣaḥīḥ*], collection of authentic prophetic *ḥadīths* by al-Bukhārī, with commentary by al-'Asqalānī (repr., Beirut: Dār al-Kutub al-'Ilmiyyah, 1989), vol. 13, 393–96, *ḥadīth* no. 7352.

4. For a detailed discussion of this subject, see al-Mir'ashlī, *Ikhtilāf al-Ijtihād*, 116–20; Wahbah al-Zuḥaylī, *Uṣūl al-Fiqh al-Islāmī*. [The Foundations of Islamic Jurisprudence] (Damascus: Dār al-Fikr, 1986), vol. 1, 46–93. Also, note that Ibn Ḥanbal, the famous jurist, argued that the fundamental rule in these matters is permissibility, unless there is an injunction by the Qur'an or the *Sunnah* prohibiting it.

On this point, see 'Abd al-Ḥalīm al-Jundī, *Aḥmad bin Ḥanbal: Imām Ahl al-Sunnah* [Aḥmad bin Ḥanbal: Imām of the Sunnis]. Cairo: Dār al-Ma'ārif, n.d.), 264; Subḥī Maḥmaṣānī, *Muqaddimah fī Iḥyā' 'Ulūm al-Sharī'ah* [Introduction to the Revival of *Sharī'ah* Studies]. Beirut: Dār al-'Ilm li'l Malāyīn, 1962), 21.

5. Al-Mir'ashlī, *Ikhtilāf al-Ijtihād*, 116–20; al-Zuḥaylī, *Uṣūl al-Fiqh*, vol. 1, 90–93.

6. Al-Mir'ashlī, *Ikhtilāf al-Ijtihād*, 74–75; al-Zuḥaylī, *Uṣūl al-Fiqh*, vol. 2, 1069.

7. Abū Ja'far al-Ṭabarī, *Tārīkh al-Ṭabarī: Tārīkh al-Umam wa'l Mūlūk* [History of Nations and Kings] (repr., Beirut: Dār al-Kutub al-'Ilmiyyah, 1991), vol. 2, 99; al-Hāfiẓ 'Imād al-Dīn Ismā'īl Ibn Kathīr, *Al-Bidāyah wa'l Nihāyah* [The Beginning and the End] (repr., Beirut: Maktabat al-Ma'ārif, 1979), vol. 4, 116–17.

8. Muḥammad bin 'Abd al-Raḥmān Ṣadr al-Dīn, *Raḥmat al-Ummah fī Ikhtilāf al-A'immah* [Mercy to the Ummah Lies in the Disagreement of the Imāms] (repr., Beirut: Mu'assasat al-Risālah, 1994) (discussing throughout the book differences among various schools of thought on various topics, and including a bibliography on the subject).

9. See, e.g., Subḥī Maḥmaṣānī, *Falsafat al-Tashrī' fi'l Islām* [The Philosophy of Legislation in Islam], 3rd ed. (Beirut: Dār al-'Ilm li'l Malāyīn, 1961), 201; see also 'Alī Ḥaydar, *Durar al-Ḥukkām fī Sharḥ Majallat al-Aḥkām* [Gems of Jurists: Exegesis of the (Ottoman) *Majallah of Rulings*] (Beirut: Dār al-Kutub al-'Ilmiyyah, n.d.), vol. 1, 43. For more on this topic, see section V.C in this chapter.

10. See note 8.

11. See also al-Zuḥaylī, *Uṣūl al-Fiqh*, vol. 2, 1043–51, 1066, 1092–93; see also Subḥī Maḥmaṣānī, *Muqaddimah*, 30 (noting that major *imāms* discouraged others from blindly following their views and emphasized the fact that the *imāms* were human and thus capable of error); see also subsequent discussion in this section.

12. Maḥmaṣānī, *Muqaddimah*, 30 (noting that jurists discouraged others from following an *ijtihād* without knowing the reasons); ; see also al-Zuḥaylī, *Uṣūl al-Fiqh*, vol. 2, 1137–38 (noting that the majority of jurists hold that the average person is not obligated to commit to a single school of thought and she may freely change it at any time). This

state of affairs changed after some Muslim states decided to adopt the *ijtihād* of one major school of thought and codify it in its laws. The most notable state that adopted this approach was the Ottoman Empire at its later stages. It adopted the *Ḥanafī* school of thought and codified it in its family law. Many countries, such as Egypt, Lebanon, and Syria, were influenced by this choice in formulating their laws. As a result, whole countries followed a single *ijtihād*, reducing/eliminating the individual's ability to choose her own school of thought. A great example of the freedom of Muslims to choose their own *ijtihād* is the story of Imām Mālik with *al-Khalīfah* al-Manṣūr, who wanted to adopt the *Mālikī* jurisprudence for the Abbassid caliphate. Imām Mālik refused because he did not want to be responsible for the *ijtihād* choices of others. This incident is mentioned in Maḥmaṣānī, *Muqaddimah*, 30.

13. Maḥmaṣānī, *Muqaddimah*, 67 (recounting the story of Imām al-Shāfi'ī who modified his school of thought, developed in Iraq, when he moved to Egypt); see also 'Abd al-Ḥalīm al-Jundī, *Al-Imām al-Shāfi'ī* (repr., Cairo: Dār al-Ma'ārif, n.d., 193–94 (recounting same story).

14. Maḥmaṣānī, *Muqaddimah*, 67–69; see also Abū Ḥāmid al-Ghazālī, *Iḥyā' 'Ulūm al-Dīn*, vol. 1, 33 (discussing the tolerant nature of early *mujtahids* toward disagreements among them).

15. Maḥmaṣānī, *Muqaddimah*, 66–67; Taha Jabir al-Alwani. *Adab al-Ikhtilāf fi'l Islām* [The Etiquette of Disagreement in Islam] (Herndon, VA: International Institute of Islamic Thought, 1987), 47–84.

16. The reader may believe that *imāms* in Islam correspond to clergy in Christianity. This is not the case. In the traditional sense, they are simply learned people whose views Muslims may choose to adopt. In the United States, the term "*imām*" usually refers to someone hired by a mosque to lead prayers and provide some advice to the worshippers. It does not signal a high level of scholarship. For more on *ijtihād* and who may engage in it, see subsequent discussion. See also, e.g., Maḥmaṣānī, *Muqaddimah*, 28–29; ' Abd al-Razzāq al-Sanhūrī, *Fiqh al-Khilāfah wa Taṭawwuruhā* [Jurisprudence of *Khilāfah* and Its Development] ([Cairo]: al-Hay'ah al-Miṣriyyah al-'āmmah li'l kitāb, 1989), 191–92. See last paragraph of section III.C.

17. Al-Alwani, *Adab*, 89; see al-Mir'ashlī, *Ikhtilāf al-Ijtihād*, 88–91.

18. See *al-Mudawwanah*, the family law code of Morocco. Aḥmad al-Khamlīshī, *Al-Ta'līq 'alā Qānūn al-Aḥwāl al-Shakhṣiyyah*, [Commentary

on the Personal Status Code] (Rabat: Maktabat al-Ma'ārif, 1984), 64 (the *Mudawwanah* eliminated *wilāyat al-ijbār* [the right of the *wali*/father to compel the underage ward/daughter into marriage]).

19. Aḥmad al-Sharbāsī, *Al-A'immah al-Arba'ah* [The Four Imāms] (Beirut: Dār al-Jīl, n.d.), 41–43 (the crisis of Abū Ḥanīfah), 87–90 (the crisis of Mālik), 173–75 (the crisis of Ibn Ḥanbal); al-Jundī, *Al-Imām al-Shāfi'ī* 17–20.

20. Islam recognizes the sacred books of Judaism and Christianity as revelations from the same God.

21. Al-Mir'ashlī, *Ikhtilāf al-Ijtihād*, 59

22. Ibid., 60. Some also required freedom, presumably to ensure freedom from coercion in interpretation. However, in today's world where slavery is presumably extinct, this issue is moot. The issue of whether a person is coerced in his *ijtihād* due to other circumstances, however, remains alive.

23. Ibid., 60–61 (provides a comprehensive list that includes all factors (i)–(v) mentioned in this category); see also Kamali, Muhammad Hashim. *Principles of Islamic Jurisprudence*. Cambridge, UK: The Islamic Texts Society, 2003, 476-80.

24. The second list under (c) was required or mentioned as desirable by some, but not all, jurists. See al-Mir'ashlī, *Ikhtilāf al-Ijtihād*, 61–63 (provides a comprehensive list that includes both sets of factors in this category (c) and annotates the second part of the list indicating which jurists proposed it); see also Kamali, *Principles*, 476–80.

25. Ḥaydar, *Durar*, vol. 1, 22–23.

26. Subḥī Maḥmaṣānī, *Al-Awḍā' al-Tashrī'iyyah fī'l-Duwal al-'Arabiyyah* [Legal Systems in the Arab World], 3rd ed. (Beirut: Dār al-'Ilm li'l Malāyīn, 1965), 480; Kamali, *Principles*, 513–21; Aḥmad al-Raysūnī, *Naẓariyyat al-Maqāṣid 'ind al-Imām al-Shāṭibī* [The Theory of the Objectives of *sharī'ah* (as viewed) by Imām al-Shāṭibī] (Herndon, VA: International Institute of Islamic Thought, 2007), 137–43.

27. Qur'an 8:61. For more on this topic, see Jawdat Said, "Law, Religion and the Prophetic Method of Social Change," *Journal of Law and Religion* vol. 15, nos. 1 & 2, 83–150 (2000–2001).

28. Ḥaydar, *Durar al-Ḥukkām*, 32–33.

29. See, e.g., Maḥmaṣānī, *Muqaddimah*, 63–70, 81–93 (noting that this rule applies only to *mu'āmalāt* and not to *'ibādāt*); Maḥmaṣānī, *Al-Awḍā'*, 478; see also al-Zuḥaylī, *Uṣūl al-Fiqh*, vol. 2, 1116.

30. Ḥaydar, *Durar al-Ḥukkām*, 46; see also Maḥmaṣānī, *Muqaddimah*, 74–77.

31. Kamali, *Principles*, 240; Abū 'Abdullāh Ibn Mājah, *Sunnan Ibn Mājah* [*Sunnahs* of Ibn Mājah], verified by Muḥammad 'Abd al-Bāqī (repr., Beirut: Dār al-Kutub al-'Ilmiyyah, n.d.), vol. 2, 1303, *ḥadīth* no. 3950.

32. See Jasser Auda, *Maqasid al-Shariah as Philosophy of Islamic Law* (Washington, D.C.: International Institute of Islamic Thought, 2008), 177–78; see also Kamali, *Principles*, 242 (discussing the views of Muḥammad 'Abduh on consensus), 255 (noting that the scholar al-Dihlāwī argued that the above *ḥadīth* must be interpreted in conjunction with a second *ḥadīth*, which states: "A section of my community will continue to remain on the right path").

33. Kamali, *Principles*, 249; Abū Zahrah, *Uṣūl al-Fiqh* [Foundations of Jurisprudence] (Cairo: Dār al-Fikr al-'Arabī, n.d.), 194.

34. Note that al-Shawkānī agrees with my position. He states that there is no consensus if a single knowledgeable scholar disagrees with the rest. See Abū Zahrah, *Uṣūl*, 194, quoting al-Shawkānī; see also Muḥammad Shalabī, *Uṣūl al-Fiqh al-Islāmī* [Foundations of Islamic Jurisprudence] (Beirut: al-Dār al-Jāmi'iyyah, n.d.), vol. 1, 164–65.

35. Kamali, *Principles*, 244-45; Abū Zahrah, *Uṣūl*, 194; al-Mir'ashlī, *Ikhtilāf al-Ijtihād*, 226–32.

36. While *Shī'ī* jurists have provided such a justification as part of an overall approach to the singular role of *ahl al-bayt* in the development of Islamic education, *Sunnī* jurists have rejected this interpretation as based on controversial assumptions. For more on the issues arising in this area and a brief overview of the various positions held by scholars, see Abū Zahrah, *Uṣūl*, 184–206; Muḥammad Beltāgī, *Manāhij al-Tashrī' al-Islāmī* [Methodologies of Islamic Legislation] (Riyadh: Lajnat al-Buḥūth wa'l Ta'līf wa'l Tarjamah wa'l Nashr, 1977), vol. 2, pt. 2, ch. 4, on *ijmā'*.

37. Kamali, *Principles*, 248–49.

38. Al-Mir'ashlī, *Ikhtilāf al-Ijtihād,* 226–30; see also Abū Zahrah, *Uṣūl,* 194.

39. Abū Zahrah, *Uṣūl,* 203, quoting al-Shawkānī as rejecting the proof-value of *ijmā* ' "because God sent only one prophet. . . ."

40. Kamali, *Principles,* 266–67.

41. For more on this, see Irving Copi's discussion of analogical reasoning, in *Introduction to Logic* (1968), especially chapter 11.

42. Kamali, *Principles,* 268 (stating that jurists agree that Qur'an and *sunnah* are a valid *aṣl* (foundation) for *qiyās* but disagree on whether *ijmā'* may also be an *aṣl* for *qiyās*), 265–66 (noting groups of Muslims that questioned the validity of *qiyās*).

43. See notes 6-7.

44. Kamali, Principles, 269; Al-Raysūnī, Naẓariyyat al-Maqāṣid, 48

45. Al-Raysūnī, *Naẓariyyat al-Maqāṣid,* 18, 77; see also Ḥaydar, *Durar al-Ḥukkām,* 37 (providing one version of this principle).

46. Kamali, *Principles,* 356; al-Shāṭibī, *Al-Muwāfaqāt fī Uṣūl al-Sharī'ah,* [Concordances in the Fundamentals of *Sharī'ah*]. Reprint. Beirut: Dār al-Ma'rifah, n.d., vol. 2, 8.

47. Al-Shāṭibī, *Al-Muwāfaqāt,* vol. 2, 10; Auda, *Maqasid,* 3; see also Kamali, *Principles,* 362–65 (discussing al-Ghazālī's view of these classes).

48. Al-Mir'ashlī, *Ikhtilāf al-Ijtihād,* 119; al-Shāṭibī, *Al-Muwāfaqāt,* vol. 2, 284.

49. Al-Mir'ashlī, *Ikhtilāf al-Ijtihād,* 291–92; al-Raysūnī, *Naẓariyyat al-Maqāṣid,* 78–79.

50. Auda, *Maqasid,* 4; see also al-Shāṭibī, *Al-Muwāfaqāt,* vol. 2, 11–12 (*Taḥsīniyyāt* are about adopting the best of customs).

51. Al-Shāṭibī, *Al-Muwāfaqāt,* vol. 2, 11–12 (listing some of the better customs, including denying women the position of *imām,* and the woman's right to execute her own marriage).

52. Ibid., vol. 2, 16–18; al-Raysūnī, *Naẓariyyat al-Maqāṣid,* 140.

53. Al-Shāṭibī, *Al-Muwāfaqāt,* vol. 2, 18; al-Raysūnī, *Naẓariyyat al-Maqāṣid,* 141.

54. Al-Raysūnī, *Naẓariyyat al-Maqāṣid,* 223–25 (quoting al-Rāzī).

55. Ibid., 235–36 (quoting Abū Muḥammad Alī Ibn Ḥazm in *Al-Iḥkām fī Uṣūl al-Aḥkām* [Precision in the Foundations of Rulings] (Beirut: Dār al-Āfāq al-Jadīdah, 1983), vol. 8, 102–3); see also Kamali, *Principles*, 271.

56. Al-Raysūnī, *Naẓariyyat al-Maqāṣid*, 235 (quoting Ibn Ḥazm; see also Kamali, *Principles*, 271.

57. Al-Raysūnī, *Naẓariyyat al-Maqāṣid*, 235, quoting Ibn Ḥazm; see also Kamali, *Principles*, 271, 291.

58. Qur'an 2:185.

59. For more, see Kamali, *Principles*, ch. 12.

60. Al-Mir'ashlī, *Ikhtilāf al-Ijtihād*, 271; Kamali, *Principles*, 351–52.

4

THE ISLAMIC WORLDVIEW*

IN THE LAST TWO CHAPTERS, WE LEARNED ABOUT THE fundamental sources of Islamic law. In other words, we reduced Islamic jurisprudence to its basic building blocks. In this chapter, we will do the reverse. We will examine the grand architecture of the Islamic worldview, which encompasses our world of nature and humanity. This examination will give us a better understanding of what interpretations and laws tend to be consistent with the philosophy and spirit of Islam and which ones are inconsistent with or alien to it.

Central to this examination is the study of the foundational principle of Islam—namely, *al-Tawḥīd* (unicity of God)—and the overarching divine principle for organizing our universe—namely, that of due balance, symbolized by *al-Mīzān* (the [Divine] Scale). As will be explained below, the Universal Ordering Principle of *al-Mīzān* is transformed in the human realm into the Principle of *al-'Adl* (justice). Together, these principles provide the basics of the Islamic worldview. To facilitate our understanding of these principles, we shall turn to

*An earlier version of the chapter was published under "Divine Justice and the Human Order: An Islamic Perspective," in *Humanity before God: Contemporary Faces of Jewish, Christian and Islamic Ethics*, eds., William Schweiker et al. (Augsburg Fortress Press, 2006), 238–55.

two famous Qur'anic stories: the fall of Iblīs (Satan) and the descent of Adam, which provide us with another vantage point in our examination of the Islamic worldview.

We shall find the story of the fall of Iblīs quite instructive. It will help us understand the centrality of monotheism to Islam, and the pitfalls of *shirk* (associating partners with God). By examining Iblīs's reasoning in this story, we are able to identify a logic that can only result in conflict and destruction. Other Qur'anic *āyahs* and *ḥadīths* encourage us to move away from this logic to a life-affirming one based on the twin ordering principles of *al-Mīzān* and *al-'Adl* that promote due balance in the universe and human justice on earth. This chapter will take us through the steps that lead to this final conclusion. The story of the descent of Adam will also alert us to pitfalls facing humans in their pursuit of the just life.

So, let us start this examination by studying the foundational principle of Islam.

I. THE FOUNDATIONAL PRINCIPLE OF *AL-TAWḤĪD*

A. INTRODUCTION

The best and safest place to start this study is in the Qur'an itself because of its supreme sacred status. Through its various verses, it articulates a clear and distinct view of the universe based on a single foundational principle—namely, the Principle of *al-Tawḥīd* (the unicity of God). This view permeates various aspects of Qur'anic teaching, from the creation of Adam and the Heavens to the world of nature in its minutest details, as well as our worldly human concerns, including ethics, social relations, and commercial and constitutional matters. United by the foundational Principle of *al-Tawḥīd*, the whole universe flows effortlessly from one realm to another within a single grand architectural scheme.

Understanding this universal scheme helps us intuit good *ijtihād*. Good *ijtihād* advances the objectives of the Creator in light of the overarching divine principle that organizes our world. Jurisprudence that is conducted piecemeal, without regard to the "big picture," risks impoverishing, even distorting, the various concepts that govern the Qur'anic approach to specific areas of human existence. Yet, many commentators, including Muslim ones, believe that they can understand the Qur'an by focusing on a single verse or passage, while disregarding the others. This approach simply misses the point. It misses the fact that there is a unified worldview that permeates the Qur'an, and that makes it a seamless web of ideas, so that no verse can be properly understood except in light of the other verses. In one sense, this is not a new argument, because ancient jurists have already stated that passages in the Qur'an "explain each other."[1]

Central to the Islamic worldview is the concept of a single Supreme Being, namely God. This concept is the linchpin of all Islamic beliefs and it reverberates throughout the Islamic worldview. The Qur'an clearly states that the God of Islam is the same God as that of Christianity and Judaism, calling followers of these two religions "People of the Book."[2] It states that God is the God of Ibrāhīm (Abraham), Mūsā (Moses), 'Isā (Jesus), Muhammad, and all the other prophets of Christianity and Judaism.[3]

While the Qur'an celebrates Jesus as a major prophet of Islam, it rejects the concept of the Trinity. I shall refer to this position as "deep monotheism." *Sūrat al-Ikhlāṣ* (chapter 112) of the Qur'an is dedicated in its entirety to articulating this position. It states:

> Say: He is God, The One and Only
> God the Eternal, Absolute,
> He begetteth not,
> Nor is He begotten
> And there is none
> Like unto Him.

Furthermore, God is All-Powerful, All-Good, and All-Knowing.[4] If God wills something into being, it materializes instantaneously.[5]

The most salient attribute of God in Islam is His compassion, for God is All-Merciful, All-Compassionate. In Arabic, the words are *Raḥmān, Raḥīm*. The translation of these words is not exact. While both words are derived from *rahmah*, which means "mercy," they signify different facts about the Divine. *Raḥīm* means "merciful," and, linguistically, it is an intensive form of the attribute that could describe a human being as well. On the other hand, *Raḥmān* is a name reserved for God, and it is even more intensive and more encompassing in its meaning of "mercy" than *Raḥīm*. It is a *sui generis* type of mercy that is distinguished by God's power to create, an act of which humans are incapable.[6] This philosophical difference, like many others in the Qur'an, is literally lost in the translation.

We know that Mercy is the most salient of God's attributes because Qur'anic chapters start with this statement: "In the name of God the All-Merciful, the All-Compassionate." Further, every prayer by Muslims must start with this same statement, which is repeated many times during prayer. It is also a statement that Muslims utter when they begin any activity, such as eating, lecturing, and signing a contract. So, while every Muslim knows that his or her God is All-Powerful, All-Knowing, and All-Good, the focus of the Qur'an and the practice is specifically on God's compassion and mercy, not God's power or knowledge.

An example of God's mercy is His forgiveness of Adam's Original Sin. According to the Qur'an, Adam repented after he ate the fruit of the forbidden tree. So, God forgave Adam's weakness and accepted his repentance.[7] As a result, each descendant of Adam is born without the burden of the Original Sin. Instead, he or she starts with a *tabula rasa* that is later defined by their life choices and actions. But there will be more on this significant story in section B.2 of this chapter. We now turn to the most critical concept in Islam, which is the linchpin of the whole belief system.

B. UNDERSTANDING *AL-TAWḤĪD*

Many Muslim jurists devoted a great deal of time and effort trying to better understand the concept of the unicity of God. For example, does it describe His essence, qualities, or divinity?[8] Briefly stated, they agreed that at minimum, it transmitted to us the idea that God Himself is not a compound Being constituted of different parts, for had that been the case, He would have been dependent on the being of His parts.[9] But God is not dependent. In fact, He is the fount of all things. He is the Creator; and hence His Being is an irreducible unity in its very essence.[10]

This idea that God's Being is a single unity (i.e., it is not made up of parts) finds support in the Qur'an. It states:

> If there were in the heavens and earth
> Other gods besides God,
> There would have been confusion in both.[11]

The reason for the confusion is explained later in another *āyah*:

> No child did God beget
> Nor was there another god with Him:
> [had that been the case, then]
> Each God would have gone away with what he had created,
> And some would have lorded it over others. . . .[12]

Imām al-Rāzī expounds on this thought and offers a variety of arguments to support the unicity of God. In one argument, he notes that had there been two divine beings or gods, each would have divine attributes, such as being omnipotent and omnipresent. But this situation is logically impossible. For, if one of the gods wills something contrary to the will of the other, then one of their wills or both will be limited by the will of the other.[13] This means that one (or both) of them is not omnipotent. Furthermore, we cannot avoid the conflict by assigning them different spaces or time zones, because a god is supposed to be omnipresent.[14]

The above discussion is intended to give the reader a feel for the deep monotheism in Islam called *al-Tawḥīd*. It has significant consequences for the human order on earth. Since God is the one and only

Supreme Being, it follows that there exists no will superior to Him. To deny this by word or action is to fall into *shirk*, that is, to associate (false) partners with God. The literature makes it clear that such partners need not be the god of the idol worshippers in pre-Islamic Arabia. It could be something more subtle, such as wealth or power, an idea that we will expound upon in the next section. In brief, anyone who is led by these "idols" to defy God's Will, is subjectively declaring them to be superior to that Will. This is the heart of *shirk*. As we shall see in the next section, according to the Qur'an, Iblīs (Satan) attempted to do just that and suffered dire consequences.

1. The Fall of *Iblīs*

The story of Iblīs's downfall is instructive on the issue of *shirk*. It is recounted in more than one place in the Qur'an. Before examining it, let us note that in relating this and other Qur'anic stories, we need to remember that, as mentioned in Chapter 2, these stories transmit to the reader in a narrative form important principles expressly articulated elsewhere in the Qur'an. They provide a more accessible method of learning for those who are not legally inclined.

According to the Qur'an, God told the angels that he was placing (creating) a vicegerent on earth.[15] Understanding this to be a reference to human beings, the angels objected, saying: "Will you place in it one who will make mischief and spill blood while we celebrate your praises and glorify your name?"[16] And God replied: "I know what you do not know."[17] Scholars have pondered over this reply, which appears to signal the promise of a humanity that will ultimately stand up for peace, justice, and harmony.

The idea that the human being was chosen by God as His vicegerent on earth was taken very seriously by jurists. They noted that this appointment carried with it a very heavy responsibility/burden (called *taklīf*) of promoting harmony (internal and external), building civilizations, developing this earth, and repairing it. In short, the appointment made humans responsible ethical beings and stewards of this earth.[18] Corruption was viewed by jurists as the result of a departure from God's guidance and laws.[19] After all, divine laws were promulgated in the public interest.

In light of these facts, the rest of this story becomes especially significant. God told the angels that he was creating the human being (Adam) from clay. He then ordered the angels to prostrate themselves to that human being once He formed him in due proportion, and breathed into him of His spirit.[20] Despite their initial misgivings about the violent nature of human beings, the angels obeyed God's order.[21] Iblīs, on the other hand, simply refused to obey. God then asked Iblīs:

> O Iblīs, what prevented you from prostrating yourself
> To one whom I have created with My hands?
> Are you haughty or are you one of the high and mighty?[22]

Iblīs's answer was very clear. He could not possibly prostrate himself to Adam for:

> I am better than him.
> You created me from fire
> and created him from clay.[23]

In other words, Iblīs subscribed to a hierarchy of being in which his kind, which was created from fire, ranked higher than Adam's kind, which was created from clay. Significantly, it is this hierarchy that led Iblīs to disobey God's explicit order even though God breathed into Adam of His spirit.

Two important questions arise in connection with this story: (1) why did Iblīs believe so strongly in that hierarchy (i.e., that fire was superior to clay), giving no weight at all to the fact that God breathed into Adam of His spirit? And (2) even if this hierarchical ordering was correct, why did Iblīs think that he could defy an express divine order? Let us turn to the first question first.

For the first question, Iblīs provides no answer. But in explaining his act of disobedience to God, it became clear that Iblīs had subscribed to a hierarchy of being that matched his arrogant view of himself. He did so knowing that this hierarchy was not quite accurate, given the fact that God breathed into humans of his spirit. So, it was

Iblīs's arrogance ("I am better than him") that blinded him to the full picture in Adam's creation.

Iblīs's arrogance led him to commit two major errors, even if we were to assume that the hierarchy was somehow correct on the material level. First, Iblīs ignored the divine breath in Adam and reduced the situation to a simple comparison between fire and clay. Second, Iblīs accorded his favored hierarchy more validity than a direct order from God. By doing so, Iblīs fell into *shirk* (i.e., associating other gods with God). The hierarchy became the "idol" to which he was beholden. By following this other master, Iblīs's decision to defy God implicitly denied God's omnipotence, even His supremacy. This situation did not happen because of Iblīs's weakness or forgetfulness, but because of an overt and conscious arrogant choice by Iblīs to hold the hierarchy and its corollary as superior to God's express Will. Thus, the hierarchy became his new idol. Iblīs fell into *shirk*.

The famous scholar Abū Faḍl al-Alūsī (d. 1854) offered a critique of Iblīs's hierarchy and his related superiority argument. He noted, first, that fire is not better than earth because each of them is part of the four basic elements that God created, the other two being water and air.[24] Each of these elements has properties not shared by the other three, but are necessary in the creation. Second, the material of which the two were created is not a sufficient indicator of who is nobler. After all, God breathed into Adam of His spirit and made him His vicegerent on earth.[25] Therefore, Iblīs's refusal to prostrate himself to Adam, despite the direct divine order, is a major sin, according to al-Alūsī.

Al-Rāzī noted that Iblīs also committed a logical error in his argument. He engaged in faulty application of *qiyās* (reasoning by analogy).[26] The general rule he derived from his false hierarchy was that a superior being should not prostrate himself to or serve an inferior one. Basing his reasoning on this rule, Iblīs used *qiyās* to reach the specific conclusion that he should therefore not prostrate himself to Adam. This, al-Rāzī pointed out, was the first use of *qiyās* ever, and it was misapplied by Iblīs because he did not understand that a divine order has precedence over all other considerations, even *qiyās* and general rules.[27] But why did Iblīs not understand this? Because his judgment was clouded by his arrogance and the hierarchy/idol he adopted to validate it.

God tells us in the Qur'an that *shirk* is the only sin He would not forgive.[28] So, God cursed Iblīs and expelled him, saying: "Get down from here. It is not for you to be arrogant here. . ."[29] Defiance of the divine in this story was the fruit of the poisonous tree—namely, Iblīs's arrogance, bolstered by the hierarchy he chose to idolize. Arrogance, therefore, appears very early on in Islamic thought as a major sin, and humility as a major virtue.

After his fall, Iblīs asked God for respite until Judgment Day. He wanted to lie in wait for the children of Adam to prove to God that they were no better than him.[30] In other words, *Iblīs* still "did not get it." He continued his old arrogant ways of thinking in terms of destructive hierarchies. God gave *Iblīs* the respite, but gave a fair warning to human beings, "O children of Adam! Do not let Satan seduce you."[31] This respite and warning are significant because in Islam there is no inherited Original Sin. Adam sinned but was forgiven.[32] The respite and divine warning set the stage for the duplication on an individual basis of the test faced by Adam in the Garden of Eden. In this arrangement, every human being has her own test in life, and the free will to make a choice.

Commenting on the story of the fall of Iblīs, the medieval scholar Imām al-Ghazālī viewed it as a continuing lesson to be understood within the context of one's own society and era. Interpreting the story within his own social context, al-Ghazālī noted that a rich man who believed that he was better than a poor man, or a free man who thought he was better than a slave, or a white man who believed he was better than a red or black, man, was succumbing to Iblisi logic.[33] For it is *Iblīsī* logic that creates vain hierarchies that move us away from piety and righteousness and lead us into idolatry and sin. This important lesson is repeated throughout the Qur'an and the *ḥadīth* in more direct forms.[34] Most popular is the *ḥadīth* of the Prophet delivered at his last pilgrimage to Makkah. He told the crowds of worshippers: "Oh People, your God is One, your father [Adam] is one, So, no Arab is better than a non-Arab nor is a red person better than a black one, nor is a black person better than a red one, except with regard to piety."[35]

In a world of temptation and false hierarchies, humility thus becomes an important virtue in Islam.[36] It is this humility that permitted renowned medieval Muslim jurists to shy away from flatly asserting the validity of their conclusions. Instead, they always concluded their arguments with the phrase *wallāhu a'lam* (God knows best) and developed an etiquette of difference among them that resulted in a free and active market of ideas, where scholarly critiques could be quite incisive, yet respectful and humble.

For us today, the story of Iblīs points to two ways of being in our world: (a) a vain and arrogant way, based on false worldly hierarchies rooted in differences such as those of wealth, race, ethnicity, or gender; and (b) a humble way, based on the recognition that we are all God's creatures, and He alone is the Supreme Being.

The Qur'an, however, is not oblivious to differences among people. Indeed, it recognizes these differences and the problems they create among us when it states:

> It is He Who has made you (His) vicegerents on earth: He has raised you in ranks, some above others: that He may try you in the gifts He has given you . . .[37]

In other words, we are on trial (*ibtilā'*) in this world, and those among us who feel superior to others because of our worldly goods or characteristics succumb to *Iblīsī* logic and fail the test of God.

2. The Descent of Adam

The story of the fall of Iblīs is not complete without the story of the descent of Adam. The drama surrounding this event is familiar to most. But in the Qur'an, the story is slightly but significantly different from that in the Bible. So, let us recount it in some detail.

The Qur'an says that God told Adam and his wife to dwell in the Garden and enjoy its fruits as they wish, so long as they do not approach the forbidden tree.[38] He also gave Adam the following warning:

> Oh Adam! Verily this [Iblīs] is an enemy,
> To you and your wife:

So do not let him get you both out of the Garden,
So that you land in misery.
There is therein [in paradise] sufficient provisions
For you not to go hungry or naked,
Nor to suffer from thirst or the heat of the sun.[39]

But, as the Qur'an says, Adam was weak and forgetful, and Iblīs, his enemy, saw an opportunity to seduce the couple.[40] He wanted to show God that humans were no better than him. Stirring their desire for more than what they already had, Iblīs whispered to Adam and Eve: "Shall I lead you to the Tree of Eternity and a Kingdom that never decays?"[41] Their answer is now history. According to the Qur'an, Adam and Eve both succumbed to the temptation and ate the fruits of the forbidden tree, thus incurring God's wrath.

Two features of the Qur'anic version of the story are of interest. First, the Qur'anic story does not accuse Eve of tempting Adam. They were both seduced by Iblīs. Furthermore, Eve was not a passive bystander in the story. Rather, she was an equal partner with Adam in the offence. As the Qur'an states:

So, they both ate of the tree,
And so their nakedness appeared to them. . . .
Thus did Adam disobey his Lord
And allow himself to be seduced.[42]

Second, why did Adam and Eve listen to Iblīs when he had refused to prostrate himself to Adam earlier and when God had warned them against him? For one, Iblīs swore to them that he was giving them earnest advice.[43] Being in a state of innocence, they believed his lie. Also, *Iblīs* used their mortal human nature and flaws against them. In the Qur'anic story, the forbidden tree was that of "Eternal Life and a Kingdom that never decays." Iblīs led Adam and Eve to believe that immortality and eternal power were within their reach if they only ate from that tree. Their overwhelming desire for these two attributes overcame their reason. In the process, it exposed their weak will that made them forget the divine warning. As the Qur'an points out, "he [Adam] forgot, and we found on his part no firm resolve."[44]

However, in the Qur'an, the story does not end there. Adam repented, and God forgave him.[45] After that, God sent Adam, Eve, and Iblīs to earth. He repeated to Adam and Eve the warning that Iblīs is their enemy, and assured them that those of their descendants who follow God's Guidance should have no fear or grief. He then followed this with yet another assurance and warning:

> Oh Children of Adam! We have bestowed raiment
> Upon you to cover your shame,
> As well as to be adornment to you . . .
> Oh Children of Adam! Let not Iblīs seduce you,
> In the same manner he got your parents out of the Garden,
> Stripping them of their raiment, to expose their shame:
> For he (Iblīs) and his tribe watch you from where you cannot see them. . . .[46]

The first part of the passage suggests that the descent to earth may not have been a punishment to Adam and Eve.[47] Some jurists have argued that it was simply a fulfillment of the promise that God would place a vicegerent on earth.[48] But it did set up the conditions for testing each of the children, as the parents were tested. At the same time, God issued a warning to these children, as he did to their parents.[49] Those who heed it and follow God's Guidance would have nothing to fear.

Examples of this challenge on earth are recounted in the Qur'an. They include the crisis of Sarah in her old age. She thought that she would never be able to have a progeny with Ibrāhīm. In other words, her test was to deprive her of children who would carry her line and give her the closest thing on earth to immortality. What would she do about it? Would she cling to Ibrāhīm? Would she be angry at God's Will? Sarah, who is viewed in the Qur'an and predominantly in the Muslim religious literature as a righteous woman, chose a better, selfless way. She sent Hājar (Hagar) to Ibrāhīm. She passed that test. As a reward, God gave her Isḥāq (Isaac).

Hājar (Hagar) had her own test too. After bearing a son for Ibrāhīm—his only son for some time—she was uprooted by Ibrāhīm from her second home and taken to a barren land by Ibrāhīm in fulfillment of a divine order to him. There he left her and their infant with no water and few provisions.[50] Hājar accepted her fate with dignity and deep faith that God would take care of them.[51] Despite her love for her infant and deep concern about their safety, she too did not cling to Ibrāhīm against God's will. She let him go in peace. Her faith and journey are celebrated annually by Muslims in their pilgrimage.

Incidentally, nothing in the Qur'an indicates that Sarah was jealous or wanted to be rid of Hājar and Ismā'īl (Ishmael). Yet, according to al-Rāzī, some Qur'anic scholars made this unfounded claim, which he finds unlikely.[52] Al-Rāzī notes further that it would not have been appropriate for Ibrāhīm to leave Hājar and Ismā'īl in a barren land with no food or water, simply because Sarah asked him to send them away. He could have left them instead in the more developed *Bilād al-Shām* (an area which today includes Syria and surrounding countries).

Ibrāhīm, who had waited for a very long time to have a son, was ordered by God to sacrifice his "only son" with his own hands. That is a very difficult test for mortals. Yet, Ibrāhīm passed it. He subjugated his desire for earthly "immortality" to God's supreme will. Even Ismā'īl, who Muslims believe was the one to be sacrificed because he was the only son at that point, encouraged his father to go ahead with the sacrifice, once he understood that it was Divine Will.[53]

There are many other examples of such tests in the Qur'an. But even today, the scramble for the earthly version of "immortality" and power "that does not decay" by building powerful dynasties, gathering huge fortunes, and establishing authoritarian, racist, or patriarchal dominion over others, continues. As warned, it has spread violence, destruction, and misery around the world. Worse yet, some of these actions are done in the name of religion, despite the fact that they are clearly contrary to it. But humans are weak, forgetful, and full of strong desires. On Judgment Day, God will distinguish between those who passed the test and accepted His Will, and those who failed the test and repeated their parents' mistake.

We are now prepared to derive the Qur'anic lessons associated with these two stories.

C. THE COMPLEMENTARY PRINCIPLES OF EQUALITY AND DIVERSITY

Earlier in the discussion we mentioned two ways of being:

i. a vain and arrogant way, based on false worldly hierarchies rooted in differences such as those of wealth, race, ethnicity, or gender; and
ii. a humble way, based on the recognition that we are all God's creatures and that He alone is the Supreme Being.

Note that the first way combines *Iblīsī* logic with human weakness and desire for immortality and power. It promotes destructive conflict and misery. So, we now examine the second way.

The second way is mentioned in the Qur'an repeatedly for emphasis. It is based on the equality of all humans and the supremacy of God. It leaves no room for vanity. Here is one of the *āyahs* that express this second way:

> O people! Reverence God (show piety towards God) who created you from one *nafs* and created from her (the *nafs*) her mate and spread from them many men and women; and reverence God, through whom you demand your mutual rights, and the wombs (that bore you), (for) God watches you.[54]

This *āyah* reminds us that we are all, male and female, created from the same *nafs* (soul or spirit). For those whose arrogant selves may tempt them to think that they are entitled to more rights and privileges than others, this *āyah* reminds them that God watches them. In other words, by virtue of our very creation, we human beings are all equal. I shall call this the Equality Principle.

Nevertheless, this *āyah* presents a question: If all humans are created from the same *nafs,* then why are we so different from each other? More specifically, why did God create different genders, even different races and ethnicities? Isn't human diversity the root of this problem of arrogance? Had we all been identical, the issue may not have even arisen.

We can find the answer to this question in yet another *āyah,* which reiterates the Equality Principle, but goes further to express what I shall call the Diversity Principle:

> O People! We created you from a single (pair) of a male and female, and made you into nations and tribes, so that you may know each other. Verily, the most honored of you in the sight of God is (the one who is) the most Righteous among you . . .[55]

This verse does not only emphasize the original equality of all humans, but specifies further that it includes races and ethnicities, and not just gender. It also educates us about the purpose of creating this diversity. Its purpose is to entice us to "get to know each other," to expand our horizons about humanity and the world, to build bridges of friendly communication, and to establish harmonious societies. That is the divine logic of difference, as opposed to *Iblīsī* logic.

We all know that variety is the spice of life, while conformity can be quite dull, monotonous, and boring. So, to make life more interesting for us, God created beautiful differences among humans in gender, in color, in language, and in other ways. These differences are, in one important sense, "cosmetic" because they do not hinder full communication among us. Underlying all of them is the same concept of humanity. Their role is not to lead us into erecting *Iblīsī* hierarchies that advance conflict and domination. Rather, it is to enrich the lives of each one of us through constructive communication that leads to cooperation and harmony. After all, the one hierarchy that the Qur'an legitimizes is based on righteousness that brings us closer to God and to each other. Incidentally, righteousness is a standard that cuts across our differences. Any one of us can strive for and achieve it. Arrogance has no place in this second way.

The Prophet exemplified these complementary principles in his own life and example. Almost fifteen hundred years ago, his position on the question of race was already very clear. The Prophet appointed Bilāl, an Ethiopian freed slave, as the *mu'adhdhin* (one who calls to prayer).[56] That was an important position, and it required Bilāl to go up to the top of the *Ka'bah* to perform the *Adhān* (call for prayer). Two men from the Prophet's noble tribe of Quraysh were scandalized by this choice. One of them, *al-Ḥārith bin Hishām*, was quite upset, saying: "Will this black slave be calling for prayer on top of the *Ka'bah*?!"[57] But *al-Ḥārith* was soon to learn the Islamic way of human equality.

The Prophet was undeterred by the objections of Quraysh. He even informed the *Ṣaḥābah* that Bilāl would lead those entering paradise.[58] He also encouraged marriage between his noble cousin and a freed slave.[59] After members of Quraysh embraced Islam, the Prophet congratulated them, repeating his message of equality. He said: "O kin of Quraysh, God has removed from you the arrogance of *Jāhiliyyah* (pre-Islamic era) and its patriarchal dynastic pride (*ta'aẓẓumuhā bi-l-ābā'*). People are of Adam, and Adam is of dust."[60]

The Prophet's position on gender was also very clear. He treated all women with respect. At home, he never raised his voice in anger or hand in violence, nor did he ask anyone to bring him a cup of water.[61] He cut meat in the kitchen, helped with childcare, and repaired his shoes.[62] He married a woman twenty years his senior and loved her, keeping her memory alive after her death.[63] He then married a woman much younger than him and loved her deeply, too.[64] He also educated her in the religion. She became a major source of *ḥadīth* and jurisprudence.[65]

The Prophet's example in relating to women outside his home in the public arena was also instructive. For example, at the dawn of Islam when the Prophet was still in Makkah, seventy-three men and two women gave the Prophet their *bay'ahs* (a form of voting or expressing allegiance).[66] The two women were Nasībah bint Ka'b and Asma' bint 'Amr. The two women's *bay'ahs* were given and accepted on the same terms as those of the men.[67] The men and women then elected twelve representatives of their tribes to discuss various matters with the Prophet. On another occasion, a delegation of Arab women met with the Prophet and gave him their *bay'ah* on behalf of other Arab women. This "women only" *bay'ah* was also accepted by the Prophet, who conversed with the women to clarify the bases of their commitment to his leadership. Some Muslims are not even aware that this event is mentioned in the Qur'an.[68] Others who are familiar with this verse persist in depriving Muslim women of their political rights because, as I was told by one Muslim parliamentarian, "this is our culture." Yet according to Islamic jurisprudence, a cultural rule may be adopted as law only if does not violate basic Islamic principles. Barring Muslim women from politics flatly contradicts the Qur'an itself!

The two *bay'ah* events mentioned above established two important principles: (1) that *bay'ah* is a basic principle on which the Islamic model of governance is based, and (2) that women share in that system on equal footing. The second principle flows from the Qur'anic statement that both genders were created from the same *nafs* and that the most favored in God's sight is the one who is most pious.[69] The events also make clear that, from the first moment of revelation, women played an important role. After all, Khadījah, the wife of the Prophet who stood by his side and supported him, was the first Muslim.

We will be discussing the gender issue in greater detail in Chapters 5, 6, and 7, both from a Qur'anic and Prophetic perspective. It is sad, however, to note that those who claim to follow the *sunnah* of the Prophet today do not seem to follow its substantive aspects. They tend to be ready to emulate his dress or appearance, but not his treatment of others. Their treatment of others is usually governed by their patriarchal cultural baggage.

II. THE UNIVERSAL ORDERING PRINCIPLE OF *AL-MĪZĀN*

GOD'S CREATION, THE QUR'AN TELLS US, WAS NEVER haphazard.[70] Everything God created was in accordance with *al-Mīzān* ([Divine] Scales). In one verse, we are told that the "firmament was raised high and He set up *al-Mīzān*, so that you may not transgress [due balance according to] *al-Mīzān*."[71] In another passage, the natural laws of *al-Mīzān* are described further: Neither the sun is permitted to overtake the moon, nor the night may outstrip the day, and each swims along in its own orbit.[72] Closer to home, the Qur'an tells us that "the earth we have spread out (like a carpet); set thereon mountains firm and immovable; and produced therein all kinds of things in due balance."[73]

Thus, the mathematical features that govern the constellations, gravity, and other similar forces of attraction and repulsion that stabilize the heavenly bodies are all part of God's overarching design, for it balances and harmonizes the universe into a beautifully integrated whole. In other words, God's principle of *al-Mīzān* permeates the heavens and the earth. This is why the Qur'an repeatedly states that all of God's creations—even fruits, vegetation, and the sea and its contents—are miraculous signs for those who ponder.[74] It exhorts us to look at nature and admire God's creation, for God's miracles are evident to those who ponder.[75] This Qur'anic worldview gave rise to the golden age of Islamic science and philosophy in medieval times, and led to the invention of algebra and algorithms; significant advances in medicine, physics, and astronomy; and ultimately to the development of alchemy, the predecessor of chemistry.[76]

This unity between physics and metaphysics, inanimate and animate, is crucial for the Islamic worldview. There is no schism between the spiritual and the material, between science and religion. One leads to the other; all are ways of knowing God. This state of affairs is a direct consequence of *al-Tawḥīd*, since the unicity of the universal ordering principle reflects the unicity of God Himself. This argument is suggested in the Qur'an itself when we are told that had there been more than one god, each god would have set his creation apart from those of the others, and some gods would have acted superior to other gods.[77] The result would be a universe radically different from ours, one that is, at best, fragmented, and, at worst, in continuous conflict or chaos.

On the other hand, the Qur'anic worldview anchored in *al-Tawḥīd* is based on a single overarching universal ordering principle symbolized by *al-Mīzān*. This principle provides our universe with due balance and harmony. It is clear from the various Qur'anic verses that *al-Mīzān,* according to which the heavens and earth were ordered, is the same *al-Mīzān* that is supposed to govern human relationships. The very verse quoted above about the firmament being raised high moves directly from talking about *al-Mīzān* in the context of nature to talking about it in human context. It enjoins us humans not to "transgress [due balance according to] *al-Mīzān*." Indeed, the word *al-Mīzān* was repeated twice in that short passage, once for each context for emphasis. Clearly then, according to the Qur'an, a single concept of balance and harmony orders the whole universe of creation from the grandest to the most humble.

As an ordering principle, *al-Mīzān* manifests itself differently in different contexts. For example, in nature, it manifests itself in the laws of nature. But in the human context where humans are the vicegerents of God on earth, and are endowed with reason and free will, *al-Mīzān* manifests itself as an ethical ideal to be realized through free human choices.[78] This ideal is articulated for us in the Qur'an as a set of values, guidelines, and laws designed to promote justice, peace, and harmony among us and in this world. They educate us about the virtuous, balanced, and happy life and about harmonious relations with others. As importantly, they educate us about other matters relating to this world, such as our treatment of animals and the environment. Commitment to this ethical ideal becomes the measure of the person in the second and final test of humanity after the fall. On the Day of Judgment, our deeds as vicegerents on earth will be measured by *al-Mīzān* (here, the scales that weigh our good deeds).

We are told that the one who has light weights (for lack of good deeds) will be among the losers.[79]

The Qur'an tells us that this momentous burden of being stewards of this earth was not imposed on us unilaterally. Rather, the human being (Adam) was offered this earthly trust by God at the beginning of creation, and he chose to accept it, binding in the process not only himself but also his progeny.[80] This acceptance bound the whole human race, and not just Adam, as God's vicegerent on earth. We have thus inherited this trust and, along with it, the burden of stewardship, which ought to be guided by God's ethical and legal principles. This is a heavy burden for each of us, especially in light of the *Iblīsī* challenge.[81]

As we mentioned earlier, the angels were concerned about the creation of Adam because his progeny would spill blood on earth.[82] But the "pious will" discharges its responsibilities towards this trust by promoting a world order that reflects God's design of harmony and balance on earth. This is why God responded to the angels' concern with the simple answer: "I know what you do not know." This answer gives humanity hope that, in God's vast knowledge, in the end we will do what is right. We will opt for a human world order that fosters balance and harmony, rather than oppression, domination, and conflict. This world order, according to the Qur'an, is one of *al-'Adl* (balance, justice). We now turn to the study of this concept.

In one passage, the Qur'an addresses Prophet David specifically, stating:

> O David! We did indeed make you a vicegerent on earth, so judge thou among people in truth and justice, and do not follow your desires, for they will mislead you from God's path.[83]

In another, it addresses the believers generally, saying:

> O you who believe! Stand out firmly for God, as witnesses to fair dealing, and let not the hatred of others towards you

> make you swerve away from justice. Be just! That is next to piety: and fear God for God is well-acquainted with all that you do.[84]

The contrast in these verses is between one's inclinations and desires on the one hand, and God's principles of truth and justice on the other. This choice between the two is a difficult one, but if the human being is to shoulder his responsibilities towards his divine trust, then he must rise above his baser inclinations and follow the path of *al-'Adl*. The Qur'anic concept of *al-Mīzān* is so intertwined with this concept that many commentators and translators use them interchangeably.[85] Put differently, the Principles of *al-Mīzān* and *al-'Adl* are two manifestations of the same principle as applied to two different domains—one governed by laws of nature, and the other by free will. This principle is central to the divine plan that permeates the universe. Emphasizing its scope and fundamental nature, the Prophet said: "The Heavens and Earth were established on the basis of *al-'Adl*."[86]

Thus, in the domain of free will, the ordering principle of *al-Mīzān* becomes an ideal choice achievable through the pursuit of *al-'Adl*. But the Islamic concept of *al-'Adl* is not one of basic retributive justice; otherwise, it would not foster balance and harmony. Rather, it is a full-bodied concept that includes, in the final analysis, forgiveness and restorative justice, elements that can, in fact, result in a balanced and harmonious world. *Al-'Adl* in the human context becomes the means by which the universal ordering principle of *al-Mīzān* is realized in the human sphere. It extends this principle to society, the state, family, self, and even other beings and nature. It reaches down even into our daily transactions and governs them with rules of justice and fairness so that we may not "transgress [due balance according to] *al-Mīzān*."

According to the Qur'an, God transmitted these rules of justice and fairness to us repeatedly through past messengers who came with the Book and *al-Mīzān* so that people may stand forth in justice.[87] Ignoring these messages and upsetting *al-Mīzān* creates chaos, imbalance, injustice, and oppression. This is why the Qur'an is very succinct in its directive: "Be just."[88] Furthermore, "if you judge among people, then judge justly,"[89] even if one of the parties involved is a relative of yours.[90] Upsetting the balance creates catastrophes in the natural world, and oppression and tyranny in society. Thus, we must strive for the proper balance in each case, to avoid wreaking havoc on our lives and those of others.

III. MORE ON THE CONCEPT OF *AL-'ADL*

FROM THE ABOVE DISCUSSION, WE CAN DISTINGUISH SEVERAL meanings of the concept of *al-'Adl.* One important general meaning is that of balance and proportionality. This meaning is most salient when we discuss the concept of *al-Mīzān* in its universal manifestation. For example, this is the meaning implicit in the Prophet's saying, "the Heavens and Earth were erected with *al-'Adl.*"[91] A more specific meaning is that of justice as fairness, or giving each his due.[92] This meaning arises uniquely within the human context because humans have free will and can choose to be unjust. In other words, *al-'Adl* in its specific meaning does not articulate a binding law of nature. Rather, it offers an ideal for a free human will that may fall short of this ideal.

In society, *al-'Adl* is manifested in large part through the Equality and Diversity Principles. This was the lesson of the story of Iblīs. *Iblīsī* logic focused on differences and nurtured behavior that creates oppressive hierarchies, injustice, and conflict, leading to chaos in the world. Qur'anic logic, as expressed in the above-quoted verse, cast differences in a positive light, as an inducements to communication and understanding.

This Qur'anic logic, however, provides mere guidance. After all, the Qur'an states clearly: "Let there be no compulsion in religion."[93] Through the divine gift of free will, we have been empowered to espouse or reject Qur'anic guidance. Hence human relations could move away from the Equality and Diversity Principles through bad choices. For example, one could be seduced to espouse *Iblīsī* logic in the public arena. If espoused, it would become a suitable foundation for an authoritarian, racist, classist, or patriarchal society in which both destructive hierarchies and conflict are rampant. Our earthly world took the first turn toward that logic when Cain killed Abel, his righteous brother.

Cain was the elder, yet God accepted Abel's sacrifice and rejected Cain's. Upset by this situation, Cain "resolved" it by killing Abel. In other words, he asserted his belief of superiority over Abel by wiping him off the face of the earth. Thus, he became one of the "losers" who espoused *Iblīsī* logic.[94] Cain soon discovered the futility of his victory.[95]

Witness the similarity in this analysis with that of Hegel's Master-Slave dialectic.[96] It starts with the "master" viewing himself as the "I" or "the Essential Consciousness" and the "slave" as the "Inessential Other." After a series of attempts to sublate this Other, the "master" discovers that he has become dependent on the slave. The tables have turned, and, in the end, this untenable situation is resolved through understanding that we are all part of the same consciousness.[97]

Yet, because of the human condition of weakness and forgetfulness, we continue to repeat Cain's mistake either by killing the Other or superseding the Other's will through the use of economic, military, or other types of oppressive power. Often, we discover the error of our ways after the fact, as Cain did; yet humanity continues to repeat these errors. Over time, the world we live in has become quite troubled and human relations have frayed at the edges. The question becomes, "How do we now change a world of defective human relationships into one that satisfies *al-Mīzān*?" This is a question that the Qur'anic revelation addressed when it was revealed about fifteen hundred years ago.

The Qur'an answers this question not by calling for a revolution—that is, change through the use of force—but by calling for gradual change, or change through persuasion, education, and personal and social development. To help this change along, it provides incentives, rationales, and injunctions. This approach gives humans time to reconsider their views and change their hearts. An imposed change only leads to frustration, resentment, and ultimately further conflict, a situation contradictory to the ideal of the universal ordering principle of *al-Mīzān*.

This Qur'anic approach is best illustrated by its call for change with respect to the treatment of three of the most vulnerable segments of the population at the time of the revelation (and today): orphans, women, and slaves.[98] The Qur'an encourages Muslims to treat these three groups with special kindness and provides protections for orphans and women as well as significant incentives for freeing slaves.[99] Further, it introduces a system of mutual responsibility according to which everyone is responsible for those less fortunate than him or her. The line of responsibility is described in detail so that those closest to the disadvantaged person will have the strongest responsibility initially, but if they and others down the line fail or are unable to help, then in the end the state becomes responsible for helping its citizens.[100] In this system, no person is left behind, and everyone's humanity is recognized.

Additionally, the system of *zakāt* (tithing) provides the underpinning of this arrangement, and is further enhanced by the concept of *ṣadaqah* (alms). While the Qur'an recognizes private property and the fact that God gives some of us much more than others, it is very emphatic about the importance of sharing our financial blessings with others.[101] It calls the *ṣadaqah* a loan to God, and asks: "Who is the one who will loan God a beautiful loan [that is, one without interest] so that God would multiply it for him and he will have [also] a noble reward?"[102]

In fact, a major rationale for the prohibition of usury appears to be that of preventing the oppression of the poor and the exploitation of their need for one's personal gain. While usury may be financially rewarding, it does foster frustration and enmity within society, as opposed to cooperation, balance, and harmony, features indicative of a state of *al-'Adl*. The Qur'an reminds us that humans tend to be stingy and unwilling to readily part with their money, even for good deeds.[103] It teaches that those who are able to overcome their stingy selves are the successful ones.[104] For these reasons, and in the spirit of fostering equal human dignity, Muslim jurists recommended that a *ṣadaqah* be given secretly, so that neither the giver nor the recipient knows the other's identity. In today's world, such modesty is becoming, under our laws, increasingly impossible.

The concept of *al-'Adl* also applies to conduct that goes beyond the scope of our social and inter-human contexts. For example, it applies to human conduct toward animals and the environment. Those who ignore it risk loss, chaos, harm, and even punishment in the afterlife. A famous story from the time of the Prophet is that of the woman who locked up a cat and starved it. When the Prophet found out about it, he said that the woman would go to hell because she did not feed the cat, nor did she let her roam to be fed by God's bounty.[105] In another story, a thirsty man in the desert found a well. So he climbed down to quench his thirst. When he finished drinking and climbed up, he found a very thirsty dog. The man went back into the well, filled his shoe with water, climbed up and let the dog drink from it until the dog quenched his thirst. The Prophet said that the man was going to heaven.[106] There is a plethora of such stories about the Prophet relating to chickens, ants, donkeys, and various other animals, all emphasizing the fact that we will be asked about our treatment of them on Judgment Day.[107] So, from the outset, Muslims took animal rights seriously. For example, around fourteen hundred years ago, *Khalīfah* 'Umar let it be known that Islamic law prohibits the maltreatment of animals, killing them, or using them for purposes other than those for which they were created. 'Umar also stated that he (in Madinah) would be responsible for a mule in Iraq who stumbled because 'Umar had not fixed the road.[108]

The concept of *al-'Adl* also applies to human irrigation policies and conduct toward nature and the environment. Since this is a vast topic, we shall refer to it here briefly. For example, the Prophet said that a Muslim who plants a tree will be rewarded for his action anytime a person, a bird, or an animal eats from it.[109] He also said that on Judgment Day, if someone has a seedling in his hand, he should go ahead and complete planting it if he can.[110] The Prophet had extensive statements about the importance of sharing water,[111] and *Khalīfah* 'Umar developed important irrigation policies, guided by prophetic *ḥadīths* and designed to restore neglected agrarian lands.[112]

The broad war-time instructions given by *Khalīfah* Abū Bakr, who was the first *Khalīfah* to succeed the Prophet, are famous among Muslims till this day. Addressing his army, he said:

> Do not betray, nor hold a grudge. Do not be treacherous and do not defile bodies of the dead. Do not kill a child, nor an elderly person nor a woman. Do not cut down a tree nor burn it, and do not cut a fruit-bearing tree. Do not kill a lamb, nor a cow nor a camel except to eat it. You will pass by people who have secluded themselves in hermitages. Leave them to what they have secluded themselves for . . .[113]

IV. FINAL OBSERVATION

SOME MUSLIM INDIVIDUALS, GROUPS, AND GOVERNMENTS are severely ignoring Qur'anic principles in favor of accumulation of power, oppressive cultural customs, and patriarchal interests. This state of affairs may be attributed in part to ignorance of Islam coupled with a decline in piety. The absence of proper religious education opens the door to confusion and worse. The "worse" is falling into *Iblīsī* behavior, based on arrogance, extremism, and the use of power. Domestic violence, honor killings, and terrorist acts are all examples of this behavior.

Politically, Muslim societies have tolerated forms of individual and collective oppression that are unthinkable within the Qur'anic worldview. Yet Muslim societies continue to claim and believe that they are being guided by the light of the Qur'an. One possible explanation for this discrepancy is the historical and compounded ignorance of Qur'anic teachings. For centuries, authoritarian Muslim rulers hired jurists to provide distorted interpretations of Qur'anic verses that served their interests. These jurists were referred to as "the *Sulṭāns'* jurists."[114] They were willing to please the ruler even at the cost of distorting the word of God. As such, they engaged in *shirk*, for they allowed the ruler's will to supersede that of God. After all, God has warned us:

> Those who conceal the clear (Signs) We have sent down, and the Guidance, after We have made it clear for the people in the Book,—on them shall be God's curse, and the curse of those entitled to curse.[115]

So, in appeasing the rulers, these jurists succumbed to *Iblīsī* logic, and, as a result, created a great deal of confusion and pain among Muslims.

Later, colonialism erected a barrier between many Muslims and the language of the Qur'an. Orientalists who came along and wrote about Islam brought their own biases and worldviews into their research. These developments compounded the initial problem of ignorance and led to a generation of Muslims who wanted to be pious but just did not know how. They became vulnerable to extremists peddling their intolerant views as "true Islam." These views ultimately resulted in a great deal of strife, bloodshed, destruction, and hatred in the world, especially within Muslim countries. None of this is consistent with Islamic values nor with *al-'Adl* or *al-Mīzān.*

What is needed today is for young Muslims to learn about the Qur'anic worldview, with its twin ordering principles of *al-'Adl* and *al-Mīzān.* These principles apply to every aspect of our lives and require us to promote justice and harmony in this world.

NOTES

1. See, e.g., Ṣubḥī al-Ṣāliḥ, *Mabāḥith fī 'Ulūm al-Qur'ān* [Research in Qur'anic Studies] (Beirut: Dār al-'Ilm li'l Malāyīn, 13th print, 1981), pt. 4, ch. 2, 299–312, explaining this concept.

2. Qur'an 3:64.

3. The most inclusive reference to the prophets of Islam is in *āyah* 4:163–64, which states:

> We have sent you inspiration,
> As we have sent to Noah and the Messengers after him
> We sent inspiration to Abraham, Ishmael, Isaac, Jacob,
> And the descendants, to Jesus, Job, Jonah, Aaron,
> And Solomon, and to David We gave the Psalms.

And Messengers, whose stories We already told you about,
And others We have not,
And to Moses God spoke directly

4. Here are some examples from the Qur'an, which is full of references to all these divine attributes. On omnipotence, see, e.g., 2:165 (God is the one and only god and he is all-powerful), 18:39 (God is omnipotent), 59:23 (He is the one and only, omnipotent and supreme), 3:26 (He is omnipotent and beneficent). On God's omniscience, see 32:6 (God is omniscient; He knows all things, hidden and apparent), 49:16 (God is omniscient), 87:7 (God is omniscient), 40:19 (God knows when eyes deceive and knows what is hidden in the hearts). On God's beneficence, see 1:1 (and the beginning of every one of 61 *sūrahs*, stating that God is all-merciful, all-compassionate), 2:37 (God forgave Adam because He is all-merciful), 2:143 (God is full of kindness and is merciful), 4:25 (God is forgiving and merciful), 9:5 (God is forgiving and merciful).

5. Qur'an 3:47.

6. Muḥammad Fakhr al-Dīn al-Rāzī, *Tafsīr al-Fakhr al-Rāzī* [Exegesis of al-Fakhr al-Rāzī] (repr., Beirut: Dār al-Fikr, 1981), vol. 1, 237–39.

7. Qur'an 2:37, 20:122.

8. Al-Rāzī, *Tafsīr*, vol. 4, 170–88 discusses the various points of view.

9. Ibid., vol. 4, 188.

10. Ibid., vol. 4, 187–93; see also Abū Faḍl al-Alūsī, *Rūḥ al-Ma'ānī* [The Spirit of Meanings] (repr., Beirut: Dār al-Kutub al-'Ilmiyyah, 1994), vol. 1, 428.

11. Qur'an 21:22.

12. Qur'an 23:91.

13. Al-Rāzī, *Tafsīr*, vol. 22, 151–52.

14. Ibid., vol. 22, p.151–52.

15. Qur'an 2:30.

16. Qur'an 2:30.

17. Qur'an 2:30.

18. See, e.g., Niẓām al-Dīn al-Ḥasan bin Muḥammad bin Ḥusayn al-Nīsābūrī, *Tafsīr Gharā'ib al-Qur'ān* [Explaining the Unusual in the Qur'an], which is included in the margin of Abū Ja'far al-Ṭabarī's

Jāmi' al-Bayān fī Tafsīr al-Qur'ān [Comprehensive Exegesis of Qur'anic Interpretation] (repr., Beirut: Dār al-Ma'rifah, 1978), vol. 1, 156–57 (exploring the meaning of "*Khalīfah*"); al-Alūsī, *Rūḥ al-Ma'ānī*, vol. 1, 222; al-Rāzī, *Tafsīr*, vol. 1, 180.

19. See, e.g., Niẓām al-Dīn al-Ḥasan al-Nīsābūrī (defining "corruption on earth") in al-Ṭabarī, *Tafsīr*, vol. 1, 157.

20. Qur'an 15:28–29.

21. Qur'an 2:30–34.

22. Qur'an 38:75.

23. Qur'an 38:76, 7:12, 15:33.

24. In *Rūḥ al-Ma'ānī*, Abū Faḍl al-Alūsī argues that Iblīs's hierarchy is a false one because each element God created in nature has its own properties not shared by the other three (earth, fire, water, and air). Al-Alūsī, *Rūḥ al-Ma'ānī*, vol. 8, 329.

25. Al-Alūsī, *Rūḥ al-Ma'ānī*, vol. 8, 329.

26. Al-Rāzī, *Tafsīr*, vol. 14, 36–37.

27. Ibid., vol. 8, 330 (noting that this *Iblīsī* use of *qiyās* led some jurists to reject the rule.); see also vol. 14, 36–37.

28. Qur'an 4:48, 4:116.

29. Qur'an 7:13, 15:33–35, 38:74–78.

30. Qur'an 7:14–16.

31. Qur'an 7:27.

32. Qur'an 2:37.

33. Abū Ḥāmid al-Ghazālī, *Iḥyā' 'Ulūm al-Dīn* [Reviving Islamic Studies] (repr., Egypt: Muṣṭafā al-Bābī al-Ḥalabī Press, 1939), vol. 3, 326–60, esp. 338–43.

34. For example, see the story in the Qur'an about the vain man who told his friend: "I have more wealth than you do, and more power in (my following of) men." Then he entered his lush garden in this state, and said to his friend: "I do not think this will ever perish." Qur'an 18:32–35. His friend tried to point out to him the problem with his statement and the *shirk* it entailed, but the vain man persevered in his attitude. The next day, the garden was in ruins and he sorely regretted his *shirk*. Qur'an 18:42–43. There are also many *ḥadīths* about vanity. For example, the Prophet said: "A person who has the weight of a mustard seed of vanity in his heart will not enter para-

dise." Al-Ghazālī, *Iḥyā'*, vol. 3, 342. Also, the Prophet said: "A person who shows modesty to God, is lifted [in stature] by Him." Ibid., vol. 3, 330.

35. Aḥmad Ibn Ḥanbal, *Al-Musnad* [The Supported (*Ḥadīths* of Aḥmad)], in *Al-Fatḥ al-Rabbānī*, ed. Aḥmad al-Banna (Cairo: Dār al-Shihāb, n.d.), vol. 19, 228.

36. Qur'an 31:18.

37. Qur'an 6:165 (another interpretation of the first part of this verse is that "He made you succeed one another on earth . . .").

38. Qur'an 2:35.

39. Qur'an 20:117-18.

40. Qur'an 20:115.

41. Qur'an 20:120. Al-Alūsī mentions the view that Adam and Eve wanted to become like the angels, not dependent on drink and food. They also wanted to avoid death and have continuous existence. In that, it is argued, they did not commit *kufr* (i.e., they did not disbelieve in God). Other jurists, he notes, did not think that Adam and Eve believed Iblīs. Rather, it was desire that overcame them both. Al-Alūsī, *Rūḥ al-Ma'ānī*, vol. 8, 340–41. Al-Alūsī notes that Ibn 'Abbās and Yaḥyā Ibn Kathīr read the full verse to refer to *Malikayn*, which means two monarchs, and not *malakayn*, which means two angels. Ibid. This reading also fits with the reference to a Kingdom that never decays.

42. Qur'an 20:121.

43. Qur'an 7:21.

44. Qur'an 20:115.

45. Qur'an 2:37.

46. Qur'an 7:26–27.

47. See, e.g., al-Rāzī, *Tafsīr*, vol. 3, 28, arguing that the descent to earth was not a punishment for Adam and Eve, because God had already forgiven them. Rather, it was a fulfilment of the promise to have a vicegerent on earth.

48. Ibid., vol. 3, 28; see also *āyah* 2:30 on this promise.

49. Qur'an 7:27.

50. Qur'an 14:37.

51. Al-Rāzī, *Tafsīr*, vol. 19, 139, saying that Hājar asked Ibrāhīm: "To whom are you leaving us?" He answered: "To God," and then asked God to take care of them. Qur'an 14:37.

52. Al-Rāzī, *Tafsīr*, vol. 19, 139. Note that, as mentioned in chapter 5, section II.A.1, it has been claimed that explanations providing stories about Creation, Eve, Hājar, and others, which have no basis in the Qur'an, may have been influenced by biblical scholarship of neighboring Christian and Jewish tribes.

53. Qur'an 37:102.

54. Qur'an 4:1.

55. Qur'an 49:13.

56. 'Izz al-Dīn Ibn al-Athīr al-Jazarī (d. 1232), *Usud al-Ghābah fī Ma'rifat al-Ṣaḥābah* [Lions of the Forest in Knowing the *Ṣaḥābah*] (repr., Beirut: Dār al-Kutub al-'Ilmiyyah, n.d.), vol. 1, 415–6; see also Khālid Muḥammad Khālid, *Rijāl Ḥawl al-Rasūl* [Men around the Prophet] (Beirut: Dār al-Jīl, 1996), 90–93.

57. Abū al-Ḥasan al-Wāḥidī al-Nīsābūrī, *Asbāb al-Nuzūl* [Occasions of the Revelation] (Damascus: Dār Ibn Kathīr, 1988), 326 (stating that this incident is the reason for the revelation of *āyah* 39:13 discussed above); see also Ibn Qayyim al-Jawziyyah, *Zād al-Ma'ād* [Provision of the Hereafter] (Beirut: Mu'assasat al-Risālah, 1994), vol. 3, 409.

58. Ibn al-Athīr, *Usud*, 417.

59. For the story, see al-Alūsī, *Rūḥ al-Ma'ānī*, vol. 21, 203; see also al-Qurṭubī, *Al-Jāmi' li Aḥkām al-Qur'ān* [Compilation of Qur'anic Rulings] (reprint, Beirut: Dār Iḥyā' al-Turāth al-'Arabī, 1985), vol. 1, 186.

60. Ibn Qayyim al-Jawziyyah, *Zād al-Ma'ād*, vol. 3, 407; see also Zayd bin 'Alī al-Wazīr, *Al-Fardiyyah: Baḥth fī Azmat al-Fiqh al-Fardī al-Siyāsī 'ind al-Muslimīn* [Individualism: Research on the Crisis of Political Individualist Jurisprudence of the Muslims], (McLean, Virginia: Yemen Heritage and Research Center, 2000), 62.

61. Al-Ghazālī, *Iḥyā'*, vol. 2, 354–55, 360–61.

62. Ibid., vol. 2, 354–55.

63. Ibn Hishām, *Al-Sīrah al-Nabawiyyah* [Biography of the Prophet] (repr., Beirut: Al-Maktabah al-'Ilmiyyah, n.d.), vol. 1, 187; 'Abd al-Ḥalīm Abū Shuqqah, *Taḥrīr al-Mar'ah fī 'Aṣr al-Risālah* [The

Liberation of Women in the Age of the Message] (Cairo: Dār al-Qalam li'l Nashr wa'l Tawzī', 2002), vol. 1, 190–92.

64. Al-Ghazālī, *Iḥyā'*, vol. 2, 45; Sa'īd Fāyiz al-Dakhīl, *Mawsū'at Fiqh 'Ā'ishah Umm al-Mu'minīn* [Encyclopedia of the Jurisprudence of 'Ā'ishah Mother of the Believers] (Beirut: Dār al-Nafā'is, 1989), 32 (henceforth *al-Mawsū'ah*); see also 'Abd al-Ḥalīm Abū Shuqqah, *Taḥrīr*, vol. 1, 226–27.

65. Al-Dakhīl, *al-Mawsū'ah*, 91–732; Abū Shuqqah, *Taḥrīr* vol. 1, 200–11.

66. Ibn Ḥanbal, *al-Musnad*, vol. 20, 269; al-Wazīr, *al-Fardiyyah*, 49, citing Ibn Hishām.

67. Al-Ḥāfiẓ 'Imād al-Dīn Ismā'īl Ibn Kathīr, *Al-Bidāyah wa'l Nihāyah* [The Beginning and the End] (repr., Beirut: Maktabat al-Ma'ārif, 1979), vol. 3, 150–61 (describing two *bay'ahs* by men, two women participating in the second. He says that the *bay'ah* of the men was on the same terms as that of the women. He was referring to a *bay'ah* given exclusively by a group of women to the Prophet, which is mentioned in the Qur'an itself. Qur'an 60:12; see also Abū Ja'far al-Ṭabarī, *Tārīkh al-Ṭabarī: Tārīkh al-Umam wa'l Mulūk* [History of Nations and Kings] (repr., Beirut: Dār al-Kutub al-'Ilmiyyah, 1991), vol. 1, 559 (describing the basis of one *bay'ah*).

68. Qur'an 60:12. When I mentioned the *bay'ah* of women in a Muslim television interview, the interviewer tried to correct me and suggest that it was mentioned in *ḥadīth* and not Qur'an! I am sure many Muslim women are not aware of this story and its significance to their political rights. This is one reason why religious education for Muslim women is crucial.

69. See informative discussion of women's political rights in early Islam by al-Wazīr, *al-Fardiyyah*, 49.

70. Qur'an 25:2.

71. Qur'an 55:7–9.

72. Qur'an 36:40.

73. Qur'an 15:19.

74. See, e.g., Qur'an 55:11–13, 19–23.

75. See, e.g., Qur'an 55:5–25, 16:65–69, 29:43–44, 23:12–22 (enumerating God's miracles).

76. See, e.g., Seyyed Hossein Nasr, *Science and Civilization in Islam* (New York: Barnes & Noble, 1968).

77. Qur'an 23:91.

78. Some jurists rejected the claim that human beings are endowed with free will. The famous school of *al-Mu'tazilah* was one of those schools that upheld the principle of freedom of will. However, the *al-Jabriyyah* school of thought argued that a human is no more capable of a free act than a stone is capable of moving. For a detailed discussion of the various schools of thought on this topic, see Muḥammad bin 'Abd al-Karīm bin Aḥmad Abū al-Fatḥ al-Shahrastānī, *Kitāb al-Milal wa'l Niḥal* [The Book of Sects and Creeds] (repr., Cairo: Maktabat al-Anglo-Miṣriyyah, 1977), 49, 87. See also Muḥammad Abū Zahrah, *Al-Madhāhib al-Islāmiyyah* [Islamic Schools of Thought] (Cairo: al-Maṭba'ah al-Namūdhajiyyah, n.d.), 170–97.

79. Qur'an 7:9.

80. There is a lot of disagreement about the meaning of the "Trust" referred to in the Qur'an. See, e.g., al-Rāzī, *Tafsīr*, vol. 25, 235–36 (providing various interpretations ranging from the literal to the spiritual); see also 'Ā'ishah 'Abd al-Raḥmān (better known as Bint al-Shāṭi'), *Al-Qur'ān wa Qaḍāyā al-Insān* [The Qur'an and Human Affairs] (Dār al-'Ilm li'l Malāyīn, 1982), 72 (listing and assessing the various meanings); al-Qurṭubī, *Al-Jāmi'*, vol. 14, 254–55.

81. Qur'an 7:16, 15:39, 38:82.

82. Qur'an 2:30.

83. Qur'an 38:26.

84. Qur'an 5:8.

85. See, e.g., Muḥammad Ibn Manẓūr, *Lisān al-'Arab* [The Tongue of Arabs] (repr., Beirut: Dār Iḥyā' al-Turāth al-'Arabī, 1992), vol. 15, 290–91.

86. Al-Alūsī, *Rūḥ al-Ma'ānī*, vol. 14, 101 (explaining that *al-Mīzān* in *āyah* 55:7 refers to the most effective and masterful system where everyone was given their due and the world became orderly).

87. Qur'an 57:25.

88. Qur'an 5:8, 4:58.

89. Qur'an 4:58.

90. Qur'an 6:152.

91. Al-Alūsī, *Rūḥ al-Ma'ānī*, vol. 27, 101; see also Murtaḍā Muṭahharī, *Al-'Adl al-Ilāhī* [Divine Justice]. Qum: Al-Dār al-Islāmiyyah li'l Nashr, n.d.), 67.

92. See Muṭahharī, *Al-'Adl al-Ilāhī*, 66–88.

93. Qur'an 2:256.

94. Qur'an 5:30.

95. Qur'an 5:31.

96. G.W.F. Hegel, "Lordship and Bondage," *The Phenomenology of Mind* (New York: Harper, 1967), 229–40.

97. Ibid., 236–37.

98. We cannot ignore sexual slavery as a serious problem in today's world.

99. For verses encouraging and praising those who take care of orphans, see Qur'an 2:83, 2:177, 2:215, 2:220, 4:36; see also Muḥammad Abū Zahrah, *Al-Tanẓim al-Islāmī li'l Mujtama'* [Islamic Organization of Society] (Cairo: Dār al-Fikr al-'Arabī, n.d.), 50–51. On women, see chapters 5 and 6 on gender. On treating slaves well and providing incentives to free them, see Qur'an 4:92, 5:89, 90:13; see also Subḥī Maḥmaṣānī, *Muqaddimah fī Iḥyā' 'Ulūm al-Sharī'ah* [Introduction to the Revival of *Sharī'ah* Studies]. Beirut: Dār al-'Ilm li'l Malāyīn, 1962), 192–94 (on the Islamic system for eliminating slavery by providing many avenues for freedom; and quoting the Prophet that "one who slaps or hits a slave must free him").

100. See, e.g., Abū Zahrah, *Al-Tanẓīm*, 140–47.

101. Qur'an 2:177, 51:19, 70:24–25, 93:10.

102. Qur'an 57:11.

103. Qur'an 4:37, 47:38, 57:24, 59:9, 64:16.

104. Qur'an 59:9, 64:16.

105. Muslim al-Nīsābūrī, *Ṣaḥīḥ Muslim bi Sharḥ al-Nawawī*, with Explanation by Muḥyī al-Dīn Abū Zakariyyā al-Nawawī (repr., Beirut: Dār Iḥyā' al-Turāth al-'Arabī, n.d.), vol. 14, 240.

106. Muslim, *Ṣaḥīḥ*, vol. 14, 241–42.

107. See, e.g., Muslim, *Ṣaḥīḥ*, vol. 17, 228–30 (prohibiting using a "life" [a living animal] as an object; prohibiting the tying down of chickens and pigeons and using them for target practice, prohibiting

the branding of animals in the face); vol. 15, 29–31 (prohibiting burning of ant hills and of killing birds wantonly).

108. 'Alī al-Ṣallābī, *Sīrat Amīr al-Mu'minīn 'Umar Ibn al-Khaṭṭāb* [The Biography of the Commander of the Faithful 'Umar Ibn al-Khaṭṭāb] (Beirut: Dār al-Ma'rifah, 2004), 170.

109. Muḥammad al-Bukhārī, *Ṣaḥīḥ al-Bukhārī* [The Authentic Prophetic *Ḥadīths*], in al-'Asqalānī's *Fatḥ al-Bārī: Sharḥ Ṣaḥīḥ al-Bukhārī* [Divine Enlightenment: Explanation of al-Bukhārī's *Ṣaḥīḥ* (collection of authentic prophetic *ḥadīths* by al-Bukhārī, with commentary by al-'Asqalānī)] (repr., Beirut: Dār al-Kutub al-'Ilmiyyah, 1989), vol. 5, Book 41 on Plowing and Agriculture, p. 3; see also Ibn Ḥanbal, *al-Musnad*, vol. 15, 10–11 (about this *ḥadīth* and several others in the same vein).

110. Ibn Ḥanbal, *al-Musnad*, vol. 23, 309.

111. Al-Bukhārī, *Ṣaḥīḥ*, vol. 5, 40–44; see also Ibn Ḥanbal, *Al-Musnad*, vol. 15, 132–34.

112. Al-Bukhārī, *Ṣaḥīḥ*, vol. 5, Books 41, and Book 42 irrigation agreements. See also Muḥammad Beltāgī, *Manhaj 'Umar Ibn al-Khaṭṭāb* [The Method of 'Umar Ibn al-Khaṭṭāb]. Reprint. Cairo: Dār al-Salām, 2003), 172–73.

113. Al-Ṭabarī, *Tārīkh*, vol. 2, 246.

114. See al-Wazīr, *Al-Fardiyyah*), 360–62.

115. Qur'an 2:159.

5

In the Garden: Gender and the Qur'anic Worldview

In Chapter 4, we introduced the Qur'anic worldview and the overarching principles on which it is based. In this and the next chapter, we shall focus on the Islamic worldview on gender relations. We shall provide an analysis based on the Qur'anic revelation, the *sunnah* of the Prophet, and traditional juristic sources. Given the number of *ḥadīths* on gender-related issues attributed to the Prophet, this study is only the beginning of a long-term project. Nevertheless, our analysis herein will expose cultural patriarchal influences that underlie the current legal understanding of gender relations in Islam.

As part of this study, we shall explore further the Equality Principle with respect to gender and assess challenges to its validity claimed to be rooted in the Qur'an and *sunnah.* We shall also study *āyahs* and *ḥadīths* that have been cited as establishing the superiority of men over women, and that have provided traditional jurisprudential support for current Muslim family laws in various countries.

I. WOMEN SPEAK OUT

WE SHOWED IN CHAPTER 4 THAT, ACCORDING TO THE QUR'AN, the divine hierarchical ordering of humans is based on *taqwā* (piety). We also showed that the alternative ordering rooted in arrogance resulted in false and oppressive hierarchies. They also led to error or worse—*shirk*. Following up on that discussion, we start this chapter with a famous incident in Islamic history that took place in public between an old woman and the powerful head of the Islamic state. The incident shows that in the early days of Islam, women had a strong voice in the public square when heads of state still observed a hierarchy of piety.

During the *khilāfah* (caliphate) of 'Umar, young men complained about the large amounts of *mahr* (marital gift) women were demanding then.[1] Afraid that such a trend might discourage men from getting married, *Khalīfah* 'Umar announced in the mosque that he was going to place an upper limit on the amount of *mahr*. An old woman rose from the back of the mosque and said to 'Umar: "God gives us and you prohibit it."[2] She then cited a clear Qur'anic verse establishing that the amount of *mahr* can be quite high.[3] Umar immediately responded: "A woman is right and a man is wrong."[4] He then abandoned his proposal.

Incidentally, the woman was quite on point. *Mahr* is purely the woman's right in Islamic law. She is entitled to set the amount or type of *mahr* as she desires, and once she receives it, she can do with it as she pleases, including donating it.[5] If it is monetary, she may decide to use it to start her own business, or invest it for a later time when she may need it. As such, it becomes the woman's safety net, given to her by a freely consenting prospective husband as a gift (*niḥlah*).[6] Today, unfortunately, fathers sometimes appropriate their daughters' *mahrs* and husbands sometimes pressure their wives into waiving the delayed part of the *mahr*, leaving the woman financially defenseless.[7] We shall discuss this matter in greater detail in a future volume.

The story of 'Umar and the unknown old woman also underlines the fact that the Muslim "head of state" is a servant of God and of the people, not an authoritarian ruler who exercises dominion over his people. This democratic view, incidentally, applies not only to the state, but also to any type of hierarchy in society. For this reason, Muslims have no "church hierarchy," but only *'Ulamā'* (scholars) and jurists.[8] As noted earlier, true *'Ulamā'* and jurists are modest about their own views, recognizing that only God knows the truth with certainty.

Khalīfah 'Umar, the *'Ulamā'*, and other Muslims learned humility through the example of the Prophet. An example relevant to this discussion is mentioned in the Qur'an itself in "*Sūrat al-Mujādilah*" ("The Arguing Woman"). Khawlah bint Tha'labah came to the Prophet to complain about her husband Aws.[9] She loved him dearly and they had young children. One day, after she finished praying, Aws approached Khawlah sexually and she turned him down. He got upset with her, and used words indicating *ẓihār*, an oppressive form of pre-Islamic divorce. Distraught, Khawlah went to the Prophet to ask whether she was indeed divorced under this pre-Islamic form. *Ẓihār* freed her husband from financial obligations toward her and from child support, throwing her into poverty and the children into chaos. The Prophet was moved by her situation, but did not have a solution for this problem. Existing laws rendered her divorced. According to narrations, the Prophet kept repeating "*ḥurrimti 'alayh*" (meaning that she was no longer Aws's wife.)[10] While he was telling her this, Khawlah lifted her hands to heaven and pleaded with God for help. Narrators tell us that as she was pleading, the face of the Prophet clouded up and a revelation descended upon him. He then called Aws and asked him to explain what made him act that way. Aws wondered why the Prophet was asking, and the Prophet recited to him the four *āyahs* that had just been revealed to him on this subject. They start with:

> God has indeed heard (and accepted) the statement
> Of the woman who is arguing with you concerning her husband
> And is pleading with God;
> And God hears your dialogue
> For God hears and sees all.[11]

The rest of the four *āyahs* then condemned and abolished this form of pre-Islamic divorce. It also provided the husband with three alternatives to atone for his behavior before he could return to his wife: freeing a slave, fasting two consecutive months, or feeding sixty poor people. Aws informed the Prophet that he could not atone under any of these conditions because of his financial and physical condition. The Prophet then gave him money to feed the poor.

In this story, the woman argued even with the Prophet himself about her situation. And God heard the argument and helped her. Following the revelation that prohibited this form of divorce, the Prophet was then able to help her out. Nowhere in the whole story is there any intimation of the Prophet being offended by the woman arguing with him. God and the Prophet both heard her anxious voice.

This prophetic behavior, characterized by humility and respect for everyone, including women, was further emphasized by other incidents. It is well known, for example, that women complained that men were dominating meetings with the Prophet. So, women requested separate meetings exclusively for themselves. The Prophet accepted their request and held these "women only" meetings.[12]

Another well-known fact about the Prophet is that he helped female slaves in doing their chores whenever possible. It is narrated that female slaves used to take his hand and lead him into town, where he would help them complete their tasks.[13]

A famous saying of Prophet Muhammad that has inspired many Muslim women over the ages is "Women are the *shaqā'iq* of men."[14] According to *Lisān al-'Arab* and even popular understanding, this *ḥadīth* means that women are the peers of men, and are like them in nature and ethics.[15]

Since these early days of Islam, piety has retreated in our societies and has been gradually replaced by arrogance. We now live in a world awash with hierarchies based on every conceivable criterion. Among these modern criteria are color, wealth, gender, ethnicity, size, and age. One of the most pernicious hierarchies of which we have become acutely aware is patriarchy. At its worst, it has cost many innocent women their lives, and visited unspeakable misfortunes upon many others. Repudiating it is the focus of this chapter and Chapters 6 and 7.

II. Gender and the Qur'anic Equality Principle

We noted in Chapter 4 that, according to the Qur'an, we were all created from the same *nafs* (soul), male and female, nations and tribes. We cited the following *āyah* in support of our argument:

> O People! We created you from a single (pair) of a male and female, and made you into nations and tribes, so that you may know each other. Verily, the most honored of you in the sight of God is (the one who is) the most righteous among you . . .[16]

We also cited the prophetic *ḥadīth* that all people are equal regardless of their color, origin, or ethnicity.[17]

We shall now return to the Equality Principle and argue more explicitly that it includes women. This is not an obvious claim to most Muslims, given centuries of patriarchal interpretations that have viewed women as inferior to men. These interpretations found great support in the story of the creation of Eve from Adam's rib—but what does Islam really say about this story?

A. Was Eve Created from Adam's Rib?

Generally, traditional literature states that Eve was created from Adam's rib to keep him company.[18] For example, according to al-Ṭabarī's (d. 923) version of the story, after Iblīs was expelled from paradise, it became Adam's dwelling. But he walked around feeling lonely for not having a companion. He fell asleep at one point, and when he woke up, he found sitting near his head a woman that God created from his rib. He asked her, "What are you?" She said, "A woman." He said, "Why were you created?" She said, "So that you find tranquility in me."[19]

There are two issues with this story. They appear to attribute to Eve an inherently inferior status to that of Adam by virtue of two separate factors:

i. The mode of Eve's creation (i.e., being created derivatively from Adam's rib); and,
ii. The purpose for her creation (she was created so that Adam could find tranquility in her).

Rejecting the claim in (i) does not necessarily imply rejecting the claim or its implications in (ii). So, we should approach them separately.

1. The Claim That Eve Was Created from Adam's Rib

Al-Ṭabarī's account of the above conversation between Adam and Eve is quite detailed. It creates the impression that he based it on solid Islamic sources. However, in one passage, al-Ṭabarī attributes his knowledge of this story to some *ṣaḥābīs* without naming them.[20] In another passage, he attributes it to what has been narrated by "the People of the Book and the Torah."[21] It appears that the People of the Book with whom al-Ṭabarī was communicating transmitted to him only the account of gender creation mentioned in Genesis II. They left out the more egalitarian account mentioned in Genesis I: 26–27. Yet, as we shall see below, the last part of the Genesis I account, which mentions the simultaneous creation of both male and female, is closer (but not identical) to the Qur'anic *āyahs*, the Islamic worldview, and some established Islamic jurisprudence, than the more popular account in Genesis II.

Al-Ṭabarī does not attribute this story either to the Qur'an or the *ḥadīth*. That is not accidental. There is nothing in either one about the creation of Eve that supports this story.[22] So, let us focus on the Qur'anic account of gendered creation first, and then turn to the *ḥadīth*. According to the Qur'an, both genders were created from the same *nafs*. On its face, this statement provides a clearly egalitarian gender-creation story. But jurists who disagree with this analysis quote another *āyah* from the Qur'an, which states in partial translation:

He created you (all)
From a single *nafs*
Then *ja'ala minhā*,
Zawjahā. . . .[23]

We shall refer to this *āyah* as the Creation *Āyah*. We have left some Arabic words untranslated so that we can examine them in greater detail.

Traditional scholars translate this Creation *Āyah* as follows:

> He created you (all)
> From a Single Person
> Then created from *him*,
> *His* mate. . . .[24]

Unfortunately, this translation is neither a pure nor an accurate *linguistic* translation of the Creation *Āyah*. Rather, it is a *translation combined with an interpretation* that harkens back to the "Adam's rib" creation story mentioned by al-Ṭabarī. In other words, this translation is based on the assumption that Eve was created from Adam's rib. Given this assumption, the word *nafs* (soul) is interpreted by the translator to refer to Adam. Consequently it is translated as "single person," which is assigned a masculine gender, despite the fact that this assignment reverses the gender of all the key words in the passage. For example, the word *nafs* has linguistically a feminine gender. The word *min* means "from," while *minhā* means "from her." *Minhā* has grammatically a feminine gender because it refers to the *nafs*. This translation has changed it into "from him." The word *zawjahā* (meaning "her mate") also has a feminine gender because it also refers to the *nafs*. This translation has changed it into "his mate." So, the translation begins turning into an interpretation very early on when it starts by interpreting the word "*nafs*" as "single person"—namely, Adam. It does so despite the fact that Adam's name was not mentioned either in this *āyah* or anywhere else in the Qur'an in connection with the gender creation story.

This initial interpretation in turn forces a complete reversal of the genders of the Arabic words in the *āyah* in order to make them consistent with it. The non-Arabic reader has no way of knowing what happened in the translation. Consequently, she would view the *āyah* as evidence in support of the "Adam's rib" story. But as we have shown, the "Adam's rib" translation/interpretation goes beyond what the *āyah* actually says.

Before further discussion, we caution the reader against over-interpreting our linguistic critique here. We are not arguing that the original linguistic gender of the words carries special significance to the creation story. We are only arguing that the total gender reversal in the translation of the passage would not have occurred had the translator not implicitly adopted the story that Eve was created from Adam's rib.

To drive this point further home, consider the first part of *āyah* 40:17. It says the following:

> That Day [Day of Judgment] will every *nafs* be requited for what [it/she] *kasabat* . . .

The verb *kasaba* means to earn. It refers here to the *nafs*, which as we mentioned earlier has linguistically a feminine gender. So, the Arabic language requires that the verb *kasaba* has a matching feminine gender, and it does—*kasabat*, which literally means "she earned." But note the traditional full translation of this passage:

> That Day will every *nafs* be requited for what *it* earned . . .[25]

Here the proper matching gender in the *English* language translation was used, as opposed to a masculine one, as in the translation of the Creation *Āyah* above (or a feminine one, to match the Arabic). The pronoun "it" was used here because there was no underlying theory that forced the translator to interpret *nafs* as referring to a male.

Having established an interpretational bias in the translation of the Creation *Āyah*, let us now examine that *āyah* more carefully. For, while gender identifications in it are linguistically indisputable, they are not necessarily jurisprudentially significant. So, let us continue our analysis. To help the reader follow this discussion, we repeat here the Creation *Āyah*:

> He created you (all)
> From a single *nafs*
> Then *ja'ala minhā*,
> *Zawjahā*. . . . [26]

According to the famous Egyptian scholar Imām Muḥammad Rashīd Riḍā (d. 1935), the phrase *ja'ala minhā zawjahā* does not mean that God created Eve from the particular *nafs* or person of Adam.[27] That, he points out, is the story in Genesis. Had that story not been there, this interpretation would not have crossed the Qur'anic reader's mind.[28] Riḍā cites an alternative interpretation provided by the famous al-Rāzī. So, let us examine al-Rāzī's commentary on this *āyah*.

Al-Rāzī provides two possible interpretations of the Creation *Āyah*. The first is the traditional Biblical one. While the details may vary, the basic version states that Eve was created from Adam's left rib, or the shortest of his left ribs, while he was sleeping.[29] When he woke up, he saw Eve and liked her because she was created from a part of him. Those who hold this view support it further by referring to a *ḥadīth*, of various versions, which will be discussed in the next section. We note that neither the Qur'an nor the authentic *ḥadīth* speaks about creating Eve during Adam's sleep or from his rib—shortest left one or any other.[30]

As a distinguished scientist, al-Rāzī points to the scientific inaccuracy of the story. He notes that the ribs on our left side are not one rib less than those on the right.[31] He also provides the following critique of the traditional interpretation: "Since God was able to create Adam in the beginning, what makes us say that He created Eve from a part of Adam? Why don't we also say that He also created Eve in the beginning?"[32]

According to al-Rāzī, the second possible interpretation of the Creation *Āyah* was suggested by Abū Muslim al-Aṣfahānī (d. 934). Under this interpretation, the phrase *ja'ala minhā zawjahā* does not mean that Eve was created from the body of Adam. Rather, it means that God created Eve of the same *jins* (i.e., nature, kind, or substance) as Adam, thus making the two a pair.[33] With *āyah* 30:21 about good spousal relations in mind, al-Rāzī argues that sharing the same *jins* makes it more likely that the pair would find tranquility in each other.[34] (After all, they were both created from one and the same *nafs*.) Al-Alūsī, who rejects this interpretation, nevertheless mentions an argument in its favor. He reports that some scholars have argued that had Eve been created from Adam's body, then Adam would have been copulating with himself, a thought that was obnoxious to these scholars.[35]

Arguing in favor of the second interpretation, both Riḍā and al-Rāzī refer to other *āyahs* in the Qur'an that have a similar grammatical construction but an unambiguous meaning. They include *āyah* 3:164, which states:

> God sent to the believers a prophet *min anfusihim.*[36]
>
> [Note that *anfus* is the plural of *nafs,* while *min anfusihim* means "from themselves."]

They note that this similar wording and construction cannot be interpreted to be about the creation of the Prophet "from" his people. One interpretation al-Rāzī provides is this: It is a statement by God that the Prophet He sent was of the same *jins* (kind, nature, substance) as his people. He did not send them an angel, for example.[37]

For these and similar reasons, Riḍā concluded that the Creation *Āyah* cannot possibly be interpreted as referring to the creation of Eve from Adam's rib unless the interpreter is willing to ignore the grammatical construction of the verse, as exhibited in other *āyahs* in the Qur'an. Riḍā remarks: "If someone has established that Eve was created from Adam's rib, then he is not compelled to impute this meaning to this *āyah*, thus excluding it from the shared meaning it has with the other *āyahs* of similar construction in the Qur'an."[38] Riḍā's comment provides a good example of correcting interpretation errors by using the Qur'an to explain itself.

Al-Rāzī also addresses a major criticism of the interpretation that Eve was created (independently) from the same *jins* as Adam. Critics argue that this interpretation implies that God created human beings not from a single *nafs* but from two, contrary to the Qur'anic *āyahs.*[39] Al-Rāzī notes that this criticism misses the mark. Referring back to *āyah* 3:164 quoted above, as well as several similar ones, he notes that the word *min,* occurring in the phrase *min anfusihim,* does not mean creation "*from* their (multiple) *nafs* (or souls)." Rather, it refers here to the *objective* of the creation, which started with Adam and followed with Eve from the same substance.[40] Al-Rāzī then remarks: "Since it has been established that God is capable of creating Adam from clay, then he is also capable of creating Eve from clay. What purpose does it serve to create her from a rib of Adam?'"[41]

Riḍā, who quotes al-Rāzī's second interpretation approvingly, mentions two additional possible interpretations of the Creation *Āyah* suggested by other jurists and scientific researchers. Both interpretations focus on the fact that the word *nafs* has a female gender and the word *zawj* (as in *zawjahā*—i.e., her mate) has a masculine gender.[42] (Note that *zawj* in the Arabic language could refer to either gender, but in this context it was assigned a masculine gender because it referred to the mate of the linguistically feminine gendered *nafs*.)

Focusing on the gendered language of the phrase *ja'ala minhā zawjahā* in the Creation *Āyah*, Riḍā suggests in the first interpretation that the male was created from the female. As evidence, he cites *āyah* 7:189, emphasizing its gendered language. It states that God created us from a single *nafs*, and created or made from her—that is, that *nafs*—"her" mate in order that *he* (meaning the mate) may dwell with *her* in tranquility.[43] The second interpretation mentioned by Riḍā views the *nafs* as being initially a hermaphrodite being, which divided later into the two gendered beings through parthenogenesis.[44]

The above discussion shows that al-Rāzī and the other respectable jurists were troubled by the traditional "rib" interpretation for theological and linguistic reasons unrelated to women's rights. In the process of explaining their critiques, these major jurists debunked the claim that Eve was created from Adam's rib, and rejected Qur'anic interpretations that embrace it.

The adoption of the Genesis II account had a cumulative effect on Islamic jurisprudence and laws because it permeated and colored the interpretation of other *āyahs*, such as *āyahs* 4:1, 30:21, and 16:72, all of which use the same language, and were thus interpreted similarly by traditionalists.[45] These interpretations fortified creation accounts like those of al-Ṭabarī quoted in section 2.A.1 of this chapter, and planted deep roots for the Genesis II story about the creation of Eve in Qur'anic *tafsīr* and prophetic *ḥadīth*. Under this interpretation, women became the only group in the human family that was deemed a priori inferior to another group—namely, men—by virtue of their *derivative* creation. Clearly, the Equality Principle on gender crumbles under this interpretation. This result, however, is inconsistent with the divine overarching Principle of *al-'Adl* discussed in Chapter 4 and with other parts of the Qur'an and *ḥadīth* as we understand them.

2. Final Remarks about the Claim That Eve Was Created from Adam's Rib

In light of the above arguments provided by al-Rāzī, al-Alūsī, al-Aṣfahānī, Riḍā, and others with respect to this claim, we conclude that

i. there is no clear evidence in the gender creation stories in the Qur'an establishing the validity of the traditional interpretation about the creation of Eve from Adam's rib;
ii. there is strong evidence that those who embraced such interpretation were influenced by sources espousing the creation story in Genesis II; and
iii. the traditional interpretation conflicts with the overarching Islamic worldview and its Principle of Equality discussed in Chapter 4.

These are, however, initial conclusions. For clauses (i) and (ii) above are not adequate proof of the applicability of the Equality Principle to matters of gender, nor are they sufficient to vindicate it. We must also study *āyahs* in the Qur'an that some have viewed as affirming the inequality of genders. The most popular of these are discussed in Chapter 6.

Furthermore, the Equality Principle's applicability to gender must be also examined in light of the *ḥadīth*. As we mentioned in Chapter 2, the *ḥadīth* and *sunnah* shed light on the Qur'an. But *ḥadīth* is a world in itself. There are tens of thousands of *ḥadīths* and the task of assessing all those relevant to women seems almost impossible at this juncture. However, we can examine at least the *ḥadīth*, referred to above, which is usually used to support the traditional interpretation of the Creation *Āyah*.

3. *Hadīth* That the Woman Was Created from a Rib

According to al-Bukhārī (d. 870) in his *Ṣaḥīḥ*, considered by the majority of scholars as one of the most reliable sources of *ḥadīth*, the Prophet is reported to have said:

i. "The woman is *ka-l-ḍila'* [i.e., *like* a rib]. If you straighten her out, you break her. And if you enjoy her, you will enjoy her with a *'iwaj* [bent-ness] in her."[46]

Another version of the *ḥadīth* states:

ii. "Be good to women, for they were created from *ḍila'* [rib], and the most bent part of the *ḍila'* is the top part, so if you try to straighten it out, you break it, and if you leave it alone, it will remain bent, so be good to women."[47]

According to Muslim (d. 875) in his *Ṣaḥīḥ*, the other major *ḥadīth* compilation, one more version of this *ḥadīth* is narrated as follows:

iii. The woman was created from *ḍila'* and will not get straight for you in some way, so if you enjoy her, you enjoy her as bent, and if you go to straighten her out, you break her, and her breakage is her divorce.[48]

Note that there is no mention of Eve in any of these *ḥadīths*. Rather, they provide a general statement about women. Despite this glaring omission, these *ḥadīths* have been used to support the traditional story about the creation of Eve from Adam's rib. So let us study them more carefully. But before doing so, we need to remove blinders that were placed on Muslims for centuries by jurisprudential interpretations that trigger in us a Genesis-type reflex. Perhaps there is no Genesis story here. Perhaps that is why there is no explicit text in the Qur'an about it. So let us begin without these a priori assumptions, by using the same methodology we used to analyze *āyahs* and *ḥadīths* in this book.

We first note that these various versions of the *ḥadīth* were included in sections entitled "*Bāb al-Waṣāh bi'l Nisā'*" ["Section on Gently Advocating for Women"] and "*Bāb al-Mudārāt ma' al-Nisā'*" ["Section of Dealing Gently (or Kindly) with Women"].[49] Neither one of these titles suggests hostility toward women. Instead, they signal that the *ḥadīth* is somehow in favor of women. The famous commentator on *ḥadīth*, al-'Asqalānī (d.1449), says: "[The phrase] 'Be good to women' signals that 'straightening a woman out' should be attempted gently, so as not to reach a breaking point . . ."[50] He then notes that the *ḥadīth* encourages approaching women gently, and being patient with them about their "bent-ness." For a man cannot live without a woman, and enjoying her cannot take place without being patient with her.[51] So, let us examine the various versions of the *ḥadīth* with this context in mind.

Version (i) of the *ḥadīth* is different from the other two in that it uses an analogy. The woman was not created from a rib (*ḍila'*) but was "like one." So, what are the characteristics of a *ḍila'* in the Arabic language? The word *ḍila'* comes from the triliteral root *ḍ. l. '* [the last symbol represents the letter *'ayn* for those who know the Arabic alphabet]. Words derived from this root have the meaning of being strong and tough, or heavy, or having the ability to endure (as in *ḍalī'*).[52] As a verb, it can mean "being able to carry a heavy burden or execute a tough assignment" (as in *iḍḍala'a*).[53] As for the specific meaning of *ḍila'* as a rib, it is also true that compared to other body parts, such as flesh, cartilage, and fat, the rib is stronger. Ribs are strong and naturally bent or bowed to protect the heart, lungs, and other vital organs. It takes force to break them.

The analogy, then, seems to suggest that women are strong-natured and not malleable. So, if a man tries to change them by force, he will risk breakage (i.e., divorce). So, the Prophet advises men to be good to women and enjoy them by accepting them as they are.

Next we turn to the word *'iwaj*, which I translated here as "bent-ness." Traditional translations of this word provide negative-value–laden synonyms, such as "crooked." Again, according to the lexicon, the word *'iwaj* means "to have bent-ness, not to be flat or straight, as with earth or a stick."[54] A woman was called *'awjā'* if she had a child towards whom she bent to nurse.[55] Neither meaning carries the suggestion of "crookedness."

Finally, we turn to the expression in the *ḥadīth* about "straightening the rib out." As pointed out earlier, unlike a stick, a rib is naturally bent or bowed. So, part of the analogy of a rib is that it has its own natural curvature. If someone tries to go against it by force, it breaks. The analogy here is that the woman's inclinations and preferences may be different from those of her husband. The reference to the top part of the rib being the most curved appears to be a metaphor about the woman having a mind of her own. If the husband tries to "straighten her out," (i.e., force his wife to become more like him), he misses the enjoyment he could have had by accepting her for who she is. Given the meaning of *'iwaj,* there may be also a hint at some differences in nature between male and female, with females being more inclined toward caring and nurturing. A man who does not understand or respect these differences risks breaking up his marriage.

This is, then, our interpretation of the first *ḥadīth.* What about the other two *ḥadīths* that do not use the language of analogy? They state directly that women were created *min ḍila'* (from a rib). According to al-Nawawī, this phrase utilizes the literary form of *tashbīh* [simile].[56] Al-Albānī agrees with this explanation because, he says, there is no *ḥadīth* that establishes that Eve was created from Adam's rib.[57]

In another part of his multi-volume work, al-Rāzī studies an *āyah* that has a grammatical structure identical to that of the *ḥadīth* under discussion.[58] Here are the *ḥadīth* and *āyah* next to each other:

a. The woman was created from *ḍila'* . . .
b. The human being was created from *'ajal* . . .[59]

The word *'ajal* means "haste." Al-Rāzī provides several possible interpretations of this *āyah,* one of which is of special significance to us. He notes that the famous Arab grammarian, al-Mubarrad (d. 898), said that this *āyah* is stated in the *mubālaghah* (intensive emphasis) literary form to emphasize the fact that humans are creatures of haste.[60]

They rush into things.[61] Al-Mubarrad analogizes this *āyah* to another one, which says:

c. God created you from *ḍa'f* . . .[62]

The word *ḍa'f* means "weakness," and the *āyah* means that God created us weak.

Al-Alūsī presents several interpretations of *āyah* (b) above, which states that the human being was created from haste. Among them is one that harkens back to creation stories. It claims that God created Adam hastily at the end of the day.[63] Another explains the *āyah* this way: Humans are so impatient, it is as if they were created from hastiness itself. So, the *āyah*, al-Alūsī continues, is really emphasizing hastiness in human nature, traits, and behavior. Calling this a more likely interpretation, al-Alūsī then quotes several scholars who said that the *āyah* is talking about our human nature, because hastiness is inseparable from it.[64] This interpretation is interesting for us because we could use the same logic to interpret *ḥadīths* (ii) and (iii) above (which state that women were created from "rib"). After all, these two *ḥadīths* have structures similar to that of *āyah* (b) (which says that human beings were created from "hastiness"). We would then conclude that the two *ḥadīths* do not provide a description of the substance of which Eve was created. Rather, they used *tashbīh* (simile) to express a thought about women. This conclusion harmonizes the two latter *ḥadīths* with the first *ḥadīth* mentioned in this section.

Al-Nawawī seems to agree. He points out that nothing in the formulation of *ḥadīth* (i) above about women's creation means that the woman was created from Adam's rib, as some had suggested, nor was there in the authentic *sunnah* anything to intimate this.[65] Rather, al-Nawawī argues, this explanation was based on the second chapter of Genesis.[66] He then agrees with other scholars that the creation of Eve was not from Adam himself, but from the same *jins* of which Adam was created.[67] As stated earlier, this interpretation makes all versions of the *ḥadīth* on this matter consistent with each other. After all, the very first version stated, "The woman is *ka-l-ḍila'*." Its use of the letter *ka* (for analogy) clearly analogizes the woman to a *ḍila'*. It does not reduce her to one. In discussing this version of the *ḥadīth*, we already explained the meaning of this analogy.

Earlier in this section, we showed that the Equality Principle does not contradict the Creation *Āyah* in the Qur'an because there is no clear statement in the Qur'an that Eve was created from Adam. We have now also shown that the Equality Principle does not contradict any authentic *ḥadīth* on the subject. The third step is to show that *āyahs* in the Qur'an that have been traditionally explained as implying or asserting the inferiority of women have been misconstrued. The most popular of those will be discussed below. But as a matter of practicality, let me note that there are some *āyahs* and many more *ḥadīths* that have been interpreted for centuries as implying woman's inferiority to man. It is practically impossible to go systematically through all of them here. That is a long-term project. In this book, I will simply address the most salient challenges to the Equality Principle and show them to be misdirected, misinterpreted, or simply wrong.

However, before we turn to these Qur'anic *āyahs*, we still have one more task to complete in this section. The previous discussion addressed only the "Adam's rib" story. It did not address the second claim, mentioned in section II.A at the beginning of this chapter—namely, that God's very purpose in creating Eve was for Adam to find tranquility in her. In other words, Eve's very creation and existence was to address Adam's needs. Hence, her existence was secondary and inferior to his. We turn now to this claim.

B. The Claim That Eve Was Created as Adam's Inferior

Unfortunately, jurisprudential progress in this area has been quite slow and it has seriously affected the interpretations of Qur'anic *āyahs* and of *ḥadīth*. The great al-Rāzī, who debunked the "rib" creation story, was no exception. Witness his discussion of the following *āyah*:

> And among His signs is this,
> That He created for you mates *min anfusikum*,
> *Li taskunū ilayhā*.[68]

The distinguished Qur'anic translator, Yūsuf 'Alī, translates this *āyah* as follows:

> And among His signs is this,
> That He created for you mates from among yourselves,
> So that you may dwell in tranquility with them.

Al-Rāzī mentions that some scholars have interpreted the above *āyah* to mean that Eve was created from Adam's body. As mentioned earlier, he rejects this interpretation, arguing that the correct intended meaning is that God created women from the same *jins* as men.[69] However, in further explaining this *āyah*, al-Rāzī focuses on the words "He created for *you*." Influenced by the purported "garden conversation" between Adam and Eve, he interprets "you" to refer to men alone. As a result, al-Rāzī commits a grave error. He says that women were created for the same reason animals, plants, and other things of utility were created. Women, he says, were created for "us" [men] and to "complete the blessings" given to "us."[70] He adds that women were "weak and silly" like boys. These words make clear that although al-Rāzī rejected the "rib" creation theory, he remained prisoner of the account of the "garden conversation" mentioned by al-Ṭabarī and others, as well as his patriarchal culture.

For example, reading this *āyah* without the distorting effects of the "rib theory" and the "garden conversation," one could reasonably conclude that women were exceptional human beings who had powers superior to those of men, because men need the women's strength and company to become tranquil! But, that is not the Qur'anic logic either. As we argued earlier, both the Qur'an and *ḥadīth* assert the equality of all human beings. The *āyah*, actually, has a more profound and beautiful meaning about male-female relationships than the unfortunate one understood by al-Rāzī or the "exceptionalist" one proposed above. It will be discussed below as embodying the Harmony Principle governing the relationships between men and women.

Given all the great works of al-Rāzī and his usually insightful interpretations, we can only repeat what Ibn 'Arabī (d. 1240), another major scholar, said about Imām al-Bukhārī when the latter committed a similarly grave patriarchal error: "*Yā lahā hafwatun min 'ālim bi-l-Qur'ān wa'l sunnah*! [What an error by a scholar knowledgeable in Qur'an and *sunnah*!]"[71]

Thus, it is a breath of fresh air to read about the view of the well-known scholar al-Qaffāl (d. 976) narrated by al-Rāzī himself. Commenting on *āyah* 7:189, which is also about human creation from the same *nafs*, al-Qaffāl argues that the *āyah* means that God created everyone from one *nafs*, and made of its *jins* (nature, kind, substance) a mate *equal in humanity* [emphasis added].[72] Relying on his own scholarly thinking, al-Rāzī endorsed al-Qaffāl's view as a credible interpretation. Thus, al-Rāzī came close to identifying the correct interpretation of this *āyah*, but extra-religious factors (patriarchal culture) prevented him from getting there.

It is worth noting that before and after al-Qaffāl, there have been many attempts at purging Islamic scholarship from extra-religious patriarchal cultural influences. The most celebrated attempts by men included Riḍā and several modernists. Unfortunately, a lot more needs to be done, and this is one step in that direction.

To sum up, there is no *āyah* in the Qur'an stating that women are inferior to men. There are, however, *āyahs* and *ḥadīths* that have been interpreted that way. We shall study in Chapters 6 and 7 two *āyahs* and a *ḥadīth* that are often quoted as asserting or implying the inferiority of women.

III. THE QUR'ANIC HARMONY PRINCIPLE

On the question of gender specifically, the Qur'an states:

> And among His signs is this, that he created for you mates from among yourselves, so that you may dwell in tranquility with them, and He has put love and mercy between your (hearts): Verily in that are signs for those who ponder.[73]

I will refer to this *āyah* as the Harmony Principle.* The thought contained in it is repeated in various forms in the Qur'an, an indication of its significance.[74] Consequently, we may justifiably conclude that it articulates a basic general principle about proper gender relations: They are relations between mates created from the same *nafs* that are intended to provide these mates with tranquility and are to be characterized by affection and mercy. Such relations leave no room for oppressive hierarchies, gendered or otherwise, which result only in strife, subordination, and oppression, characteristics abhorred by Islam.[75]

The Prophet's example in his own household illustrates this Harmony Principle. In the absence of an oppressive family structure, his private relationships were based on open communication and mutual respect. 'Ā'ishah, his young wife, blossomed and felt free to think, argue, and disagree with the Prophet repeatedly. They treated each other with tender affection and kindness, and the Prophet nurtured 'Ā'ishah's young mind while at the same time integrating her into the life of the Muslim community where she played an important role. The Prophet told 'Ā'ishah that he always knew when she was annoyed with him. In those instances, she referred to God as the God of Abraham; otherwise, she referred to Him as the God of Muhammad.[76] When 'Ā'ishah's father heard her argue with the Prophet, he tried to strike her.[77] 'Ā'ishah hid behind the Prophet, who admonished her father for his behavior. The Prophet himself was a model "modern" husband and father, never asking anyone to wait on him and participating in household chores and childcare.[78] His great love and respect for 'Ā'ishah and Khadījah, even after the latter's death, as well as his daughter Fāṭimah, are well documented in history books.[79]

NOTES

1. 'Alī al-Ṣallābī, *Sīrat Amīr al-Mu'minīn 'Umar Ibn al-Khaṭṭāb* [The Biography of the Commander of the Faithful 'Umar Ibn al-Khaṭṭāb]

---

*An earlier version of this discussion appeared in Azizah al-Hibri, "Islam, Law and Custom: Redefining Muslim Women's Rights," *American Journal of International Law and Policy*, vol. 12, no. 1, 20, 26–27 (1997).

(Beirut: Dār al-Ma'rifah, 2004) (citing Ibn Kathīr's *Tafsīr*) and al-Bayhaqī's *Sunan*, 107.

2. Al-Ṣallābī, *Al-Sīrah*, 107.

3. Qur'an 4:20.

4. Muḥammad Fakhr al-Dīn al-Rāzī, *Tafsīr al-Fakhr al-Rāzī* [The Exegesis], (Beirut: Dār al-Fikr, 1985), vol. 10, 14. 'Umar then commented: "Everyone is more knowledgeable in jurisprudence than 'Umar." Al-Ṣallābī, *Al-Sīrah*, 107.

5. Muḥammad Abū Zahrah, *Muḥāḍarāt fī 'Aqd al-Zawāj wa Ātharih* [Lectures in the Marriage Contract and Its Consequences] (repr., Cairo: Dār al-Fikr al-'Arabī, 1971), 203 (noting that *mahr* is a right of the woman and she gets full control over it once she receives it, but that her *wali* (guardian) has the right to object to a low *mahr* and have it increased).

6. Qur'an 4:4.

7. Social custom made it possible for men to deliver *mahr* in a "prompt" installment at the time of marriage and a "delayed" instalment usually due upon death or divorce. See Abū Zahrah, *Muḥāḍarāt*, 205.

8. This may be confusing to the reader given media references to Muslim "clergy." In fact, scholars only present their *ijtihād* on a certain matter and the average Muslim then decides whether to adopt or reject it.

9. Al-Rāzī, *Tafsīr*, vol. 29, 250–51.

10. See al-Rāzī, *Tafsīr*, vol. 29, 250–51; Abū 'Abdullāh al-Qurṭubī, *Al-Jāmi' li Aḥkām al-Qur'ān* [The Comprehensive Compilation of Qur'anic Rulings] (repr., Beirut: Dār Iḥyā' al-Turāth al-'Arabī, 1985), vol. 17, 270; Abū Ja'far al-Ṭabarī, *Jāmi' al-Bayān fī Tafsīr al-Qur'ān* [Comprehensive Exegesis of Qur'anic Interpretation] (repr., Beirut: Dār al-Ma'rifah, 1978), vol. 28, 2.

11. Qur'an 58:1–4.

12. Aḥmad al-'Asqalānī, *Fatḥ al-Bārī: Sharḥ Ṣaḥīḥ al-Bukhārī* [Divine Enlightenment: Explanation of al-Bukhārī's *Ṣaḥīḥ* (collection of authentic *ḥadīths* of the Prophet)] (repr., Beirut: Dār al-Kutub al-'Ilmiyyah, 1989), vol. 13, 362; see also 'Abd al-Ḥalīm Abū Shuqqah, *Taḥrīr al-Mar'ah fī 'Aṣr al-Risālah* [The Liberation of Women in the Age of the Message] (Cairo: Dār al-Qalam li'l Nashr wa'l Tawzī', 2002), vol. 2, 171.

13. See, e.g., this story as recounted by Abū Ḥāmid al-Ghazālī, *in Iḥyā' 'Ulūm al-Dīn* [Reviving Islamic Studies] (repr., Egypt: Muṣṭafā al-Bābī al-Ḥalabī Press, 1939), vol. 2, 361 (he would also go with widows and the poor and help them complete the tasks they needed done); see also Abū Shuqqah, *Taḥrīr*, 91.

14. Aḥmad Ibn Ḥanbal, *Musnad Aḥmad* [The Supported (*Ḥadīths* collected by) Aḥmad]. In *Al-Fatḥ al-Rabbānī*. Edited by Aḥmad al-Banna. Cairo: Dār al-Shihāb, n.d., vol. 2, 116.

15. Muḥammad Ibn Manẓūr, *Lisān al-'Arab* [The Tongue of the Arabs] (repr., Beirut: Dār Iḥyā' al-Turāth al-'Arabī, 1992), vol. 7, 166. The lexicon also provides a meaning based on the theory that Eve was created from Adam, but we have discounted that theory as being un-Islamic. We also recognize that some *ḥadīths* attributed to the Prophet are either false or erroneously interpreted as misogynistic. But as stated in this chapter, we cannot address the whole body of *ḥadīth* in this book. We are focusing here only on those relevant to the specific topic under discussion.

16. Qur'an 49:13.

17. I once found an old version of this *ḥadīth* at a Columbia University library, and it referred to women as well. But I have not been able to locate it again.

18. See, e.g., al-Ḥāfiẓ 'Imād al-Dīn Ismā'īl Ibn Kathīr, *Al-Bidāyah wa'l Nihāyah* [The Beginning and the End] (repr., Beirut: Maktabat al-Ma'ārif, 1979), vol. 1, 74 (quoting Eve as telling Adam that she was created so that he could find tranquility in her); see also al-Qurṭubī, *Al-Jāmi'*, vol. 1, 301.

19. Abū Ja'far al-Ṭabarī, *Tārīkh al-Ṭabarī: Tārīkh al-Umam wa'l Mūlūk* [History of Nations and Kings] (repr., Beirut: Dār al-Kutub al-'Ilmiyyah, 1991), vol. 1, 69.

20. Al-Ṭabarī, *Tārīkh,* vol. 1, 69. Other historians, such as Ibn Kathīr, name in passing some *ṣaḥābīs* as sources of this account, but do not attribute it to the Prophet. See Ibn Kathīr, *Al-Bidāyah wa'l Nihāyah*, vol. 1, 74.

21. Al-Ṭabarī, *Tārīkh,* vol. 1, 69.

22. See Muḥammad Naṣruddīn al-Albānī, *Silsilat al-Aḥādīth al-Ḍa'īfah wa'l Mawḍū'ah* [Series of Weak and Fabricated *Ḥadīths*]

(Riyadh: Maktabat al-Ma'ārif, 2004), vol. 13, pt. 2, 1138 (noting that Abū al-Shaykh, a commentator on these *ḥadīths*, did not notice that they did not contain Eve's name).

23. Qur'an 39:6.

24. 'Alī's translation of *āyah* 39:6 uses "his mate" as an interpretation of *zawjahā*. But his interpretation is better than the one provided here in that it replaces "from him" with "of like nature." As we shall see later, this is a significant difference.

25. See, e.g., Yūsuf 'Alī's translation of this passage.

26. Qur'an 39:6.

27. Muḥammad Rashīd Riḍā, *Tafsīr al-Qur'ān al-Ḥakīm* [Exegesis of the Noble Qur'an], known as *Tafsīr al-Manār* (henceforth *Tafsīr al-Manār*) (repr., Beirut: Dār al-Ma'rifah, n.d.), vol. 4, 330.

28. Ibid., 330.

29. Al-Rāzī, *Tafsīr*, vol. 9, 167. For the traditional interpretation, see, e.g., Jalāl al-Dīn al-Suyūṭī (d. 1505), *Al-Durr al-Manthūr fī-Tafsīr al-Ma'thūr* [Scattered Gems in Transmitted Exegesis] (repr., Beirut: Dār al-Kutub al-'Ilmiyyah, 2000), vol. 2, 206. See also al-Ṭabarī, *Tārīkh*, vol. 1, 70; Ibn Kathīr, *Al-Bidāyah wa'l Nihāyah*, vol. 1, 74; al-Qurṭubī, *Al-Jāmi'*, vol. 1, 301–2.

30. See al-Albānī, *Silsilat al-Aḥādīth*, vol. 13, pt. 2, 1138–40.

31. Ibid.

32. Al-Rāzī, *Tafsīr*, vol. 9, at 167.

33. See Yūsuf 'Alī, *Qur'an Translation*. He got this part of the translation right. See also al-Rāzī, *Tafsīr*, vol. 25, 111.

34. Al-Rāzī, *Tafsīr*, vol. 25, 111; *Riḍā, Tafsīr al-Manār*, vol. 4, 330 (referring to al-Rāzī's view about Eve being created of the same nature as Adam). *Āyah* 30:21 says: "And among His signs is this: that he created for you mates from among yourselves that you may dwell in tranquility with them . . . ."

35. Abū Faḍl al-Alūsī, *Rūḥ al-Ma'ānī* [The Spirit of Meanings] (Reprint, Beirut: Dār al-Kutub al-'Ilmiyyah, 1994), vol. 2, 392.

36. *Āyah* 3:164 states that "God did confer a great favor on the believers when He sent them an apostle from among themselves." Another *āyah* 9:128 states: "Now has come to you an apostle from amongst yourselves."

37. Al-Rāzī, *Tafsīr*, vol. 16, 241; ibid., vol. 9, 167; Riḍā, *Tafsīr al-Manār*, vol. 4, 330. See also Muḥammad al-Shangīṭī, *Aḍwā' al-Bayān fī Īḍāḥ al-Qur'ān bi'l Qur'ān* [Explanatory Lights in Clarifying the Qur'an by the Qur'an] (repr., Beirut: Dār al-Kutub al-'Ilmiyyah, 2006), vol. 3, 241.

38. Riḍā, *Tafsīr al-Manār*, vol. 4, 330–2. Riḍā also mentions that Imām Muḥammad 'Abduh joins him in subscribing to al-Rāzī's second interpretation.

39. Al-Rāzī, *Tafsīr*, vol. 9, 167.

40. Ibid.

41. Ibid.

42. Nevertheless, even with the masculine gender, the word could still linguistically refer to a female. Riḍā however focuses on the literal interpretation.

43. Riḍā, *Tafsīr al-Manār*, vol. 4, 331.

44. Ibid.

45. *Āyah* 4:1 states: " Oh people, reverence your God who created you from a single *nafs* and created *minhā* its mate . . . ." For the translation of *minhā*, see the discussion in the text. See also *āyah* 30:21, which says: "And among His signs is this, that he created for you mates from among yourselves . . . ." *Āyah* 16:72 says: "And God made for you mates from among yourselves . . . ." Note that the phrase *min anfusikum* has been translated here as "from among yourselves." Linguistically, *anfus* is the plural of *nafs*, and "*anfusikum*" *means* "your *anfus*." For more discussion of this topic, see the text of this section.

46. Muḥammad al-Bukhārī, *Ṣaḥīḥ al-Bukhārī* (The Authentic Prophetic *Ḥadīths*), in *Fatḥ al-Bārī: Sharḥ Ṣaḥīḥ al-Bukhārī* [Divine Enlightenment: Explanation of al-Bukhārī's *Ṣaḥīḥ*], ed. and commentary Ibn Ḥajar al-'Asqalānī (repr., Beirut: Dār al-Kutub al-'Ilmiyyah, 1989), vol. 9, 313, *ḥadīth* no. 5184.

47. Ibid., vol. 9, 314.

48. Muslim al-Nīsābūrī, *Ṣaḥīḥ Muslim bi Sharḥ al-Nawawī* [The Authentic *Ḥadīths* [as collected by] Muslim, with Explanation by Muḥyī al-Dīn Abū Zakariyyā al-Nawawī] (repr., Beirut: Dār Iḥyā' al-Turāth al-'Arabī, n.d.), vol. 10, 57.

49. Al-Bukhārī, *Ṣaḥīḥ*, vol. 9, 313–15; also in Muslim, *Ṣaḥīḥ*, vol. 10, 57.

50. Al-'Asqalānī, *Fatḥ al-Bārī*, vol. 9, 316.

51. Ibid.

52. Muḥammad Murtaḍā al-Zabīdī, *Tāj al-'Arūs min Jawāhir al-Qāmūs* [The Bride's Crown of the Lexicon's Jewels] (repr., Beirut: Manshūrāt Dār Maktabat al-Ḥayāt, n.d.), vol. 5, 434.

53. Ibid.

54. Al-Zabīdī, *Tāj al-'Arūs*, vol. 2, 78.

55. Ibid., vol. 2, 80; Ibn Manẓūr, *Lisān*, vol. 9, 456.

56. Abū Zakariyyā al-Nawawī, *Riyāḍ al-Ṣāliḥīn* [The Meadows of the Righteous] (repr., Beirut: Mu'assasat al-Risālah, 1992), 161 n 3.

57. Al-Albānī, *Silsilat*, vol. 13, pt. 2, 1140.

58. Muḥammad Fakhr al-Dīn al-Rāzī, *Tafsīr*, vol. 22, 171–72.

59. Qur'an 21:37.

60. Al-Rāzī, *Tafsīr*, vol. 22, 172.

61. See, e.g., 'Alī, *Qur'an Translation*.

62. Qur'an 30:54.

63. Abū Faḍl al-Alūsī, *Rūḥ al-Ma'ānī*, vol. 17, 47. Incidentally, al-Rāzī mentions this interpretation as well, in his *Tafsīr*, vol. 22, 171.

64. Al-Alūsī, *Rūḥ al-Ma'ānī*, vol. 17, 47.

65. Al-Nawawī, *Riyāḍ al-Ṣāliḥīn*, 161 n3.

66. Ibid.

67. Ibid.

68. Qur'an 30:21.

69. Al-Rāzī, *Tafsīr*, vol. 25, 111. It is hard to accuse al-Rāzī of being partial to women, when in the prior passage, on the same page, he argues that women were created for men's comfort, like animals and plants. But see the next endnote and related text.

70. Al-Rāzī, *Tafsīr*, vol. 25, 111.

71. Muḥyī al-Dīn Ibn 'Arabī (d. 1148), *Aḥkām al-Qur'ān* (repr., Beirut: Dār al-Ma'rifah, 1987) vol. 1, 418.

72. Al-Rāzī, *Tafsīr*, vol. 15, 61. As translated by Yūsuf 'Alī, *āyah* 7:184 states:

> It is He who created you from a single person
> And made his mate of like nature in order
> That he may dwell with her (in love)

73. Qur'an 30:21.

74. See, e.g., Qur'an 7:189, 39:6; Badr al-Dīn al-Zarkashī, *Al-Burhān fī 'Ulūm al-Qur'ān* [Proof in Qur'anic Studies] (Beirut: Dār al-Jīl, 1988), vol. 1, 29; see also al-Suyūṭī, *Al-Itqān*, vol. 1, 35, citing al-Zarkashī (on the significance of Qur'anic repetition).

75. See Farīda Bennānī, *Taqsīm al-'Amal Bayn al-Zawjayn* [Division of Labor between Spouses]. Marrakesh: Silsilat Manshūrāt Kulliyyat al-'Ulūm al-Qānūniyyah wa'l Iqtiṣādiyyah wa'l Ijtimā'iyyah, Jāmi'at al-Qāḍī 'Ayyāḍ, 1992) 13–14 (noting that Muslim patriarchal societies used the concept of *qiwāmah* to create a hierarchical structure within the family, headed by the husband). She also argues that such hierarchy contradicts the basic principle of gender equality revealed in the Qur'an. Ibid., 27–29.

76. Al-Bukhārī, *Ṣaḥīḥ al-Bukhārī*, in *Fatḥ al-Bārī*, vol. 9. 407, *ḥadīth* no. 5228; see, e.g., Akram Ḍiyā' al-'Umarī, *Al-Sīrah al-Nabawiyyah al-Ṣaḥīḥah* [The Authentic Biography of the Prophet] (Riyadh: Maktabat al-'Ubaykān 1995), vol. 2, 648; 'Umar Riḍā Kahālah, *A'lām al-Nisā' fī 'Ālamayy al-'Arab wa'l Islām* [Prominent Women in the Arab and Muslim World] (Beirut: Mua'ssasat al-Risālah, 1977), vol. 3, 14–15.

77. Abū Ḥāmid al-Ghazālī, *Iḥyā' 'Ulūm al-Dīn* [Reviving Religious Studies] (repr., Egypt: Muṣṭafā al-Bābī al-Ḥalabī Press, 1939), vol. 2, 44–45.

78. Al-Ghazālī, *Iḥyā'*, vol. 2, 354; see also Abū al-Ḥasan al-Nadawī, *Al-Sīrah al-Nabawiyyah* [The Prophetic Biography] (Jeddah: Dār al-Shurūq, 1977) 370; al-'Umarī, *Al-Sīrah*, vol. 2, 644–45.

79. Indeed, all the *Sīrah* (the Prophet's biography) books acknowledge the Prophet's love to his family. See, e.g., al-'Umarī, *Al-Sīrah*, vol. 2, 646–47; Sa'īd Fāyiz al-Dakhīl, *Mawsū'at Fiqh 'Ā'ishah Umm al-Mu'minīn* [Encyclopedia of the Jurisprudence of 'Ā'ishah Mother of the Believers] (Beirut: Dār al-Nafā'is li'l Ṭibā'ah wa'l Nashr wa'l Tawzī' 1993) 51–52; Muḥammad Sa'īd Mubayyiḍ, *Mawsū'at Ḥāyāt al-Ṣaḥābiyyāt* [The Encyclopedia of *Ṣaḥābī* Women] (Qatar: Dār al-Thaqāfah, 1990), 531–41 (on the Prophet's love for 'Ā'ishah); 626–27 (on the Prophet's love for his daughter Fāṭimah), 325–30 (on the Prophet's continued love and loyalty to his wife, Khadījah, even after her death).

6

Mirror, Mirror on the Wall: Gender and Interpretation*

Islam is often stereotyped in the West as oppressive to women. Part of the problem is generated by individuals who cite specific *āyahs* to support this view without full understanding of the correct interpretations of these *āyahs* within the overall context of the Qur'an. Another part is generated by pernicious patriarchal regimes in other parts of the world that deny women's rights under the guise of religion. A third part is rooted in the huge body of uncontested patriarchal jurisprudence inherited over a period of centuries. If we are to improve the condition of Muslim women in the public sphere and within their families, this can only be achieved through proper education about their rights. Let me share a story about this with the reader.

*Parts A and B of this chapter were published in "Islam, Law and Custom: Redefining Muslim Women's Right," *American University Journal of International Law and Policy* vol. 12, no.1 (1997), 1–44.

Patriarchal popular culture in various Muslim societies propagates the view that *āyah* 4:34 states that men are "superior" to women. I grew up hearing this *āyah* being cited repeatedly by men who could hardly call themselves devout. The effect on the average woman, who has no jurisprudential abilities, is devastating. On one of my lecturing tours abroad, I held a private meeting with a group of non-Arabic speaking Muslim women. I asked them to tell me in earnest whether they thought Islam was patriarchal. Some thought so, citing this particular *āyah*, but adding sadly that if that was God's Will, then they would simply accept it. I was very touched by the piety of these women, who were Western educated and not outwardly religious. I then explained to them that the word "superior" was not part of the Arabic meaning of the *āyah*, but rather a patriarchal interpretation of one of its terms. After going through a brief analysis of the *āyah*, I could hear audible sounds of relief. Some women asked: "Why were we not told this before?" The answer, of course, is that perhaps more women need to be involved in Islamic jurisprudence. And this is why they are discouraged in some countries from doing so.

I. UNDERSTANDING THE MEANING OF THE COMPLEX STATEMENT

LET US NOW EXAMINE THAT PART OF *ĀYAT AL-QIWĀMAH* (4:34) that has unfairly been used to assert male superiority. We shall refer to this part as the Complex Statement to indicate that its meaning is not as obvious as it has been claimed to be. The Complex Statement has been translated as follows:

i. Men are the protectors and maintainers of women, because God has given the one more (strength) than the other, and because they support them from their means . . .[1]

This modern translation unilaterally resolves important issues left open by the original Arabic language. So, as usual, we now provide a partial translation that preserves key Arabic words that occur in the original passage:

ii. Men are *qawwāmūn* over women *bimā* God *faḍḍala* some of them over others, and *bimā* they support them from their means. . . .

Our partial translation signals that major issues revolve around the meaning of the three words that remained untranslated. They are *qawwāmūn, faḍḍala,* and *bimā*. We shall discuss them in sequence. The discussion will land us into the midst of the interaction between culture and language.

A. Classical Arabic Language and Society

Focusing on the first word, we note that *qawwāmūn* is a masculine plural form (also used when referring collectively to both genders) of the singular masculine derivative deverbal noun[2] *qawwām* and that *qiwāmah* is the infinitive form of that noun. It would help the reader to know that

a. most Arabic derivative deverbal nouns have a triliteral root (one consisting of three radical (that is, root) letters)[3]; and
b. Arabic derivative deverbal nouns generally derive their basic meanings primarily from two sources:
   i. the meaning of the root verb, and
   ii. the applicable derived form of the root verb.

For example, the nouns *qawwāmūn*, *qawwām*, and *qiwāmah* are all derivative deverbal nouns, derived from the same triliteral root verb. The root is *q.w.m*, pronounced *qawama* and later transformed into *qāma*. The root word has a literal meaning of "standing up." Related words have meanings of "straightening out" things and "holding steadfast to things." More figuratively, it has the meaning of "preservation and betterment" or "taking care of things."[4] It also has the meaning of "getting up" (as in getting up to do something). The infinitive of *qāma* is *qiyām*, a word reflected in the phrase *Yawm al-Qiyāmah*, the Day of Resurrection (or Judgment, when everyone "gets up" or is raised from the dead).[5] The noun *qā'im*, the masculine form for the one who engages in *qiyām* (i.e., the one who stands up, oversees, takes care of, or straightens things out) is also derived from *qāma*.

Furthermore, the words *qā'im* and *qayyim*, while sharing the same root verb, are derived from different derived forms of the triliteral verb. Each one of these numerous forms provides a different shade of meaning to a permutation of the root word. *Qā'im*, for example, is modeled after the noun *fā'il* (doer), the subjective form modeled after the derived verb form *fa'ala*, a basic and oft-used form meaning "to do." *Qayyim*, which is modeled after a different derived verb form, refers to the head of a tribe or leader of a community (*sayyid*)—that is, the one who takes care of his people's affairs.[6] The feminine form of the word is *qayyimah*.[7] In some Arabic dialects, the *qayyim* of a woman is her husband because he takes care of her affairs.[8] This linguistic observation is a cultural one, as well; it points to some prevalent customs in some tribes, which were in turn reflected in their use of the Arabic language.

Another linguistic cultural indicator arises from the meaning of *qawm, nomen verbi* of *qāma*.[9] According to a well-regarded ancient dictionary, Arabs disagreed on whether this Arabic word meant "people" or "men." Ibn al-Athīr (d. 1233), observed that the word used to mean "people," but then changed its meaning over time to refer only to "men."[10]

Incidentally, as pointed out in Chapter 2, the word *nās* (people), which is used repeatedly in the Qur'an, had a similar history. But the following story about the Prophet settles its meaning. 'Amr ibn al-'Āṣ asked the Prophet: "Whom do you love most of all the *nās*?" He responded: "'Ā'ishah." 'Amr then asked: "And of the men?" He answered: "Her father."[11]

Such linguistic issues remind us that the Qur'an was revealed in the pre-Islamic Age of *Jāhiliyyah* (the Age of Ignorance) to a people who used to practice female infanticide. Men married a large number of wives, inherited their fathers' wives as chattel, and denied women any inheritance.[12] There were pockets of less patriarchal tribes and some fortunate independent women, but the Qur'anic revelation came to slow down and roll back a patriarchal system that was on the ascent. This is why the Qur'anic revelation that men and women were created from the same *nafs* would have been a radical departure from the existing thinking. Also, given the radical worldview introduced by the Qur'an, it was necessary to combine it with the Qur'anic philosophy of gradualism to insure a peaceful transformation.

Returning to our linguistic study, we focus on the word *qawwām*, which is one of the variations derived from the triliteral verb *qāma*, (whose original form is *qa.wa.ma*). This specific form suggests intensity in the degree of "doing" referred to by the root verb, but it shares with other words derived from the same root verb a similar meaning.[13] So, *qawwām* has been variously interpreted by dictionaries and commentators to mean "head," "leader," "protector," "care-taker," and "advisor."[14] All these synonyms cluster around the core meaning of the root word and its derivatives, namely that of care-taking and straightening things out. This is quite a wide range of meanings, covering a broad spectrum of relationships. Coupled with one's social understanding of these relationships, the meanings can range from the most hierarchical and patriarchal to the most co-operative and democratic. Meanings with strict hierarchical significance tended to be found in older commentaries. They have been reified and carried, often uncritically, into modern jurisprudential interpretations.

One old Arabic dictionary defines the related word *qiyām*, specifically in the context of the *āyah*, as "having the meaning of preservation and betterment."[15] Another old dictionary defines the related word *qayyim* as "one who manages people's affairs, leads and straightens them out."[16] The difference between *qawwām* and *qayyim* is again a matter of degree, not scope. The first reflects an even greater intensity in discharging one's responsibilities than the second.

Two observations are in order. First, as may have become clear from earlier discussion, the term *qayyim* (and even the term *qawwām*) is not specific to gender relations. In fact, it is used just as often to describe the relation of the ruler to the people.[17] In both contexts, however, the interpretation of the word was influenced by the social and political realities of the time. For example, al-Zabīdī (d. 1790), notes in his dictionary that men are *qawwāmūn* over women in matters to which *women may not* attend.[18] This interpretation refers to a patriarchal *social* bar on women's activities. Modern patriarchal interpretations are more likely to claim a *natural* bar when they state that men are *qawwāmūn* over women, because men are physically stronger.[19]

Furthermore, dictionary meanings of *qayyim* and *qawwām*, whether relating to gender or politics, are open to hierarchical authoritarian interpretations. So, where a society was authoritarian, it made sense that interpreters colored these meanings with their own authoritarian perspectives.[20] But even in those societies, some scholars, such as Niẓām al-Dīn al-Nīsābūrī, recognized that men's *qiwāmah* was based on *faḍl* (as explained below), not on "subjugation, overreaching and oppression."[21] As the world changed, some modern interpreters have tried to expunge from the word its authoritarian meaning.[22] In this chapter, I shall further this effort by examining the actual practice of the Prophet Muḥammad in Madinah. After all, as the leader of the Muslims there, not to mention their Prophet, he was *qawwām* over their affairs.

In exercising *qiwāmah* over the people of Madinah, the Prophet engaged in consultation. Except in matters of revelation, wherever others had more expertise or were more convincing, he deferred to their judgment.[23] His leadership was collective, not authoritarian. More importantly, upon being chosen the leader, the Prophet executed with the people of Madinah a political charter that was tantamount to a bill of rights for all the citizens, Muslim and Jewish alike.[24] The Charter of Madinah defined the relationship between the State and the citizens. That relationship was based on constitutional Qur'anic guarantees, such as *bay'ah*, *shūrā*, and the right to privacy. The Charter articulated important additional rights, such as freedom of belief, the right to due process, and the prohibition of guilt by association.[25] In short, the Prophet was selected to be *qawwām* over a democratic political system designed to safeguard the *maṣlaḥah* (public interest) of the citizens there. Such a system is antagonistic to an authoritarian one based on the sheer power of the ruler and his own interests.

Given the Prophetic political model, one might ask whether there is an analogous familial model. In fact, one may wonder, why should the man be the one who is *qawwām* in a family? Is not that what patriarchy is in part about? Why cannot the woman be *qā'imah* or *qawwāmah* over the affairs of her family, even over her husband? The answer to these questions will require further careful examination of the Complex Statement.

The next word I would like to highlight in the Complex Statement is the verb *faḍḍala*. It is usually translated as meaning "being superior to or better."[26] Linguistically, *faḍḍala* derives from the root word *f.d.l* or *fadala*, which indicates a "remainder," "excess," or "left over." The derived transitive verb form *faḍḍala* usually means to favor someone over another—for example, by giving that someone "something extra" that distinguishes him or her from another.[27] At this point, I ask the reader to resist concluding prematurely that the Qur'an therefore states that men and women are essentially different, and that men are superior to women because God endowed them with "something extra," such as strength. That is in fact the patriarchal conclusion; mine is different. Later discussion will place the word *faḍḍala* in the Complex Statement in its proper context and provide its full accurate meaning.

The word *bimā* is the most complex and crucial word in this passage. Linguistically, it is composed of two parts: *bi* and *mā*. *Bi* is a connector with more than one meaning. Among the most prevalent meanings of *bi* are: (a) one that conveys a relation of causality (*sababiyyah* or *'illiyyah*); (b) one which conveys circumstantiality (*ẓarfiyyah*); (c) one which conveys a quantity which is less than all (*tab'īḍ*); and, finally, (d) one that conveys instrumentality (*isti'ānah*), so that what comes after the *bi* becomes "an instrument for realizing what precedes '*bi*,' and that we are told is the most common meaning of '*bi*.'[28] *Mā* acts here as a pure connector (*mawṣūlah*) but may have at times a more enhanced meaning (indicating a *maṣdar*, or *nomen verbi*).[29] It is used to refer to other than rational beings (such as things).[30]

The critical meaning, then, of *bimā* revolves mostly around the *bi* segment. As a result, *bimā* could mean: (a) "because"; (b) "in circumstances where"; (c) "in that which," a meaning which indicates *tab'īḍ* (i.e., a portion or a part of but not the whole); or (d) instrumentality. Looking back at the above translation, we can now revise it to read:

iii. Men are [advisors/providers of guidance] to women [because/in circumstances where/in that which] God made some of them different from some others and [because/in circumstances where/in that which/by virtue of what] they spend of their own money . . .

We are now ready to discuss the apparent conflict between the Harmony Principle and the Complex Statement. A basic rule of Islamic jurisprudence is the following: Where *āyahs* appear to conflict, they must be carefully studied in search of a meaning that makes them consistent with each other.[31] Another basic rule states that one way to resolve apparent conflict between *āyahs* is to check the scope of each.[32] If one is general and the other is particular, then the second may be an exception to or a carve-out from the first.

Here, the Qur'anic *āyah* that articulates the Harmony Principle is clearly general. It has no qualifiers, *provisos*, or carve-outs. It is also repeated in similar forms in the Qur'an.[33] The Complex Statement is different in structure. In stating what appears to be a general statement, namely that "men are *qawwāmūn* over women," the Complex Statement immediately provides an explanation. The explanation acts as a *limitation* upon the apparently general statement (*takhṣīṣ* of the *'āmm*) by specifying the reasons (*'illahs*) or circumstances (as indicated by the various meanings of *bimā*) that would entitle a male to be *qawwām*.[34] These include differences between some males and some females.[35]

The elements of this limitation are two. The first part of (ii)—namely, that men are *qawwāmūn* over women—is a general statement. But it is operative only: (1) where God has endowed a male (in a certain circumstance or at a certain time) with a feature, ability, or characteristic that a particular woman lacks and presumably needs in that circumstance or at that time, *and* (2) that male is maintaining that particular woman financially. Only under *both* of these conditions may the man presume to offer guidance, leadership, or advice to the woman. The first element is important for explaining why the *qiwāmah* of the male is acceptable at all, the second element is important for limiting that role to the man who is already taking care of the woman as her provider (if the woman is indeed being provided for). Otherwise, she may be faced with droves of men who want to provide unsolicited advice (*fuḍūliyyūn*).

The Qur'an clearly indicates that not all men satisfy both conditions. For one, the *tab'īḍī* meaning of *bimā* mentioned above suggests that the reference in the *āyah* is to a part of a group, but not the whole. The remaining text of the *āyah* reinforces this view when it explicitly uses the word *ba'ḍahum*, which means "some." More precisely, the remainder of the Complex Statement speaks of "some" whom God *faḍḍala* over "some" others.[36] (Note that the broad linguistic Qur'anic construction bears also the interpretation that God *faḍḍala* some men over some other men and women and *faḍḍala* some women over some men and other women.) This explicit use of *ba'ḍahum* in the second part of the Complex Statement reinforces the *tab'īḍī* meaning of the whole Complex Statement, since *tab'īḍ* was indicated at least once, and perhaps twice, in it.

In other words, the Qur'an was describing (not prescribing) in this *āyah* a situation akin to the traditional one existing at the time, where many women were financially dependent on men. In those circumstances, the *āyah* informs us, God gave the men who support these women the *taklīf* (i.e., the responsibility, not the privilege) of offering them (and them alone) guidance, leadership, and advice in those areas in which these men happen to be more qualified, informed, or experienced.[37] To put it differently, the man occupies the role of *qawwām* with respect to certain women in his family only if he meets simultaneously two stipulations: maintenance *and* superior knowledge or skill in the matters in relation to which he is exercising his *qiwāmah*, and then only against the background of the general rules of democratic relations exemplified by the Prophet in Madinah. Otherwise, it would be hard to reconcile this *āyah* about familial gender relations with the Qur'anic ideal, which is infused with tranquility, affection, and mercy.

Clearly, the ability of the man to exercise *qiwāmah* depends to a large degree on the needs and abilities of the women in his family. A working wife who completed her engineering degree and works in a construction company may have better skills than her husband (say, a poet) in construction engineering, even if she is being supported by him. If the couple decides to build a house, the husband would be wise to defer to his wife's expertise and not argue that he has *qiwāmah* over her by virtue of his gender. On the other hand, a husband married to a housewife who has never ventured much into the outside world is *qawwām* over her interests, but not without her informed consent. These two examples reveal one source of the male temptation for keeping women in the home, uneducated and severed from public life. This temptation is further stained by hierarchical *Iblīsī* logic.

In short, the Complex Statement is a *limitation upon*, not a license for, patriarchal men who would want to interfere in the lives of women, even in the absence of one or both of these conditions. (Incidentally, the same is true of the rest of *Āyat al-Qiwāmah*.) Men are simply not *qawwāmūn* over independent women or women they do not support. This fact has not been explicitly recognized by most jurists;[38] for this reason, a husband can still prevent his wife from leaving the house or working without his permission, even if he is not supporting her. This is perhaps what al-Zabīdī meant when he stated in his dictionary that "'men are *qawwāmūn* over women' means that men take care of matters to which *women may not* attend."

Thus, the passage that has been used for so long as the cornerstone of the patriarchal claim that men are superior to women turns out not to be about superiority at all. First, had God wanted to express the idea of "gender superiority," God would have used Arabic words that better express this idea, such as *afḍal*, *aḥsan*, and *mutafawwiqūn 'alā*. But the Qur'an eschewed all these words in favor of *qawwāmūn*, a word that has the meaning of "caretaking." This fact alone should be food for a great deal of thought, since as we all know, every word, even letter, in the Qur'an has its significance.[39] Second, the *āyah* does not even state that men take care of women. It only states that men have the obligation to take care of women in cases where two specific circumstances obtain *at the same time*: financial support by the male candidate for *qiwāmah*, *and* greater capability by that male in the area where the *qiwāmah* is needed. It is very important to recognize that neither one of these two circumstances constitutes either a gender-specific characteristic or a permanent deficiency. Both can be changed in time, if desired, in a fair and equitable society that does not discriminate against women. The foundations of such a society have already been articulated in the Qur'an itself, especially on the matter of gender relations. Thus, the limitations in Complex Statement represent a gradualist approach at transforming the consciousness of *Jāhiliyyah* men about women and gender relations. This Qur'anic approach of reformation by limitation and education is used elsewhere in the Qur'an and is part of its overall gradualist philosophy of change.

B. Further Thoughts

Although this interpretation differs from that offered by traditional jurists, our analytic method is, as usual, based on traditional religious and linguistic sources. In that sense, it does not constitute a departure from tradition. It *is* a traditional interpretation. As proof, I offer a similar (but not identical) interpretation of *bimā* offered by the famous jurist al-Rāzī.[40]

Al-Rāzī focused on the meaning of *bimā* in the second part of *Āyat al-Qiwāmah,* which will be discussed in another work. As translated, this second phrase states:

> iii. Righteous women are devoutly obedient and guard in (the husband's absence) *bimā* God guarded.[41]

Al-Rāzī argued that *bimā* in the phrase "*bimā* God guarded" had one of the following two meanings:

> a. *Bimā* may mean "that which," where *mā* acts as a pure connector.

Al-Rāzī then explained that given this meaning of *bimā,* phrase (iv) means that women are to guard the husband's rights *in exchange for that which* God guarded of women's rights against their husbands.[42] Notice that al-Rāzī's interpretation of *bimā* does more than merely connect the two parts of (iii). As he himself observes, it expresses also causality (*sababiyyah*) between them through the use of the locution "in exchange for."

b. *Bimā* may be *maṣdariyyah.*

Under this category of Arabic grammar, according to al-Rāzī, the Complex Statement means either "women guard their husband's rights *because* (*sababiyyah*) God helps women succeed in their effort (*bi tawfīqi llāh*)" or "*women guard their husband's rights because* (circumstantial) they guard (i.e., obey) God's orders by obeying their husbands."[43] Thus al-Rāzī, too, provides at least two meanings of *bimā* in this context, one of causality and another of circumstantiality.

In addition to al-Rāzī, as I showed earlier, my analysis is supported by several standard dictionaries.[44] In other words, there is nothing extraordinary about the linguistic analysis I provided for *bimā* in the Complex Statement. The problem arises only when this analysis is taken seriously and an interpretation is based on it. At that point, the fundamentally limiting scope of the Complex Statement (whether causal, circumstantial, or *tab'īḍī*) becomes apparent, a matter which, as shown earlier, most traditional jurists ignored or dismissed.

Our linguistic analysis shows that the Complex Statement makes perfect sense. Indeed, if our conclusion is correct, the Statement about the *qiwāmah* of certain women over certain men under similarly specified conditions would also make sense from the theoretical point of view. Such a Statement, however, would not have addressed any existing conditions in need of limitation at the time of revelation. Nevertheless, when at one point it became necessary to speak of a symmetrical responsibility for guidance and *protection* between men and women, the Qur'an did not hesitate. It said of male and female believers, that some of them are *walis* of some of the other male and female believers.[45] Thus, it is important to emphasize this *āyah* as a compassionate egalitarian foundation for gender relations in today's Muslim societies.

The Complex Statement was revealed in an authoritarian/patriarchal society that the Prophet was attempting to civilize and democratize. Consequently, it should be viewed for what it really is. It is a *limitation* on men that prevents them from assuming automatically (as many did then) oppressive authoritarian roles with respect to women. At most, the Complex Statement tells them that they can guide, lead, and advise only these women they support financially and then only when one more condition obtains.

This result is also consistent with the established juristic view that a woman may include in her marriage contract stipulations that would give her greater rights and freedoms within the marriage, including the right to divorce.[46] Such stipulations usually modify the traditional balance within the family in favor of the wife, thus detracting from the male's claimed "superiority" or authority. For this reason, these stipulations are widely resisted, and when accepted, they are often kept secret. Many commentators (including women) argued that the stipulations were either invalid, "unnatural," or acceptable only to inferior men.[47]

Despite its limiting structure, the Complex Statement has been misused by some traditional jurists to build an edifice of patriarchal oppression within the family.[48] This structure has destroyed for many women all tranquility and imposed upon them loss of basic liberties of such a nature and to such an extent as to make them wards, virtual slaves, and prisoners in their own homes and marriages.[49] Traditional jurisprudence ignored totally the limitational aspect of the Complex Statement and instead generalized it as a right and a privilege belonging to *all* men, even in cases where God clearly favored some women over some men with brains, skills, wealth, and other gifts.

C. Final Remarks

The traditional approach of jurists towards the issue of *qiwāmah* of men was generally two-pronged. As we saw earlier, one prong was based on the argument that God had favored all men over all women by endowing them with more brains, brawn, and money. This interpretation is quite narrow and was significant in days when physical power was necessary for survival. The rise of industrial and informational technology has led to societies that have depended more on brain than muscle and have opened the door to the education and employment of women. While these societies are not yet fully gender equitable, they have established two facts: (1) physical power has been replaced by technological or "smart" power, which has leveled the playing field for people of disparate physical abilities, and (2) women are as intellectually capable as men. These facts reveal the wisdom of the structure of the Qur'anic *āyah*, as well as the philosophy of change in the Qur'an.

With respect to the wisdom of the structure of the Qur'anic *āyah*, as argued earlier, the first part is closely tied to a *'illah* (cause). It is a known juristic principle that a rule revolves around its *'illah* and is suspended when the *'illah* disappears.[50] Based on this principle, *Khalīfah* 'Umar stopped payment of alms to *al-mu'allafati qulūbuhum*, although the Qur'an explicitly ordered such payments.[51] 'Umar argued that there was an implied *'illah* underlying that Qur'anic injunction that was no longer present. The first part of *Āyat al-Qiwāmah* is structured so that the *'illah* is explicitly stated in its second part. It consists of the two conditions for establishing *qiwāmah*. In our society, one and sometimes both parts of the *'illah* are absent. This means that *qiwāmah* cannot be established in their absence.

Some patriarchal jurists may argue that the absence of the *'illah* for *qiwāmah* in our American society only shows that our society is in need of reform. Where women become equal to men, they observe, the family structure is damaged, the family suffers, and children do not receive proper upbringing. A family needs a head. In his absence, drugs and violence infect our society. This argument is based on an authoritarian view of life that is inconsistent with basic Islamic principles. It is also too simplistic in terms of its analysis of the problems plaguing our American society. More importantly, if God did not mean for women to have their improved status, God would not have given them the brains and skills to do so. Furthermore, God the Almighty would have stated out flatly in the Qur'an that women are inferior to men and must submit to them. There is no such statement in all of the Qur'an, yet the Qur'an repeatedly states the thought contained in the Harmony Principle.

Now that our societies have realized the falsehood of the general patriarchal proposition about the inferiority of women, men can no longer rely on it to claim automatic *qiwāmah* over a woman. Also, in a world more inclined toward democratic relations, a man who does have such *qiwāmah* must also understand that exercising *qiwāmah* is a (perhaps temporary) duty and not a privilege (pending a possible change in circumstance). Furthermore, it is a duty based on consent and consultation, and is rooted in the Qur'anic Harmony Principle. This is the path that was followed by the Prophet and, after him, by many pious jurists in their own personal relationships. It is time that we make it our path as well.

II. THE OTHER *ĀYAH*: MEN HAVE A *DARAJAH* OVER WOMEN

The discussion of the Complex Statement will not be complete without a discussion of another *āyah* that is used as further support for the proposition that men are superior to women. *Āyah* 2: 228 says towards the end:

> Women shall have rights similar to those against them, according to what is equitable: But men have a degree (of advantage) over women.

The full *āyah* explains some rules relating to a form of divorce initiated by men (forms of divorce that are available to women will be discussed in a later work). Under this scenario, the Qur'an gave the man an opportunity to change his mind and reverse his decision within a certain period of time. This fact reflects again Qur'anic wisdom in recognizing that husbands often divorce their wives in anger only to regret it later. In this *āyah,* the Qur'an states that these wives have rights "similar" to the rights [men have] against them, according to what is equitable, but that the men have a degree (of advantage) over them. It seems obvious that the degree referred to in this context is the ability of men, not shared by women in this specific circumstance, to rescind the divorce initiated by the men themselves.[52] Some jurists, however, generalized this statement to say that men are "a degree" above women, or that this degree is a reference to the fact that men maintain women, the "weaker sex."[53] This sort of interpretation reflects the same patriarchal thinking underlying the hierarchical interpretation of the Complex Statement.

Generally, many traditional jurists not only espoused a patriarchal model of gender relations, but they actively worked at making it a universal reality by passing restrictive laws that were highly detrimental to women. They utilized the stereotype of the woman in their culture as emotional, dependent, and weak, and used their legal power and religious prestige to assert the automatic *qiwāmah* of all men.[54] This unjust approach defeated the limitational purpose of the Complex Statement. Their interpretation of the Complex Statement was based on a biased patriarchal interpretation of that *āyah*, an oppressive behavior toward women, and the supplementation of Qur'anic law with a stereotype that harbored a deep contradiction with the Qur'anic Harmony Principle as stated in several *āyahs*. Consequently, thoughtful Muslims should no longer accept that interpretation, and Muslim women must rediscover the truth of the Qur'anic Equality Principle in order to achieve liberation and freedom without guilt.

To be able to reach this challenging goal, Muslim women must formulate a strategy for change. In this strategy, the dramatic increase in the number of women seeking legal and religious education must rank very high. This fact becomes especially clear when we turn to a discussion of *ḥadīth*. There are numerous alleged *ḥadīths* that denigrate women. Revisiting them with fresh eyes is a very demanding task, requiring decades of hard work. To complete the discussion in this chapter, however, we shall select one *ḥadīth* for the next chapter that many Muslim men have quoted to their wives.

NOTES

1. This is Yūsuf 'Alī's translation with no modifications. 'Abdullāh Yūsuf 'Alī, *The Meaning of the Holy Qur'an* (Beltsville, MD: Amana Publications, 2004).

2. Refers to a noun derived from a verb. W. Wright, *A Grammar of the Arabic Language*, 3rd ed (Cambridge: University Press, 1933), 106.

3. Ibid., 29, 106.

4. Muḥammad Murtaḍā al-Zabīdī (d. 1790), *Tāj al-'Arūs Min Jawāhir al-Qāmūs* [The Bride's Crown of the Lexicon's Jewels] (repr., Beirut: Manshūrāt Dār Maktabat al-Ḥayāt, n.d.), vol. 9, 37; Muḥammad Ibn Manẓūr, *Lisān al-'Arab* [The Tongue of Arabs] (repr., Beirut: Dār Iḥyā' al-Turāth al-'Arabī, 1992), vol. 11, 354, 357–59; Wizārat al-Awqāf wa'l Shu'ūn al-Islāmiyyah (of Kuwait), *Al-Mawsū'ah al-Fiqhiyyah* [The Jurisprudential Encyclopedia] (Egypt: Dār al-Ṣafwah, 1993), vol. 34, 76 (the difference between a *qayyim* and a *waṣiyy* is that the former is usually in charge of collecting and preserving wealth but not managing it, while the latter has these responsibilities but also acts like an agent).

5. Al-Zabīdī, *Tāj al-'Arūs*, vol. 9, 37; Ibn Manẓūr, *Lisān*, vol. 11, 362.

6. Al-Zabīdī, *Tāj al-'Arūs*, vol. 9, 37; Ibn Manẓūr, *Lisān*, vol. 11, 359.

7. Al-Zabīdī, *Tāj al-'Arūs*, vol. 9, 37; Ibn Manẓūr, *Lisān*, vol. 11, 359.

8. Al-Zabīdī, *Tāj al-'Arūs*, vol. 9, 35, 37; Ibn Manẓūr, *Lisān*, vol. 11, 359.

9. Al-Zabīdī, *Tāj al-'Arūs*, vol. 9, 34; Ibn Manẓūr, *Lisān*, vol. 11, 361.

10. See Ibn Manẓūr, *Lisān*, vol. 11, 361, quoting Ibn al-Athīr.

11. According to al-Zabīdī, the word *nās* is derived ultimately from the word *ins*, which refers to "human beings." Al-Zabīdī, *Tāj al-'Arūs*, vol. 4, 98–99; see also Muḥammad al-Bukhārī, *Ṣaḥīḥ al-Bukhārī* [The Authentic Prophetic *Ḥadīths*], in al-'Asqalānī's *Fatḥ al-Bārī: Sharḥ Ṣaḥīḥ al-Bukhārī* [Divine Enlightenment: Explanation of al-Bukhārī's *Ṣaḥīḥ*], collection of authentic prophetic *ḥadīths* by al-Bukhārī, with commentary by al-'Asqalānī (repr., Beirut: Dār al-Kutub al-'Ilmiyyah, 1989), vol. 7, 22, *ḥadīth* no. 3662.

12. There is a reference to these pre-Islamic ways of mistreating women in the Qur'an 4:19. See also Niẓām al-Dīn al-Ḥasan bin Muḥammad bin Ḥusayn al-Nīsābūrī, *Tafsīr Gharā'ib al-Qur'ān* [Explaining the Unusual in the Qur'an] published in the margin of Abū Ja'far al-Ṭabarī's *Jāmi' al-Bayān fī Tafsīr al-Qur'ān* [Comprehensive Exegesis of Qur'anic Interpretation] (repr., Beirut: Dār al-Ma'rifah, 1978), vol. 28, 207; Muḥammad Rashīd Riḍā, *Tafsīr al-Qur'ān al-Ḥakīm* [Exegesis

of the Noble Qur'an], known as *Tafsīr al-Manār* (repr., Beirut: Dār al-Ma'rifah, n.d.), vol. 4, 345–46.

13. See, e.g., Abū Ḥayyān al-Gharnāṭī, *Al-Baḥr al-Muḥīṭ* [The All-Encompassing Sea (of Knowledge)] (repr., Beirut: Dār al-Fikr, 1978), vol. 3, 238; see also al-Nīsābūrī, *Tafsīr, in Jāmi' al-Bayān,* vol. 6, at 40 (stating that the form of *qawwām* indicates intensiveness, also stating that the man protects the woman like the ruler protects the people); *Al-Mawsū'ah,* vol. 34, 75.

14. See, e.g., *Al-Mawsū'ah,* vol. 34, 75–78 (stating that a *qawwām* protects the wealth and collects payments and goods, but does not exercise full management control over it; also, he is the head and most senior member of the family (*ra'īsuhā wa kabīruhā*)). But see al-Zabīdī, *Tāj al-'Arūs,* vol. 9, 37 (stating that a *qawwām* takes over full responsibility [*mutakaffil bi'l amr*], is a protector [*muḥāfaẓah*], a reformer [as in *iṣlāḥ*], and also a "leader" [*sā'is al-amr*]); Riḍā, *Tafsīr al-Manār,* vol. 5, 67 (mentions protection, caretaking, being the head of the family (*riyāsah*) and advisor (*irshād*), and overseeing); see also Aḥmad Ghandūr, *Al-Aḥwāl al-Shakhṣiyyah fi'l Tashrī' al-Islāmī* [Personal Status in Islamic Legislation] (henceforth, *Al-Aḥwāl*) (Kuwait, Jāmi'at al-Kuwait Press, 1972), 235–36 (stating that a *qawwām* is a leader (*riyāsah*), advisor (*murshid*), and overseer (*murāqabah*)).

15. Ibn Manẓūr, *Lisān,* vol. 11, 355.

16. Abū 'Abd al-Raḥmān al Farāhidī, *Kitāb al-'Ayn* [The Book of (the Letter) 'Ayn] (repr., Beirut: Mu'assasat al-A'lamī li'l Maṭbū'āt, 1988), vol. 5, 232.

17. See, e.g., al-Ṭabarī, *Jāmi' al-Bayān,* vol. 5, 37 (men are princes over women who must obey their orders); 'Abd al-Raḥmān al-Tha'ālibī, *Tafsīr* [Exegesis] (repr., Beirut: Dār Iḥyā' al-Turāth al-'Arabī, 1997), vol. 2, 229 (men are princes over women); Abū al-Qāsim al-Zamakhsharī, *Al-Kashshāf* [The Revealer] (repr., Beirut: Dār al-Ma'rifah, 2009), 234 (men are *qawwāmūn* over women ordering and prohibiting them like rulers do with their subjects); see also Muḥammad al-Kilbī, *Kitāb al-Tashīl li 'Ulūm al-Tanzīl* [The Book of Facilitation of Revelation Studies] (repr., Beirut: Dār al-Kitāb al-'Arabī, 1973), vol. 1, 140. (men are princes over women).

18. Al-Zabīdī, *Tāj al-'Arūs,* vol. 9, 34.

19. See above translation of the verse. See also Riḍā, *Tafsīr al-Manār,* vol. 5, 69 (men are stronger and more capable); *Al-Mawsū'ah,* vol. 34, 78 (quoting an older source that God favored men over women with rationality and judgment); Muḥammad 'Aqlah, *Niẓām al-Usrah fi'l Islām* [The Family System in Islam] (Amman: Maktabat al-Risālah al-Ḥadīthah, 1983), vol. 2, 17 (reasons for *qiwāmah* of men over women are divine order, physical strength, ability to make a living, more in line with the woman's nature, which is submissive towards men); Muḥammad al-Dusūqī, *Al-Usrah* [The Family] (Doha: Dār al-Thaqāfah, 1995), 158 (God gave the man physical strength, determination, and ability to work).

20. See note 17 where the various sources reflect their own prevalent cultural values in interpreting the concept of *qiwāmah.*

21. Al-Nīsābūrī, *Tafsīr* in *Jāmi' al-Bayān,* vol. 5, 40 (arguing that the verse shows that the *wilāyah* (guardianship) over women is acquired by merit, not by overpowering, overreaching, or oppression. Note that al-Nīsābūrī uses the words *wilāyah* and *qiwāmah,* interchangeably in this passage. See also al-Zamakhsharī, *Al-Kashshāf,* 234 (stating a similar thought to that of al-Nīsābūrī and using *wilāyah* in the same sense).

22. See, e.g., Riḍā, *Tafsīr al-Manār,* vol. 2, 380 (the man has a better claim on leadership because he knows best the interests of the family, has better execution power with his strength and money, and is required by law to protect and maintain the woman); ibid., vol. 5, 67 (God favored men over women at creation and gave them more power and strength); see also Aḥmad Ghandūr, *Al-Aḥwāl al-Shakhṣiyyah fi'l Tashrī' al-Islāmī* [Personal Status in Islamic Law] (Kuwait: Jāmi'at al-Kuwait Press, 1972), 235–36 (detailing ways in which men are superior to women).

23. See Tawfīq al-Shāwī, *Fiqh al-Shūrā wa'l Istishārah* [The Jurisprudence of Consultation and Seeking Advice] (Manṣūrah, Egypt: Dār al-Wafā', 1992), 131–42 (distinguishes between the two concepts, with consultation being binding, but not seeking advice; provides examples of the Prophet's consultations); 'Abd al-Ḥamīd al-Anṣārī, *Al-Shūrā wa Atharuhā fi'l Dīmuqrāṭiyyah* [Consultation and Its Impact on Democracy]. Reprint. Beirut: Al-Maktabah al-'Aṣriyyah, 2nd print, 1980), 65–76.

24. See Azizah al-Hibri, "Islamic and American Constitutional Law: Borrowing Possibilities or a History of Borrowing?" *University of Pennsylvania Journal of Constitutional Law,* vol. 1, no. 3, 511–14 (1999); see also Akram Ḍiyā' al-'Umarī, *Al-Sīrah al-Nabawiyyah al-Ṣaḥīḥah* [The Authentic Biography of the Prophet] (Riyadh: Maktabat al-'Ubaykān, 1995), vol. 2, 282–85; Muḥammad Ḥamīdullāh, *Majmū'at al-Wathā'iq al-Siyāsiyyah li'l 'Ahd al-Nabawī wa'l Khilāfah al-Rāshidah* [Collection of Political Documents of the Prophetic and Rashidi Eras] (Beirut: Dār al-Nafā'is, 1987), 57–62.

25. See al-Hibri, "Islamic and American Constitutional Law," 511–14; al-'Umarī, *Al-Sīrah,* vol. 2, 282–85; Ḥamīdullāh, *Majmū'at al-Wathā'iq,* 57–62.

26. See, e.g., Riḍā, *Tafsīr al-Manār,* vol. 5, 67; Ghandūr, *Al-Aḥwāl,* 235–36.

27. Ibn Manẓūr, *Lisān,* vol. 10, 280. Linguistically, the root verb *faḍala* refers to "the opposite of deficiency," and *fuḍlah* means "remnant." See al-Farāhidī, *Kitāb al-'Ayn,* vol. 7, 43; Ibn Manẓūr, *Lisān,* vol. 10, 281. Consequently, a secondary meaning of the word reduces *faḍḍala* to mere difference, without ascribing any value to that difference. As a result of this secondary meaning, the science of differential equations is called in many Arab universities *'ilm al-tafāḍul,*—that is, the science of difference. I do not believe that this meaning is linguistically appropriate in the context under discussion. The appropriate meaning here is the primary one of having some distinction, quality, or attribute the other does not have. But as we shall see later, this is not a reference to male superiority over women. Rather it is one of two requisite characteristics that a male must satisfy before he can even attempt to lead or even advise a woman.

28. These meanings can be found in a regular Arabic dictionary. See, e.g., Muḥammad Isbīr and Bilāl Junaydī, *Al-Shāmil* [The Comprehensive] (Beirut: Dār al-'Awdah, 1981), 235–36; see also Fakhr al-Dīn al-Rāzī, *Al-Maḥṣūl fī 'Ilm Uṣūl al-Fiqh* [The Harvest in the Study of the Foundations of Fiqh] (Beirut: Mu'assasat al-Risālah, 1992), vol. 1, 379, 381 note 3 (for the meaning of *tab'īḍ*); Badr al-Dīn al-Zarkashī, *Al-Burhān fī 'Ulūm al-Qur'ān* [Proof in Qur'anic Studies] (Beirut: Dār al-Jīl, 1988), vol. 1, 252–56 (on the *isti'ānah* and other meanings of '*bi*').

29. Isbīr and Junaydī, *Al-Shāmil*, 764. See also Abū Ja'far Aḥmad bin Ismā'īl al-Naḥḥās, *I'rāb al-Qur'ān* [Syntax of the *Qur'an*] (repr., Beirut: Dār al-Ma'rifah, 2011), 182.

30. See, e.g., Isbīr and Junaydī, *Al-Shāmil*, 765; al-Zarkashī, *Al-Burhān*, vol. 1, 533-401 (discussing the two meanings along with others), al-Rāzī, *al-Maḥṣūl*, vol. 1, 333 ("*mā*" is used for nonhumans).

31. Wahbah al-Zuḥaylī, *Uṣūl al-Fiqh al-Islāmī* [The Foundations of Islamic Jurisprudence] (Damascus: Dār al-Fikr, 1986), vol. 1, 434 (stating that the Qur'an is internally consistent).

32. Ibid.

33. See, e.g., Qur'an 7:189, 39:6, 4:1.

34. Muḥammad Shalabī, *Uṣūl al-Fiqh al-Islāmī* [Foundations of Islamic Jurisprudence] (Beirut: al-Dār al-Jāmi'iyyah, n.d), 432–64 (defining *'āmm* and *khāṣṣ* and their juristic relationship).

35. Farīda Bennānī, *Taqsīm al-'Amal bayn al-Zawjayn* [Division of Labor between Spouses]. Marrakesh: Silsilat Manshūrāt Kulliyyat al-'Ulūm al-Qānūniyyah wa'l Iqtiṣādiyyah wa'l Ijtimā'iyyah, Jāmi'at al-Qāḍī 'Ayyāḍ, 1992.), 35–36. Bennānī, among others, points out that the structure of the Complex Statement permits the interpretation that the differences referred to there are not differences between men and women, but rather between men and other men. Ibid. She argues that such differences are based on the man's ability to maintain his family. Ibid.

36. It is interesting in this regard to examine the interpretation of Riḍā in *Tafsīr al-Manār*, vol. 5, at 68–69, in which he argues that, in this case, "some" refers to the whole masculine and feminine genders as classes, not to all men and women, because there are exceptions within each gender. Ibid. In other words, like some other jurists, he interprets "some" in the *āyah* to mean "all." Ibid.

37. Bennānī, *Taqsīm*, 35, makes a similar point.

38. A survey of modern juristic books on this point reveals a serious lacuna. They discuss mutual duties and obligations of husband and wife, the duty of the husband to maintain the wife, duties of the wife towards the husband, reasons for stopping her maintenance, and legal consequences of the husband being unable to maintain his wife. Nowhere in this discussion is the Muslim woman informed that if

she is not supported by her husband, he is not *qawwām* over her, and what follows from that fact. Rather, some jurists argue that the *mahr* the husband gave his wife at marriage is sufficient to establish his *qiwāmah*. (This analysis is wrong, but that is an argument for another day about *mahr*.) In an online opinion, the Saudi scholar, Fāṭimah 'Umar Naṣīf, addressed this issue directly, stating that *qiwāmah* means that the husband fulfills his responsibilities toward the family. Short of that, he loses his *qiwāmah*. See http://www.liilas.com/vb3/t177721.html. Again, this underlines the importance of women's voices in jurisprudence.

39. See Jalāl al-Dīn al-Suyūṭī, *Al-Itqān fī 'Ulūm al-Qur'ān* [Mastery of Qur'anic Studies] (Beirut: Dār al-Nadwah al-Jadīdah, 1951), 141–79; see also Ṣubḥī al-Ṣāliḥ, *Mabāḥith fī 'Ulūm al-Qur'ān* [Research in Qur'anic Studies] (Beirut: Dār al-'Ilm li'l Malāyīn, 13th print, 1981), 313–33.

40. I also would like to suggest to those familiar with Arabic and the exact nature of the words used in the Qur'an to reflect on how the meaning of the Complex Statement would have changed had the word *limā* been used instead of *bimā* . I found it significant that it was not.

41. Qur'an 4:34.

42. Muḥammad Fakhr al-Dīn al-Rāzī, *Tafsīr al-Fakhr al-Rāzī* [The Exegesis of al-Rāzī] (better known as theGrand Exegesis) (Beirut: Dār al-Fikr, 1985), vol. 10, 92.

43. Ibid.

44. See notes 28–30 and related text.

45. Qur'an 9:71.

46. Muḥammad al-Khamlīshī, *Al-Ta'līq 'alā Qānūn al-Aḥwāl al-Shakhṣiyyah* [Commentary on Personal Status Code] (Rabat: Maktabat al-Ma'ārif, 1987), vol. 1, 322-28; Azizah al-Hibri, "Marriage Laws in Muslim Countries," *International Review of Comparative Public Policy* 4 235–36 (1992); 'Abd al-Raḥmān al-Jazīrī, *Kitāb al-Fiqh 'alā al-Madhāhib al-Arba'ah* [The Book of Jurisprudence of the Four Schools of Thought] (Beirut: Dār Iḥyā' al-Turāth al-'Arabī, 1969), vol. 4, 88; cf. Muḥammad Ibn Juzayy, *Qawānīn al-Aḥkām al-Shar'iyyah* [Laws of *Sharī'ah* Rulings] (repr., Beirut: Dār al-'Ilm li'l Malāyīn, 1979), 243

(distinguishing among the different ways by which the condition is introduced into the marriage contract and the related consequences).

47. See, e.g., Sanā' Hānī, "*Zawjī al-'Azīz Anta Ṭāliq*" [My Dear Husband You are Divorced," on <http://lahona.com/2014/04/09/17603/زوجي العزيز أنت طالق.html>, visited August 1, 2014. See also, Khawlah Hāmid, "*'Al-'Iṣmah bi Yadihā' Hal Tuṣbiḥ Amran Ṭabī'iyyan Yawman mā?!*" [The *'Iṣmah* in Her Hand "Would this Become a Normal Matter One Day?!"], http://www.amanjordan.org/a-news/wmview.php?ArtID =22539.

48. Ibid.

49. Bennānī, *Taqsīm*, 14–17 (pointing out that the basis of that edifice was the division of labor within the family). The division of labor was in turn justified by the patriarchal stereotype of women.

50. See, e.g., Al-Bardīsī, Muḥammad Zakariyyā. *Al-Aḥkām al-Islāmiyyah fi'l Aḥwāl al-Shakhṣiyyah* [Islamic Rulings in Personal Status Laws]. Egypt: Dār al-Nahḍah al-'Arabiyyah, 1965), 327–37. See also Muwaffaq al-Dīn Ibn Qudāmah, [d. 1187], *Al-Mughnī* [The Enricher/or Sufficient] (repr., Beirut: Dār al-Kitāb al-'Arabī, n.d.), vol. 8, 128–29 (lists matters in which the husband can dictate to the wife her actions, and that he can prevent her from leaving the house). A woman, called Umm Janā from Jordan, wrote to a "juristic" website on the Internet asking about the limits of her husband's *qiwāmah* and of her obedience. "Can he," she asked, "force me to work so that I am unable to continue my education? Is this a *qiwāmah* that God would accept?" Unfortunately, the answer was unresponsive. It simply restated the traditional rules.

51. Fakhr al-Dīn al-Rāzī, *Al-Maḥṣūl*, vol. 5, 207.

52. Qur'an 2:228.

53. This is one of the interpretations mentioned by al-Rāzī in his *Tafsīr*, vol. 6, 102.

54. Riḍā, *Tafsīr al-Manār*, vol. 2, 380 (arguing that this degree is one of leadership and caretaking, as stated in *Āyat al-Qiwāmah*); see also, e.g., commentary by Yūsuf 'Alī, *Qur'an Translation*, 92 n. 255; Hishām Qabalān, *Adāb al-Zawāj fi'l Islām* [The Etiquette of Marriage in Islam] (Beirut: Manshūrāt 'Uwaydāt, 1983), 190 (stating that the

degree is that of heading the family, otherwise, the spouses are equal in all rights and obligations).

55. Bennānī, *Taqsīm*, 25 (alluding to this point when she wonders whether present gender differences were not artificially produced by patriarchal manipulation of the rules and laws of society and the family); see Fāṭimah Naṣīf, *Ḥuqūq al-Mar'ah wa Wājibātuhā fī Ḍaw' al-Kitāb wa'l Sunnah* [Women's Rights and Duties in Light of the Book and Sunnah] (Jeddah: Tahāmah, 1992), 238–40, where the Saudi author argues that the husband is entitled to head his family by virtue of the natural capabilities that God endowed all men with. Among her reasons for giving men the leadership status are the following two: each organizational structure must have a head, and the husband is better suited to be that head, because of his physical strength and his role as maintainer and protector. For info on the gender Stereotype, see also Azizah al-Hibri, "Islam, Law and Custom."

7

To Prostrate Herself or Not to Prostrate, That Is the Question

In the last chapter, we illustrated how Qur'anic interpretation influenced by cultural perspectives advanced a patriarchal view of gender relations not rooted in the Qur'an itself. In this chapter we will show that a similar problem occurred with respect to the prophetic *ḥadīth*. This fact accounts for the contradictory *ḥadīths* attributed to the Prophet, some of which empower women while others are clearly misogynistic and inconsistent with the Prophet's life and example.

We have chosen for this chapter a commonly known *ḥadīth* that appears to give the husband a stature superior to that of his wife within the family, and hence it is not quite consistent with the Islamic model of family relations. In its simplest version, the *ḥadīth* states:

> If I were to order a person to prostrate himself to another, I would order the woman to prostrate herself to her husband.[1]

In other versions, the *ḥadīth* explains: "due to his great right over her."[2] Let us refer to this as the Prostration *Ḥadīth*. The full extent of its inconsistency will not become evident until we provide a thorough analysis of Islamic family law, which is the subject of a whole other book. However, we have laid sufficient grounds in this book to be able to formulate a judgment.

I. DETERMINING THE GOAL AND PROCESS

BEFORE WE EMBARK ON OUR TASK OF EXAMINING THIS *ḤADĪTH*, let us remind ourselves of why we are doing this. We are doing it because the Qur'an orders us to follow the Prophet's instructions and guidance. As pointed out in Chapter 2, *āyah* 59:7 states:

> So take what the Prophet gave you [as part of the Message]
> And what he forbade, do not engage in.

The Prophet himself emphasized this fact, and without his guidance, Muslims today would not know how to pray, perform pilgrimage, or fast, among other things. Also, as we saw in prior chapters of this book, the Prophet went beyond these basic instructions to teach us Islamic values through his words and example. He taught us about such things as human and animal rights, which were hardly a hot topic fifteen hundred years ago. He taught us about interfaith tolerance, respect and friendship, conflict resolution, ethics, and good manners. He said: "I was sent to complete *makārim al-akhlāq* (the noblest of ethics)."[3] In all of that, the Prophet was himself embodying Qur'anic values and principles. As 'Ā'ishah said: "The Qur'an was *khuluquh* [the Prophet's ethics and manners]."[4]

For all these reasons, Muslims take *ḥadīth* very seriously as an important part of their faith. Thus being able to discern an authentic *ḥadīth* from a weak or fabricated one is critical. This concern led scholars centuries ago to develop the discipline of "*ḥadīth* studies," which provided a road map of how to determine the authenticity of a *ḥadīth*. This road map includes such matters as how to investigate the soundness of the *isnād* of a *ḥadīth* (its chain of attribution to the Prophet), as well as ways of assessing the soundness of its *matn* (content or substance).

Ṣubḥī al-Ṣāliḥ, a modern scholar of *ḥadīth*, discusses the importance of properly determining the authenticity of *ḥadīth*.[5] He points out that Orientalists misunderstood the goals of *ḥadīth* studies by focusing too much on *isnād* and not enough on *matn*.[6] He notes that examining *isnād* is only one means, out of many, for reaching the goal of identifying the authentic *matn*. For this reason al-Ṣāliḥ notes that it is important to keep this goal in mind and examine the *matn* by checking it not only against the Qur'an and reliable *ḥadīth*, but also against the same *indicia* used for discovering fabrications.[7]

According to al-Ṣāliḥ, these *indicia* include grammatical errors or other linguistic defects or weaknesses in the *ḥadīth*, irrational or illogical content, content that contradicts human sensibilities, threatening language, passages that mix eloquent wording with technical terms used by certain jurists, content that appeases the ruling class, and elements not befitting the Prophet, including language that is impossible for him to have uttered.[8] All these factors are important to uncover defects in the attributed *ḥadīth* and ascertain its integrity.

It is also important to note that a defect in either the *matn* or *isnād* of a *ḥadīth* is sufficient to render it weak and unreliable. A defect in both should be fatal. In this section, to be systematically rigorous, we shall examine both the *isnād* and *matn* of the main versions of the Prostration *ḥadīth*.

Having reminded ourselves of the religious importance of and methodology used for the examination to be undertaken in this section, we turn to this task.

II. VARIOUS VERSIONS OF THE PROSTRATION *ḤADĪTH*

There are several versions of the Prostration *Ḥadīth*, with different *matns* and chains of *isnād*. This should not alarm us because the Prophet could have reiterated the *ḥadīth* on various occasions in different forms. In fact, the *ḥadīth* is narrated as having originated from quite a few well-respected *ṣaḥābīs* and even from the Prophet's wife 'Ā'ishah. Among these *ṣaḥābīs* are Mu'ādh bin Jabal, Abū Hurayrah, Anas bin Mālik, and Ibn 'Abbās, all well known in *ḥadīth* literature. For this and other reasons, most scholars judged this *ḥadīth* to be *ṣaḥīḥ*, but some others disagreed.

It is important to note that, despite its impressive pedigree, the Prostration *Ḥadīth* was not included in the most reliable compilations of *ḥadīth*—namely, *Ṣaḥīḥ al-Bukhārī* and *Ṣaḥīḥ Muslim*. However, it was included in compilations of lesser status and in works of historians and other writers. In this study, we shall focus only on versions of the *ḥadīth* included in the most reliable compilations of *ḥadīth* scholars. Even in these compilations, narrations of this *ḥadīth* appear in various forms, both with respect to *isnād* and *matn*. For our purposes in this chapter, we shall first focus on the two main versions cited in the highly respected *Musnad al-Imām Ibn Ḥanbal* (henceforth, *al-Musnad*). These two versions have also been narrated by other sources as well, often with some variation:

> First Version: While the Prophet was with a group of *ṣaḥābīs*, a camel approached him and then sank to the ground prostrating itself before him. The amazed *ṣaḥābīs* said to the Prophet that if irrational animals prostrated themselves to him, then rational human beings must have a greater reason to do the same. The Prophet answered: "Worship God [alone], and honor your brother [in faith, i.e., the Prophet himself, by following his teachings]. Had I wanted to order one person to prostrate himself to another, I would have ordered the woman to prostrate herself to her husband . . ." [Henceforth, the "Camel Version."][9]

> Second Version: Upon his return from Yemen (or Damascus), Mu'ādh bin Jabal [a *ṣaḥābī*] told the Prophet: "I saw Christians prostrating themselves to their bishops and patriarchs, and I thought that you are more deserving of being venerated." The Prophet answered: "If I were to

> order one person to prostrate himself to another, I would have ordered the woman to prostrate herself to her husband . . ." [Henceforth, the "Travels Version."][10]

The two accounts differ drastically. But again, this is no reason to dismiss either one of them or both. It is possible that the Prophet reiterated the same thought on two (or more) different occasions. So, we need to assess each one of these *ḥadīths* by the two standards discussed earlier and in Chapter 3: soundness of *isnād* and soundness of *matn*.

A. Soundness of *Isnād*

A word of warning to the reader: This section is a highly technical part of the discussion. It shows through a systematic and lengthy proof that all versions of the Prostration *Ḥadīth* considered herein have defects and, as a result, are weak and unreliable. The reader may decide to satisfy himself with this conclusion and move directly to section B of this chapter where the discussion turns on the content or substance of the *ḥadīth*.

1. First Version

General Observations

Examining the soundness of the *isnād* of the Prostration *Ḥadīth* is a challenging but rewarding task. Let us turn first to the Camel Version narrated in *al-Musnad*. Its primary source is no other than 'Ā'ishah, the wife of the Prophet, as narrated by 'Alī bin Zayd bin Gud'ān, a *ṭābi'ī* and a subsequent narrator.* The *ḥadīth*, we are informed, was not narrated *verbatim*. Rather, it was paraphrased.[11] This explains why Ibn Mājah (d. 887), another major *ḥadīth* scholar, narrates the same version of this *ḥadīth* but with slightly different wording and a similar attribution.[12] The fact that the narrated *ḥadīth* was not quoted verbatim raises questions about its original intended meaning. But this is

*A *ṭābi'ī* belongs to the generation of Muslims that followed that of the *ṣaḥābīs*.

not sufficient reason to discount the *ḥadīth* altogether because all the narrations transmitting it appear to share a similar core meaning.

Chain of Narration in the First Version

We turn now to the chain of narrators of this first version of the Prostration *Ḥadīth*. Aḥmad al-Banna (d. 1958), who commented on it, states that 'Alī bin Zayd bin Gud'ān was considered by some scholars of *ḥadīth* as being a weak link in the narration chain.[13] Incidentally, 'Alī bin Gud'ān also appears in the narration chain of this *ḥadīth* mentioned by Ibn Mājah.

A major source of information about narrators is Muḥammad Ibn Aḥmad al-Dhahabī (d. 1348), author of *Mīzān al-I'itidāl (The Scale of Moderation)*. According to al-Dhahabī, commentators regarded 'Alī bin Zayd bin Gud'ān as truthful and pious.[14] However, that was not the problem. Several commentators judged him as having one or more of the following defects: weakness in narrating, confusion later in life, reversal of *ḥadīth*, not being a reliable source, and not having a good memory.[15] Reversal of *ḥadīth* (*qalb al-ḥadīth*) is an important defect, which involves an inaccuracy either in the names of the narrators in the chain, or in matching the chain to the proper *ḥadīth*.[16] As a result, some commentators did not rely on the narrations of 'Alī bin Zayd, and weakened the *ḥadīths* narrated through him—that is, they placed them low on the ladder of authenticity.[17] We concur with their actions in light of the substantial reasons provided.

Al-Banna notes that this *ḥadīth* has been narrated through other chains.[18] This is an important comment for two reasons. First, the other narrations may have stronger *isnād* than the one under consideration. So, it is possible to establish the soundness of the *ḥadīth* in its other forms. Second, according to al-Nawawī, in certain cases, a weak *ḥadīth* that is corroborated by other chains of that *ḥadīth* (or various versions of it) that are themselves weak may acquire sufficient strength from these corroborations to move up the ladder of authenticity.[19] This is a troubling position because repetition is no substitute for soundness or authenticity. However, I would conjecture that the cases referred to by al-Nawawī are ones where jurists saw no harm in accepting the weak *ḥadīth* because it made sense and had none of the *matn* defects listed above. But this is the rub. What makes sense to one person may not make sense to another. In any case, as a result of this comment, examining the soundness of other narrations of the *ḥadīth* gains urgency.

2. Second Version

General Observations

Another chain of narration is provided by the second main version of this *ḥadīth*. The primary source of this narration is the respected *ṣaḥābī* Mu'ādh bin Jabal.[20] This version has its own two sub-versions: One refers to Yemen and the other to Damascus. Let us focus first on the Yemeni version. The commentator, al-Banna, points out that he had not come across this specific version of the *ḥadīth* anywhere else except in *al-Musnad*, but that those in the narrating chain were highly reliable.[21] Jurists do not automatically discount such *ḥadīths*. They evaluate them in light of other versions of the *ḥadīth*, if any. But before we turn to these other versions, I would like to share some observations about some narrators in the Yemeni version, including the respected *ṣaḥābī* Mu'ādh bin Jabal himself.

The personality and history of Mu'ādh bin Jabal, who is supposedly the primary narrator of this version, are not consistent with the facts of this *ḥadīth*. (We are now edging closer towards the intersection between the *isnād* and *matn*, but a more thorough discussion of the *matn* will take place later.) First, Mu'ādh was known not only for his piety, but also for his vast knowledge of the religion. The Prophet is quoted as having said about him: "Mu'ādh is the most knowledgeable person in matters of *ḥalāl* (what is permitted) and *ḥarām* (what is prohibited)."[22] Yet, according to the *ḥadīth*, Mu'ādh told the Prophet that the Christians in Yemen prostrated themselves to their bishops and patriarchs, and so he wanted to prostrate himself to the Prophet.

Now, every Muslim, young or old, knows that Muslims prostrate themselves only to God and to no one else; otherwise, they would fall into *shirk*. Why did Mu'ādh not know that? Why did he hurry back from Yemen to prostrate himself to the Prophet?

Furthermore, according to the famous historian Ibn Kathīr, who quotes al-Bukhārī, the Prophet appointed Mu'ādh as governor of

Yemen.[23] After that, the Prophet undertook his last pilgrimage to Makkah (*ḥijjat al-wadāʿ*) and died eighty-one days later. Muʿādh did not return from Yemen until after the death of the Prophet.[24] So, there would have been no occasion for Muʿādh to have the narrated conversation with the Prophet.

Chain of Narration in the Second Version

There also seems to be a problem in the chain of narration of this second version. In *al-Musnad,* the chain of narration is described is as follows:

> al-Aʿmash (last narrator named)—*ʿan*—Abū Dhubyān—*ʿan*- Muʿādh bin Jabal (primary narrator).[25]

Ibn Kathīr (d. 1373) points to another similar narrating chain about the same story. It is as follows:

> al-Aʿmash—heard—Abū Dhubyān—*ʿan*—a man from the *Anṣār*—*ʿan*—Muʿādh bin Jabal.[26]

In this second chain, al-Aʿmash narrates that he *heard* the narration from Abū Dhubyān, who narrated it *ʿan* "a man from the *Anṣār*" who narrated it *ʿan* Muʿādh.

Ibn Kathīr points out this discrepancy between the two chains of narration. Most importantly, in the second chain, we have an unknown intermediate narrator—namely, the "man from the *Anṣār*"—who was omitted from the first. The accuracy and trustworthiness of this unknown person cannot be properly assessed. For this reason, and given other factors as well, Ibn Kathīr discounts the first narration, noting that there were better sources to rely upon.[27] Here it appears that Ibn Kathīr assumed that the intermediate questionable narrator was simply omitted from the first chain to hide a weakness in it. So, Ibn Kathīr rejected the whole chain. But why would Ibn Kathīr make such an assumption?

It appears that Ibn Kathīr was being a polite critic. For, al-Dhahabī reports that the great scholar Aḥmad bin Ḥanbal himself impugned narrations by al-A'mash. He judged him to be quite *muḍṭarib*.[28] This meant that there were numerous discrepancies, in *isnād* or *matn*, between al-A'mash's narrations and those of others who were equally or more reliable, something that Ibn Kathīr delicately pointed out.

Al-Dhahabī quotes other well-known commentators who also concluded that al-A'mash's narration was unreliable. These included al-Jawzajānī, Jarīr bin 'Abd al-Ḥamīd, and Abū Dāwūd.[29] While noting the integrity and fairness of al-A'mash, some commentators even accused him of unintended *tadlīs*, of which the above discrepancy would be an example.[30] The general view was that al-A'mash's unreliability did not arise from an ill motive, but rather from lack of precision, sufficient knowledge about the situation, or *wahm* (faulty imagination or memory). This accounts for Ibn Kathīr's delicate treatment of this issue.

Regardless of the reasons for these discrepancies, there is enough evidence that narrations by al-A'mash are unreliable. So, the Yemeni version of the Prostration *Ḥadīth* will be discounted for all the above reasons, ranging from historical inconsistencies to unreliable narrations. Incidentally, there is one more historical factor: Yemen did not have a significant Christian population at that time. So, it is unlikely that Mu'ādh witnessed Christians prostrating themselves to bishops and patriarchs there. Perhaps the narrator of this version confused Yemen with Damascus. After all, there was a significant presence of Christians in Damascus, complete with bishops and patriarchs, that continues to this day. This makes the Damascene version look more promising as to its authenticity.

Ibn al-Kathīr also mentions the Damascene version. However, while the reference to Christian bishops and patriarchs there is consistent with historical facts, the story remains historically troubled. For, Mu'ādh did not go to Damascus till after the Prophet's death, where he himself then died from the plague.[31] These historical facts challenge the narration's accuracy. Also, since the Yemeni and Damascene versions share the same narrating chain, the same problems raised earlier about al-A'mash permeate this version as well. So, in short, this version suffers altogether similar historical inconsistencies and narrating defects as the Yemeni version.

But let us not be in a hurry to dismiss the Prostration *Ḥadīth* based on these two main versions in *al-Musnad*, which also overlapped with Ibn Mājah's version. Let us examine the other versions narrated in *al-Musnad*.

3. Two More Versions

These two versions were attributed to Anas bin Mālik and Ibn Abī Awfā.[32] The reason we have not identified them as "main" versions is because their *matn* is so weak as to disqualify them. The first version does not contain the story of Mu'ādh. Instead it simply repeats the core prostrating quote attributed to the Prophet, and adds to it some problematic language. The second version reverts to the story of Mu'ādh in Yemen (or Damascus) and also adds to it different problematic language.

The additional language attributed to the Prophet in these versions suffers from being impossible for him to have uttered. The words are simply not consistent with his style, linguistic expressions, refined manners, character, and thinking. For those who studied the life of the Prophet, this language appears quite foreign to his own. Lest someone views our conclusion as a purely subjective one rooted in our subconscious wish to dismiss it, we point to a similar view by scholars who approach these matters from quite a different perspective, namely a *Salafī* one.

Sheikh 'Abdullāh al-Juday', a contemporary Saudi scholar, articulated a position similar to that of Ṣubḥī al-Ṣāliḥ about detecting defects in *ḥadīths*. In his *Taḥrīr 'Ulūm al-Ḥadīth* (*Liberating Ḥadīth Studies*) he notes that early commentators identified certain signs of a defective *ḥadīth*.[33] For example, if the language attributed to the Prophet is repulsive to a critic and is not befitting a prophet, then this indicates a defect in the *ḥadīth* itself. Using flowery language, Sheikh al-Juday' notes that for a person who has immersed himself in Prophetic language, a sign of a defective *ḥadīth* is that it turns bitter in the mouth and weighs heavily on the critic. This makes it imperative for the critic to investigate the *ḥadīth* further to locate the point of error.[34] Al-Juday' cautions against understanding this position to mean that a person could reject a *ḥadīth* because it goes against his own inclinations. That is not the same, he points out, and we need to guard against it.[35] Quoting these criteria, Sheikh Muḥammad Ṣāliḥ al-Munajjid, another contemporary Saudi scholar, concludes after a lengthy analysis that the troubling language we mentioned above could not have originated from the Prophet.[36]

The fact that scholars from a very conservative tradition steeped in *ḥadīth* studies concur with our conclusion gives us comfort that we are not being swayed by inclination in this matter.

However, *al-Musnad* categorizes both versions as *jayyid* or "good."[37] This expression sometimes implies a *ṣaḥīḥ* classification, but may also imply a slightly lower status. So, we shall not stop at our observations above about the language in the *ḥadīth*. Instead, we shall forge ahead and examine the *isnād* of the first version in this set.

The chain of narration in this first version is as follows:

> Khalaf bin Khalīfah—*'an*—Ḥafṣ—*'an*—Anas bin Mālik[38]

We observe that, first, this *ḥadīth* has a *'an'anah* chain. So, we have the problem of not knowing whether the information narrated was heard directly from the previous link or not. Second, Khalaf bin Khalīfah was viewed as *ṣadūq* (truthful).[39] This description is a term of art that puts him in second rank of reliable narrators.[40] According to the scholar of *ḥadīth* Ibn Abī Ḥātim, this term does not indicate accuracy in narration. So, the narration is subject to being investigated further for accuracy.[41] Another scholar, Aḥmad bin 'Adiyy, said that he would not claim that Khalaf was not wrong in some of his narrations.[42] Furthermore, commentators noted that he had a stroke later in life and became confused.[43] Ibn Ḥanbal mentions visiting him after he became ill. He tried to talk to him, but could not understand what Khalaf was saying, so Ibn Ḥanbal stopped relying on his later narrations.[44]

So, one critical question as to the *isnād* of this *ḥadīth* becomes: When did Khalaf narrate it? This question has led to a great deal of discussion. Even today, it is being raised on the Internet by pious Muslims not necessarily concerned about women's issues as much as they are about determining the authenticity of this *ḥadīth*. However, there is a rule about such situations: when it was not known whether a *ḥadīth* was narrated before or after a narrator became confused, the rule was to reject the narration.[45] This is a wise rule in our case, because it is known that *Ṣaḥīḥ al-Bukhārī* and *Ṣaḥīḥ Muslim*, the two most reliable compilations of *ḥadīth,* did not include any version of the Prostration *Ḥadīth*, including this one.

The second version of this set has the following narrating chain:

> Ismā'īl—heard—Ayyūb—*'an*—al-Qāsim al-Shaybānī—*'an*—'Abdullāh bin Abī Awfā[46]

This is the same chain mentioned by Ibn Mājah in another version of the Travels Version included in his *ḥadīth* compilation. However, in Ibn Mājah's version, Mu'ādh actually prostrates himself to the Prophet and then explains his action.[47] This detail renders this version even less consistent with Mu'ādh's personality and his knowledge of Islam.

According to some commentators, the chain suffers from the fact that al-Qāsim al-Shaybānī was part of it. He was judged by the scholar Abū Ḥātim al-Rāzī (d. 890) as *muḍṭarib* in his *ḥadīth* and weak and, hence, not reliable.[48] Other serious scholars reached a similar conclusion.[49] Furthermore, the *isnād* in the chain is *munqaṭi'* (broken, disconnected). The story is about Mu'ādh, but the chain of narration goes back only to Abī Awfā. It does not continue to Mu'ādh. This second version has also the same historical defects mentioned in our discussion of the Yemeni and Damascene Versions.

4. Conclusion on Soundness of *Isnad* of the Prostrating *Ḥadīth* in *al-Musnad*

This completes our analysis of the soundness of *isnād* of all the versions and sub-versions of the Prostration *Ḥadīth* mentioned in *al-Musnad*. Although there are many other versions in other works that differ slightly in *isnād* or *matn*, we chose *al-Musnad* because it is the most reliable of all the works that refer to this *ḥadīth*. Yet, we found quite a few problems with these versions. To sum up, the versions of the Prostration *Ḥadīth* narrated in *al-Musnad* have one or more of these problems:

a. the version was judged "weak" by some respected scholars, based on its *isnād*;
b. it was judged *muḍṭarib* (has discrepancies with other narrators of equal or better reliability);
c. the chain of *isnād* is *munqaṭi'* (broken, not complete);
d. profile of an individual in the *ḥadīth* (Mu'ādh, in this case) is inconsistent with the content of the *ḥadīth*;
e. elements of the *ḥadīth* are inconsistent with historical facts;
f. the narrator became confused at one point, and it is unclear when that took place; and
g. the language of the version is incompatible with the language, character, style, and sensibilities of the Prophet (also a *matn* observation).

In short, in terms of soundness of *isnād* and related considerations, all the versions examined here suffer from serious defects.

5. Version in *Sunan al-Tirmidhī*

The scholar al-Tirmidhī (d. 892), who authored another respected compilation of *ḥadīths*, narrates the Prostration *Ḥadīth* in a very rudimentary form, quoting the *ṣaḥābī* Abū Hurayrah.[50] He classifies this *ḥadīth* as *ḥasan gharīb*.[51] Al-Tirmidhī's definition of *ḥasan* is a *ḥadīth* with a good chain of narrators in which no one has been accused of lying, error, or distortion. A *gharīb ḥadīth* is one with only one chain of narration having that specific wording.[52]

The classification of the *ḥadīth* by al-Tirmidhī is questionable in light of his definition of *ḥasan* and some established facts in the *ḥadīth* literature. As we know from a discussion in Chapter 2, Abū Hurayrah was corrected in his account of a *ḥadīth* about the Prophet. Here is that story again:

> Upon hearing a narration by the *ṣaḥābī* Abū Hurayrah that the Prophet said that bad omens reside in women, homes, and horses, 'Ā'ishah became quite upset. She corrected Abū Hurayrah, saying: "What the Prophet used to say was: 'In the times of *Jāhiliyyah* [pre-Islamic], people found bad omens in women, homes and animals.'"[53] It appears that Abū Hurayrah had not heard the beginning of the Prophet's sentence and narrated only the last part.

But that was not the only time 'Ā'ishah corrected Abū Hurayrah. On another occasion, she corrected his narration of a purported *ḥadīth* that says that prayer is interrupted (made void) when a woman, a donkey, or a dog passes in front of the person praying. 'Ā'ishah objected: "You analogized us to donkeys and dogs!"[54] In fact, she stated at one point, "May God show mercy to Abū Hurayrah. He misheard, so he responded erroneously."[55] 'Ā'ishah also corrected many other *ṣaḥābīs* in their narrations.[56] Some of the corrections, as we see from the example above, concerned matters relating to women. Since she was not present at all narrations, one wonders how many others she could have corrected had she been there.

So in light of 'Ā'ishah's experience with Abū Hurayrah's narration, as well as other stories that bring the accuracy of his narrations into question, we are less inclined to classify the *ḥadīth* narrated by al-Tirmidhī as *ḥasan* because its primary source is Abū Hurayrah. This demotion is especially significant because, according to various scholars, a *ḥasan ḥadīth* may be used in an argument the same way as the *ṣaḥīḥ* (valid) *ḥadīth* is used, even if it has less probative "strength."[57]

6. Version in *Sunan Abī Dāwūd*

One final version to be considered here comes from Abū Dāwūd (d. 889).[58] This time the setting is in Iraq, and the prostration is to a Persian leader. The chain of attribution is as follows:

> 'Amr bin 'Awn—was told by—Isḥāq bin Yūsuf—*'an*—Sharīk bin Ḥusayn—*'an*—al-Shu'bī—*'an*—Qays bin Sa'd[59]

Although scholars agree that Sharīk is *ṣadūq*, and some even call him *thiqah* (reliable), many well-known ones do not rely on his narration.[60] For example, al-Jawzajānī (d. 873) says that Sharīk does not memorize well, and that his narrations were *muḍṭarib*.[61] Ibn Mubārak does not accord weight to Sharīk's narrations.[62] Ibn Ma'īn says that Sharīk makes mistakes and does not perfect his narrations.[63] Abū Zur'ah says that Sharīk imagines things (*wahm*) and makes mistakes.[64] So, Sharīk is the weak link in the above chain that renders this version unreliable.

7. Conclusion on Soundness of *Isnād* of the Prostration *Ḥadīth* in Three Major Compilations

We have now examined all versions of the Prostration *Ḥadīth* narrated by *al-Musnad*, Ibn Mājah al-Tirmidhī, and Abū Dāwūd. These compilations represent the second level of reliable compilations after *Ṣaḥīḥ al-Bukhārī* and *Ṣaḥīḥ Muslim*. But the latter two did not include this *ḥadīth* at all. Also in every case we considered, we found clear reasons to impugn the *isnād* of the *ḥadīth* and, thus, weaken it.

We understand that the above versions are not the only ones in the literature. But they are the ones included in the most respected *ḥadīth* compilations. As such, they represent the strongest cases for establishing the authenticity of this *ḥadīth*. Yet, they fail to do so. While I am aware of other versions and chains of narration out there, I am not aware of any that constitute a serious challenge to our conclusions herein. Furthermore, some of these versions have already been examined and "weakened" by the Saudi scholar Dr. Suhayla Zayn al-'Ābidīn Ḥammād[65] and by Sheikh al-Rabī' bin Hādī, among others whose views I came across on the Internet.[66] Their views will be discussed in more detail later in this section.

In sum, there is no chain of narration in any version of the Prostration *Ḥadīth* discussed herein that is sound. Furthermore, several jurists have also cast doubt or weakened other versions of this *ḥadīth*. So, it is hard to conclude from this set of attribution chains that they collectively proffer sufficient corroborating evidence to strengthen the *ḥadīth* in any one of its narrated forms.

But what if we have missed the one sound *isnād* of this *ḥadīth*? Fortunately, scholars agree that even if the *isnād* of a *ḥadīth* is not impugned, if its *matn* is inconsistent with the Qur'an and *sunnah* of the Prophet, then it should be rejected. So, we turn now to the substantive discussion of the *matn* of the Prostration *Ḥadīth* and begin the second part of our assessment.

B. SOUNDNESS OF *MATN*

We shall focus on the core *matn* of the Prostration *Ḥadīth*, which states:

> If I were to order one person to prostrate one's self to another, I would have ordered the woman to prostrate herself to her husband.

From our perspective, and in light of the Equality and Harmony Principles articulated earlier in this book, there is a clear inconsistency between this core *matn* and the Qur'an and *ḥadīth*. However, this answer is *prima facie* inadequate because it appears circular. It seems to say that the *ḥadīth* contradicts the Qur'an because it contradicts our interpretation of the Qur'an. And since our interpretation is correct, then this *matn* must be rejected. How can we avoid this circular reasoning? The best way to avoid it is by setting aside for the moment our interpretation and worldview and going back to the basics. We should examine this *matn* directly on its own merits in light of the clear statements in the Qur'an and *sunnah* and not in light of our interpretation of them. It would also be best if such examination is conducted by another scholar who is unfamiliar with our interpretation.

Fortunately, other scholars have done just that. The first is the Saudi woman scholar Suhayla Ḥammād, whom I found on the Internet. In her article entitled, "The Wife's Obedience: A Corrective View," she leaves no doubt that the inconsistency between the Qur'an and the *matn* of the Prostration *Ḥadīth* is enormous.[67]

Ḥammād provides ten separate arguments in support of her position, and lists a number of *āyahs* and *ḥadīths* establishing the equality of women and men in humanity in the Qur'an. Leading these *āyahs* are ones listed previously in this book. We derived from them the Equality Principle. For example:

> O People! We created you from a single (pair) of a male and female, and made you into nations and tribes, so that you may know each other. Verily, the most honored of you in the sight of God are (the ones who are) the most Righteous among you.[68]
>
> And among His signs is this, that he created for you mates from among yourselves, so that you may dwell in tranquility with them, and He has put love and mercy between your (hearts): Verily in that are signs for those who ponder.[69]
>
> And from the *ḥadīth*:
>
> Women are the peers [or split halves] of men.[70]
>
> You are all shepherds, and are all responsible for your flock.[71]

Other *āyahs* mentioned include the following:

> And their Lord hath accepted
> Of them and answered them:
> "Never will I suffer to be lost
> The work of any of you,
> Be it male or female,
> You are members, one of another."[72]
>
> We have given Dignity to
> The Children of Adam.[73]

And women shall have rights
Similar to the rights against them,
According to what is equitable.[74]

Several additional *āyahs* are listed in support of Ḥammād's ten arguments for the equality and dignity of women in Islam. From all of these, Ḥammād concludes that the *matn* of the Prostration *Ḥadīth* in its various versions is inconsistent with the Qur'anic *āyahs* and the prophetic *ḥadīth*. It denies women what God and the Prophet have clearly stated is their right as women, as Muslims, and as human beings. Ḥammād's treatment in this article includes several other versions of the Prostration *Ḥadīth* and provides additional arguments in support of her position. In the same article, and others as well, she exposes the weaknesses in other popular *ḥadīths* and some jurisprudential interpretations.

Incidentally, Ḥammād is not alone in her conclusions about the *matn* of the Prostration *Ḥadīth*. Two Moroccan women scholars, Dr. Nādya al-Sharqāwī and Dr. Asma Lamrabet, have made similar arguments.[75] Al-Sharqāwī notes that while the message of Islam was revealed to reform society, patriarchy found ways to distort it and root itself in the religion.[76]

This is an important point to understand. Patriarchal thinking is not always the result of a conscious effort by men to subdue women. It is not a conspiracy. Rather, it is a way of looking at the world that places men at the center and women at the periphery. To that extent, it partakes of Satanic logic. Looking at the Qur'an from this perspective, it leads to hierarchical interpretations of the *Qiwāmah Ayah*, as well as the readiness to uphold the veracity of the Creation story and to believe the "garden conversation." It takes sharp logic, like that of al-Rāzī, as well as great moral strength not only to recognize the fact that this is an interested male worldview, but also to reject the privileges it offers. In this instance, we found that Sheikh al-Munajjid was indeed able to overcome social bias and recognize the weakness of the Prostration *Ḥadīth*. But he is not the only male scholar to do so. Muslim women scholars must work diligently with supporting male scholars to put an end to the distortion of our *ḥadīth* heritage.

Patriarchy has been around since the beginning of life on this earth. Patriarchal thought and hierarchical structures have had thousands of years to penetrate deep into all cultures. *Ijtihād*, *tafsīr*, and *ḥadīth* are no exception. Reversing this wave will not happen overnight. Our effort here is only one step forward.

'Ā'ishah tried hard to stand before this patriarchal avalanche, but after the death of the Prophet things were different. The Islamic rule of law was being rapidly replaced with the tribal use of force. Over the next few centuries, both men and women suffered. Scholars who refused to become a tool of the state suffered immensely. Many of them immigrated to other locations in search of greater freedom of thought. Women were squeezed out from the public sphere and their influence withered steadily. Their rights were rolled back, and religious interpretation and explanation became primarily the domain of men. This is why knowledge about the various narrators is named "*'Ilm al-Rijāl*," ("The Study of Men"). This is shocking in light of the fact that a significant part of the *ḥadīth* was originally narrated by women. Except for 'Ā'ishah, the wife of the Prophet, and other women in his household and small circle, few other women remain in the *ummah*'s (community's) memory. Somehow, not much has changed. Part of what feminist scholars in the United States protested in the 1960s, which is still going on to some extent in this 21st century, is that men quote men, not women. With the gradual exclusion of women's voices, the woman's perspective disappeared.

So, when some male scholars do not find an inconsistency between a *ḥadīth* like the Prostration *Ḥadīth* and the Qur'an, it is because they have interpreted the Qur'an through their own hierarchical perspective, which colors, interprets away, or ignores clearly egalitarian principles within it. But when some female scholars examine the same material, they do so through their own equitable worldview and come to different conclusions. This may suggest a level of subjectivity in interpretation. That is correct; it is the human condition, despite all our efforts to claim objectivity.

Subjectivity cannot be eliminated from interpretational endeavors, but it can be limited. Some Qur'anic passages are so clear on their face that it would be hard to force upon them a patriarchal interpretation. We have mentioned some of these in this book. They are used by scholars to argue that Islam is fair to women. We know that. The question is how to purge the religion from contrary influences that undercut this noble Qur'anic message. I believe this can only be done through the empowerment of women in the serious study and interpretation of religion. They could then interact with male scholars who are willing to take a fresh look at tradition. Together, they can identify and eliminate gender-related biases by either group.

I conclude this discussion with one last comment and a quote.

C. A Final Comment

Defending the Prostration *Ḥadīth*, some scholars have argued that the idea of the woman prostrating herself to her husband is not demeaning. It only honors him for all that he does for her. This explanation is refuted by the very language in the Camel Version of the *ḥadīth*. When the companions of the Prophet asked him if they could prostrate themselves to him, he answered: "Worship God and honor your brother." The Commentator explained this correctly to mean: "Prostrate yourselves only to God and do not engage in *shirk* (associating partners with God) by prostrating yourselves to another. And honor your brother (the Prophet) by following my injunctions." Those who uphold the soundness of the *matn* of this *ḥadīth* should conclude that if the Prophet did not find it fitting to honor him by having others prostrate themselves to him, it follows that no other Muslim is worthy of such a prostration either.

D. An Insightful Quote

Struggling with the challenge of establishing the authenticity of a *ḥadīth*, al-Rabīʿ Ibn al-Haytham, a *tābiʿī*, said that "a *ḥadīth* has a light like the light of day, so we recognize it, and a darkness like the darkness of night, so we reject it."[77] This Prostration *Ḥadīth* has the darkness of night.

NOTES

1. See, e.g., the various versions of this *ḥadīth* in Aḥmad Ibn Ḥanbal's *Al-Musnad* [The Supported (*Ḥadīths*)], in *al-Fatḥ al-Rabbānī*, ed. and commentary by Aḥmad al-Banna (Cairo: Dār al-Shihāb, n.d.), vol. 16, 226–28.

2. Ibid., vol. 16, 227.

3. Al-Hāfiẓ 'Imād al-Dīn Ibn Kathīr, *Al-Bidāyah wa'l Nihāyah* [The Beginning and the End] (repr., Beirut: Maktabat al-Ma'ārif, 1979), vol. 6, 35.

4. Ibn Ḥanbal, *Al-Musnad*, vol. 22, 97.

5. Ṣubḥī al-Ṣāliḥ, *'Ulūm al-Ḥadīth* [The Studies of *Ḥadīth*] (Beirut: Dār al-'Ilm li'l Malāyīn, 1959), 275–88.

6. Ibid., 283.

7. Ibid., 286.

8. Ibid.

9. Ibn Ḥanbal, *Al-Musnad*, vol. 16, 226–27.

10. Ibid., 227.

11. Ibid., 226.

12. Ibn Mājah, *Sunan Ibn Mājah* [*Sunnas of* Ibn Mājah], verified by Muḥammad 'Abd al-Bāqī (repr., Beirut: Dār al-Kutub al-'Ilmiyyah, n.d.), vol. 1, 595.

13. Al-Banna, *Al-Fatḥ al-Rabbānī*, vol. 16, 227.

14. Abū 'Abdallāh Muḥammad al-Dhahabī, *Mīzān al-I'tidāl* [The Scales of Moderation] (Beirut: Dār al-Fikr, n.d.), pt. 3, 127–28.

15. Ibid.

16. 'Uthmān bin 'Abd al-Raḥmān Ibn al-Ṣalāḥ, al-Shahrazūrī (d. 1245) *'Ulūm al-Taḥdīth* [Studies of Narration of *Ḥadīth*] (Damascus: Dār al-Fikr, 1986), 101–2.

17. Aḥmad al-Banna, *Bulūgh al-Amānī* [Realizing Wishes], an exegesis of *Musnad Ibn Ḥanbal*, in *Al-Fatḥ al-Rabbānī*, Aḥmad al-Banna, ed. (Cairo: Dār al-Shihāb: n.d.), vol. 16, 227.

18. Ibid.

19. Muḥammad Jamāl al-Dīn al-Qāsimī, *Qawā'id al-Taḥdīth* [Rules of (the Discipline) of Narration of *Ḥadīth*] (Beirut: Dār al-Nafā'is, 1987), 112, quoting Muḥyī al-Dīn Abū Zakariyyā al-Nawawī.

20. Ibn Ḥanbal, *Al-Musnad,* vol. 16, 227.

21. Al-Banna, *Al-Fatḥ al-Rabbānī* (editor separated *isnād* information from *ḥadīth*), vol. 16, 227.

22. Ṣubḥī al-Ṣāliḥ, *'Ulūm al-Ḥadīth,* 376.

23. Ibn Kathīr, *Al-Bidāyah wa'l Nihāyah* vol. 5, 99–101.

24. Ibid.

25. Ibn Ḥanbal, *Al-Musnad,* vol. 16, 227.

26. Ibn Kathīr, *Al-Bidāyah wa'l Nihāyah,* vol. 5, 101.

27. Ibid.

28. Al-Dhahabī, *Mīzān al-I'tidāl,* pt. 2, 224.

29. Ibid.

30. Ibid.

31. 'Izz al-Dīn Ibn al-Athīr al-Jazarī (d. 1233), *Usud al-Ghābah fī Ma'rifat al-Ṣaḥābah* [Lions of the Forest in Knowing the *Ṣaḥābah*] (repr., Beirut: Dār al-Kutub al-'Ilmiyyah, n.d.), v. 5, 189–90.

32. Ibn Ḥanbal, *Al-Musnad,* vol. 16, 227.

33. Muḥammad Ṣāliḥ al-Munajjid, *"Al-Islām Su'āl wa Jawāb,"* (Islam, Question and Answer), visited May 16, 2016, http://islamqa.info/ar/151353, 2, citing the views of al-Juday'.

34. Ibid.

35. Ibid.

36. Al-Munajjid, *"Al-Islām Su'āl wa Jawāb,"* 2.

37. Ibn Ḥanbal, *Al-Musnad,* vol. 16, 227–28.

38. Ibn Ḥanbal, *Fatḥ al-Bārī,* vol. 16, 227.

39. Al-Dhahabī, *Mīzān al-I'tidāl,* pt. 1, 660.

40. Ibn al-Ṣalāḥ, *'Ulūm al-Taḥdīth* [Studies of Narration of *Ḥadīth*] (Damascus: Dār al-Fikr, 1986), 122–23.

41. Ibid., 122–23.

42. Quoted by al-Munajjid in his discussion of that sub-version of the *ḥadīth.*

43. Al-Dhahabī, *Mīzān al-I'tidāl,* pt. 1, 659.

44. Ibid.

45. Ibn al-Ṣalāḥ, *'Ulūm al-Taḥdīth,* 392.

46. Ibn Mājah, *Sunan,* vol. 1, 595.

47. Ibid.

48. Suhayla Zayn al-ʿĀbidīn Ḥammād, *"Al-Ṭāʿah liʾl Zawj: Naẓrah Taṣḥīḥiyyah"* [Obedience to the Husband: A Corrective View], 9, http://dr-suhaila-z-hammad.blogspot.com/2011/10/blog-post_7705.html. For the definition of *muḍṭarib*, see al-Qāsimī, *Qawāʿid al-Taḥdīth*, 136, quoting al-Rāzī.

49. Al-Dhahabī, *Mīzān al-Iʿtidāl*, pt. 3, 376.

50. Muḥammad Ibn ʿĪsā al-Tirmidhī, *Al-Jāmiʿ al-Ṣaḥīḥ: wa huwa sunan al-Tirmidhī* [Comprehensive Compilation of the *Ṣaḥīḥ* (*ḥadīths*), and it is Sunnahs of al-Tirmidhī] (Beirut: Dār al-Kutub al-ʿIlmiyyah, 2000), vol. 2, 223.

51. Ibid., vol. 2, 223. For definition of *ḥasan gharīb* in al-Tirmidhī, see al-Qāsimī, *Qawāʿid al-Taḥdīth*, 107–8.

52. Qāsimī, *Qawāʿid al-Taḥdīth*, 108.

53. Saʿīd Fāyiz al-Dakhīl, *Mawsūʿat Fiqh ʿĀʾishah Umm al-Muʾminīn* [Encyclopedia of the Jurisprudence ʿĀʾishah Mother of the Believers] (Beirut: Dār al-Nafāʾis, 1989), 608; Ibn Ḥanbal, *Al-Musnad*, vol. 17, 198–200.

54. Muslim, *Ṣaḥīḥ Muslim*, vol. 4, 229.

55. Zainab Taha Alwani, *Dalālāt Manhajiyyah fī Qirāʾat al-Sayyidah ʿĀʾishah al-Qurʾāniyyah* [Systematic Evidence in Lady ʿĀʾishah's Qurʾanic Understanding], 9, http://www.karamah.org/articles.

56. Ibid., 10.

57. Al-Qāsimī, *Qawāʿid al-Taḥdīth*, 109.

58. Abū Dāwūd al-Sijistānī, *Sunan Abī Dāwūd* (Beirut: Dār al-Jīl, 1988), vol. 2, 250.

59. Ibid.

60. Al-Dhahabī, *Mīzān al-Iʿtidāl*, Part II, 270.

61. Ibid.

62. Ibid.

63. Ibid.

64. Ibid.

65. See Ḥammād, *"Al-Ṭāʿah,"* and other articles on her website dealing with the same topic.

66. Quoted on Sahab Salafi Network, in *"Daʿf wa Nakārat Qiṣṣat Sujūd Muʿādh liʾl Nabiy"* [The Weakness and *Nakārah* of the Story of

Mu'ādh prostrating himself to the Prophet]. "*Nakārah*" is a term of art referring to a weak *ḥadīth* narrated by a single person, on http://www.sahab.net/home/?p=727.

67. Ḥammād, "*Al-Ṭā'ah.*"

68. Qur'an 49:13.

69. Qur'an 30:21.

70. Abū Dāwūd al-Sijistānī, *Sunan*, vol. 1, 60; *ḥadīth* no. 236; see also al-Tirmidhī, *Sunan*, vol. 1, 90, *ḥadīth* no. 113.

71. Muḥammad al-Bukhārī, *Ṣaḥīḥ al-Bukhārī* [The Authentic Prophetic *Ḥadīths*], in al-'Asqalānī's *Fatḥ al-Bārī: Sharḥ Ṣaḥīḥ al-Bukhārī* [Divine Enlightenment: Explanation of al-Bukhārī's *Ṣaḥīḥ*], collection of authentic prophetic *ḥadīths* by al-Bukhārī, with commentary by al-'Asqalānī (repr., Beirut: Dār al-Kutub al-'Ilmiyyah, 1989), vol. 9, 316, no. 5188.

72. Qur'an 3:195.

73. Qur'an 17:70 (incorrect translation says "sons of Adam").

74. Qur'an 2:228.

75. Asma Lamrabet, *Women and Men in the Qur'an: Which Equality?* (Paris: Al-Bouraq, 2011), 65 (pointing out that the *ḥadīth* violates the basic principle of *al-Tawḥīd,* and stating that some scholars have found the *ḥadīth* unreliable with respect to its chain of transmission). Also, Nādya al-Sharqāwī, "*Al-Mar'ah al-Muslimah bayna'l-Taḥrīr al-Qur'ānī wa Sulṭat al-Mujtama' al-Dhukūrī*" [The Muslim Woman Between Qur'anic Liberation and the Authority of Patriarchal Society] (henceforth "Muslim Woman") (forthcoming, passage e-mailed to me by author). Al-Sharqāwī states that the *ḥadīth* is *ṣaḥīḥ*, but its *matn* contradicts the Qur'an.

76. Al-Sharqāwī, "Muslim Woman," quote from author by e-mail.

77. Aḥmad 'Umar Hāshim, *Difā'un 'an al-Ḥadīth al-Nabawī* [A Defense of the Prophetic *ḥadīth*] (Cairo: Maktabat Wahbah, 2000), 91.

Epilogue

In this book we began a long-term project of reviving *ijtihād*, and Islamic religious studies generally, to develop a serious jurisprudence suitable for our society and our historical era. Writers have been calling for jurists to take such action for some time now, but in this book, we are actually doing it. We understand that this is just a modest first step, which will be followed, God willing, by several others. But the reader must have now an idea about the complexity of this project, the many skills needed to execute it, the time it will take to complete it, and its momentous consequences. For this reason, we have approached our task with a great deal of professionalism, and have tried not to be swayed by our own special interests.

In the last couple of decades, with the rise of the Muslim population in the United States, the U.S. courts have been faced with various types of cases, especially divorce and child custody ones, where expert testimony about Islamic law was required. Unfortunately, many of these witnesses testified about custom and not religious law. As a result, some verdicts were based on faulty information about Islam and women's rights in the family, in divorce, and in the custody of children. At times, this resulted in increasing the burden on these women in transition. This is a very serious matter given the unfortunate rise in divorces. Perhaps we can address these issues in a future book. What is most important now is that the first step has been taken, and others, who have appropriate qualifications, are welcome to follow.

GLOSSARY

'afw	Forgiveness
'ibādāt	Matters of worship
'illah	Cause, *ratio*; in *ḥadīth* discussions, it can also mean a defect.
Aḥkām	Legal rulings
Al-'Adl	Justice
Al-Mīzān	Scales
Asbāb al-nuzūl	Occasions of the revelation
Āyah	A verse of the Qur'an. Also means a sign, a miracle, or magnificent creation.
Bay'ah	Expressing allegiance to a leader, a form of voting
Ḍa'īf	Weak
Ḍarūriyyāt	Necessities
Ḍila'	Rib
Gharīb ḥadīth	A *ḥadīth* with only one chain of narration having that specific wording.

Ḥadīth	Literally, means conversation. Refers to the statements of the Prophet Muhammad. May be used to refer to a single statement or to the whole body of statements made by him.
Ḥafaẓah	Those individuals who memorized the whole Qur'an.
Ḥājiyyāt	Needs
Ḥasan	Good
Ijmā'	Consensus
Ijtihād	Literally, to exert effort or endure hardship in pursuit of a goal. Also refers to exerting effort in interpreting religious text
Isnād	Chain of narration
Istiḥsān	Literally means to prefer something because it seems good (*ḥasan*)
Jins	Nature, kind or substance
Khuluq	Ethics and manners
Mahr	Obligatory gift given by a prospective husband to his prospective wife as an expression of his commitment to establishing a family. It is purely the woman's right in Islamic law.
Makārim al-akhlāq	The noblest of ethics
Maqāṣid al-sharī'ah	The objectives of *Sharī'ah*
Maṣlaḥah 'āmmah	Public interest
Matn	Content of the *ḥadīth*
Mawḍū'	Fabricated
Mu'āmalāt	Course of dealings among people
Muḍṭarib ḥadīth	Refers to numerous discrepancies, in *isnād* or *matn*, between one's narrations and those of others who are equally or more reliable.
Mujtahids	Those who engage in *Ijtihād*
Munqati' ḥadīth	Refers to a broken, or incomplete chain of narration.
Nafs	Soul or spirit
Naṣṣ	Definitive text
Niḥlah	Gift

Nizā'	Conflict
Qalb al-ḥadīth	Reversal of *ḥadīth,* is an important defect which involves an inaccuracy either in the names of the narrators in the chain, or in matching the chain to the proper *ḥadīth.*
Qiblah	The direction to which Muslims turn for prayer facing the *Ka'bah,* an ancient cubic structure built by Abraham and Ismā'īl (Ishma'el) in Makkah as the first House of God on earth.
Qiyās	Reasoning by analogy
Ṣadūq	Truthful
Ṣaḥābah	A collective term which refers to the group of *ṣaḥābīs* [singular masculine: *ṣaḥābī,* feminine: *ṣaḥābiyyah*], or companions of the Prophet. Usually it refers to those who spent some time with the Prophet and attended his gatherings, where he talked with and taught the people.
Ṣaḥīḥ	Authentic
Sharī'ah	Literally, the word means a way, path, or system (*manhaj*). It usually refers to the Islamic body of laws, but could be used also to refer, for example, to Jewish or Christian *sharī'ah.*
Shirk	Worshipping other gods with God
Shūrā	Consultation
Sunnah	Precedents set by the Prophet's words, actions and ratifications
Sūrah	A chapter of the Qur'an
Tafsīr	Exegesis or explanation of text
Taḥsīniyyāt	Luxuries
Tawḥīd	Unicity of God
Thiqah	Trustworthy
Ummah	The community of believers
Uṣūl al-Fiqh	Foundations of Islamic jurisprudence

BIBLIOGRAPHY

(Names familiar to the reader of English literature without transliteration have not been transliterated in this book.)

'Abd al-Khāliq, 'Abd al-Ghanī. *Hujjiyyat al-Sunnah* [Proof-Value of the *Sunnah*]. Beirut: Dār al-Qur'ān al-Karīm, 1986.

'Abd al-Raḥmān, 'Ā'ishah (better known as Bint al-Shāṭi'). *Al-Qur'ān wa Qaḍāyā al-Insān* [The Qur'an and Human Affairs]. Reprint. Beirut: Dār al-'Ilm li'l Malāyīn, 1982.

Abū Dāwūd, Sulaymān al-Sijistānī. *Sunan* [*Sunnahs*]. Reprint. Beirut: Dār al-Jīl, 1988.

Abū al-Fatḥ al-Shahrastānī, Muḥammad. *Kitāb al-Milal wa'l Niḥal* [The Book of Sects and Creeds]. Reprint, Egypt: Maktabat al-Anglo-Miṣriyyah, 1977.

Abū Shahbah, Muḥammad. *Difā'un 'an al-Sunnah* [A Defense of the Sunnah]. Reprint. Beirut: Dār al-Jīl, 1991.

Abū Shuqqah, 'Abd al-Ḥalīm. *Taḥrīr al-Mar'ah fī 'Aṣr al-Risālah* [The Liberation of Women in the Age of the Message]. Cairo: Dār al-Qalam li'l Nashr wa'l Tawzī', 2002.

Abū Zahrah, Muḥammad. *Al-Madhāhib al-Islāmiyyah* [Islamic Schools of Thought]. Cairo: al-Maṭba'ah al-Namūdhajiyyah, n.d.

———. *Aḥkām al-Tarikah wa'l Mawārīth* [The Laws of Legacy and Inheritance]. Reprint. Cairo: Dār al-Fikr al-'Arabī, 1987.

———. *Muḥāḍarāt fī 'Aqd al-Zawāj wa Ātharihi* [Lectures in the Marriage Contract and Its Consequences]. Reprint. Cairo: Dār al-Fikr al-'Arabī, 1971.

———. *Al-Tanẓīm al-Islāmī li'l Mujtama'* [Islamic Organization of Society]. Cairo: Dār al-Fikr al-'Arabī, n.d.

———. *Uṣūl al-Fiqh* [Foundations of Jurisprudence]. Cairo: Dār al-Fikr al-'Arabī, n.d.

Al-Albānī, Muḥammad Naṣruddīn. *Silsilat al-Aḥādīth al-Ḍa'īfah wa'l Mawḍū'ah* [Series of Weak and Fabricated *Ḥadīths*]. Reprint. Riyadh: Maktabat al-Ma'ārif, 2004.

'Alī, 'Abdullāh Yūsuf. *The Meaning of the Holy Qur'an*. Reprint. Beltsville, MD: Amana Publications, 2004.

Allison, Robert J. *The Crescent Obscured: The United States & the Muslim World*, 1776–1815. Oxford University Press, 1995.

Al-Alūsī, Abū Faḍl. *Rūḥ al-Ma'ānī* [The Spirit of Meanings]. Reprint. Beirut: Dār al-Kutub al-'Ilmiyyah, 1994.

Al-'Alwānī, Ruqayyah Ṭaha Jābir. *Athar al-'Urf fī Fahm al-Nuṣūṣ* [The Effect of Customs in Understanding Texts of Rulings]. Damascus: Dār al-Fikr, 2003.

Al-Alwani, Taha Jabir. *Adab al-Ikhtilāf fi'l Islām* [The Etiquette of Disagreement in Islam]. Herndon, VA: International Institute of Islamic Thought, n.d.

Alwani, Zainab Taha. *Dalālāt Manhajiyyah fī Qirā'at al-Sayyidah 'Ā'ishah al-Qur'āniyyah* [Systematic Evidence in Lady 'Ā'ishah's Qur'anic Understanding], 9, http://www.karamah.org/articles.

Al-Anṣārī, 'Abd al-Ḥamīd. *Al-Shūrā wa Atharuhā fi'l Dīmuqrāṭiyyah* [Consultation and Its Impact on Democracy]. Reprint. Beirut: Al-Maktabah al-'Aṣriyyah, 1980.

'Aqlah, Muḥammad. *Niẓām al-Usrah fi'l Islām* [The Family System in Islam]. Amman: Maktabat al-Risālah al-Ḥadīthah, 1983.

Al-'Asqalānī, Ibn Ḥajar. *Fatḥ al-Bārī: Sharḥ Ṣaḥīḥ al-Bukhārī* [Divine Enlightenment: Explanation of al-Bukhārī's *Ṣaḥīḥ*]. Collection of authentic prophetic *ḥadīths* by al-Bukhārī, with commentary by al-'Asqalānī. Reprint. Beirut: Dār al-Kutub al-'Ilmiyyah, 1989.

Auda, Jasser. *Maqasid al-Shari'ah as Philosophy of Islamic Law*. Washington, DC: International Institute of Islamic Thought, 2008.

Al-A'ẓamī, Muḥammad. *Dirāsāt fi'l Ḥadīth al-Nabawī* [Riyadh: Studies in Prophetic *Ḥadīth*]. Al-Maktab al-Islāmī, 1992.

Al-Banna, Aḥmad. *Bulūgh al-Amānī* [Attaining Aspirations], an exegesis of *Musnad Ibn Ḥanbal*, in *Al-Fatḥ al-Rabbānī*, Aḥmad al-Banna, ed. Cairo: Dār al-Shihāb: n.d.

Al-Bardīsī, Muḥammad Zakariyyā. *Al-Aḥkām al-Islāmiyyah fi'l Aḥwāl al-Shakhṣiyyah* [Islamic Rulings in Personal Status Laws]. Egypt: Dār al-Nahḍah al-'Arabiyyah, 1965.

Al-Bayātī, Munīr Ḥāmid. *Al-Niẓām al-Siyāsī al-Islāmī* [The Islamic Political System]. Amman, Jordan: Dār al-Bashīr, 1994.

Beltāgī, Muḥammad. *Manhaj 'Umar Ibn al-Khaṭṭāb* [The Method of 'Umar Ibn al-Khaṭṭāb]. Reprint. Cairo: Dār al-Salām, 2003.

Bennānī, Farīda. *Taqsīm al-'Amal bayn al-Zawjayn* [Division of Labor between Spouses]. Marrakesh: Silsilat Manshūrāt Kulliyyat al-'Ulūm al-Qānūniyyah wa'l Iqtiṣādiyyah wa'l Ijtimā'iyyah, Jāmi'at al-Qāḍī 'Ayyāḍ, 1992.

Al-Bukhārī, Muḥammad. *Ṣaḥīḥ al-Bukhārī* [The Authentic Prophetic *Ḥadīths*]. Included in al-'Asqalānī's *Fatḥ al-Bārī: Sharḥ Ṣaḥīḥ al-Bukhārī*. See al-'Asqalānī.

Al-Dakhīl, Sa'īd Fāyiz. *Mawsū'at Fiqh 'Ā'ishah Umm al-Mu'minīn* [Encyclopedia of the Jurisprudence of 'Ā'ishah Mother of the Believers]. Beirut: Dār al-Nafā'is, 1989.

Al-Dhahabī, Abū 'Abdallāh Muḥammad. *Mīzān al-I'tidāl* [The Scales of Moderation]. Reprint. Beirut: Dār al-Fikr, n.d.

Diouf, Sylviane A. *Servants of Allah*. New York University Press, 1998.

Al-Dusūqī, Muḥammad. *Al-Usrah* [The Family]. (Doha: Dār al-Thaqāfah, 1995)

Al-Farāhidī, Abū 'Abd al-Raḥmān al-Khalīl Ibn Aḥmad. *Kitāb al-'Ayn* [The Book of (the Letter) *'Ayn*]. Reprint. Beirut: Mu'assasat al-A'lamī li'l Maṭbū'āt, 1988.

Ghandūr, Aḥmad. *Al-Aḥwāl al-Shakhṣiyyah fi'l Tashrī' al-Islāmī* [Personal Status in Islamic Law]. Kuwait: Jāmi'at al-Kuwait Press, 1972.

Al-Gharnātī, Abū Ḥayyān. *Al-Baḥr al-Muḥīṭ* [The All-Encompassing Sea (of Knowledge)]. Reprint. Beirut: Dār al-Fikr, 1978.

Al-Ghazālī, Abū Ḥāmid. *Iḥyā' 'Ulūm al-Dīn* [Reviving Religious Studies]. Reprint. Egypt: Muṣṭafā al-Bābī al-Ḥalabī Press, 1939.

Al-Ghazālī, Muḥammad. *Kayfa Nata'āmal ma' al-Qur'ān* [How Do We Deal with the Qur'an]. Herndon, VA: International Institute of Islamic Thought, 1977.

Ḥamīdullāh, Muḥammad. *Majmū'at al-Wathā'iq al-Siyāsiyyah li'l 'Ahd al-Nabawī wa'l Khilāfah al-Rāshidah* [Collection of Political Documents of the Prophetic and Rashidi Eras]. Reprint. Beirut: Dār al-Nafā'is, 1987.

Ḥammād, Suhayla Zayn al-'Ābidīn. "*Al-Ṭā'ah li'l Zawj: Naẓrah Taṣḥīḥiyyah*" [Obedience to the Husband: A Corrective View]. Last visited May 16, 2014. http://dr-suhaila-z-hammad.blogspot.com/2011/10/blog-post_7705.html.

Hāshim, Aḥmad 'Umar. *Difā'un 'an al-Ḥadīth al-Nabawī* [Defense of the Prophetic *Ḥadīth*]. Cairo: Maktabat Wahbah, 2000.

Ḥaydar, 'Alī. *Durar al-Ḥukkām fī Sharḥ Majallat al-Aḥkām* [Gems of Jurists: Exegesis of the (Ottoman) Majallah of Rulings]. Beirut: Dār al-Kutub al-'Ilmiyyah, n.d.

Al-Hibri, Azizah. "Divine Justice and the Human Order: An Islamic Perspective," in *Humanity before God*. Minneapolis: Fortress Press, 2000.

———. "Islam, Law and Custom: Redefining Muslim Women's Rights." *American Journal of International Law and Policy* 12 (1997), 1.

———. "Islamic and American Constitutional Law: Borrowing Possibilities or a History of Borrowing?" *University of Pennsylvania Journal of Constitutional Law* 1 (1999), 492.

———. "Islamic Constitutionalism and the Concept of Democracy." *Case Western Reserve Journal of International Law* 24, no. 1 (1992), 1–27.

———. "Marriage Laws in Muslim Countries." *International Review of Comparative Public Policy* 4 (1992), 227.

———. "The Muslim Perspective on the Clergy-Penitent Privilege." *Loyola of Los Angeles Law Review* 29 (1996), 1723.

Hegel, G.W.F. *The Phenomenology of Mind*. New York: Harper, 1967.

Ibn 'Arabī, Muḥyī al-Dīn. *Aḥkām al-Qur'ān*. Reprint. Beirut: Dār al-Ma'rifah, 1987.

Ibn al-Athīr, 'Izz al-Dīn al-Jazarī. *Usud al-Ghābah fī Ma'rifat al-Ṣaḥābah* [Lions of the Forest in Knowing the *Ṣaḥābah*]. Reprint. Beirut: Dār al-Kutub al-'Ilmiyyah, reprint, n.d.

Ibn Ḥanbal, Aḥmad. *Musnad Aḥmad* [The Supported (*Ḥadīths* collected by) Aḥmad]. In *Al-Fatḥ al-Rabbānī*. Edited by Aḥmad al-Banna. Cairo: Dār al-Shihāb, n.d.

Ibn Hishām. *Al-Sīrah al-Nabawiyyah* [Biography of the Prophet]. Reprint. Beirut: Al-Maktabah al-'Ilmiyyah, n.d.

Ibn Juzayy, Muḥammad. *Qawānīn al-Aḥkām al-Shar'iyyah* [Laws of *Sharī'ah* Rulings]. Reprint. Beirut: Dār al-'Ilm li'l Malāyīn, 1979.

Ibn Kathīr, al-Ḥāfiẓ 'Imād al-Dīn Ismā'īl. *Al-Bidāyah wa'l Nihāyah* [The Beginning and the End]. Reprint. Beirut: Maktabat al-Ma'ārif, 1979.

Ibn Mājah, Abū 'Abdullāh. *Sunnan Ibn Mājah* [*Sunnahs* of Ibn Mājah]. Verified by Muḥammad 'Abd al-Bāqī. Reprint. Beirut: Dār al-Kutub al-'Ilmiyyah, n.d.

Ibn Manẓūr, Muḥammad. *Lisān al-'Arab* [The Tongue of Arabs]. Reprint. Beirut: Dār Iḥyā' al-Turāth al-'Arabī, 1992.

Ibn Qayyim al-Jawziyyah. *Zād al-Ma'ād* [Provision of the Hereafter]. Beirut: Mu'assasat al-Risālah 1994, vol. 3, 407.

Ibn Qudāmah, Muwaffaq al-Dīn. *Al-Mughnī* [The Enricher/or Sufficient]. Reprint. Beirut: Dār al-Kitāb al-'Arabī, n.d.

Ibn al-Ṣalāḥ,'Uthmān bin 'Abd al-Raḥmān al-Sharazūrī. *'Ulūm al-Taḥdīth* [Studies of Narration of *Ḥadīth*]. Reprint. Damascus: Dār al-Fikr, 1986.

Isbīr, Muḥammad, and Bilāl Junaydī. *Al-Shāmil* [The Comprehensive]. Beirut: Dār al-'Awdah, 1981.

Al-Jamal, Bassām. *Asbāb al-Nuzūl* [Reasons for the Revelations]. Casablanca: Al-Markaz al-Thaqāfī al-'Arabī, 2005.

Al-Jazīrī, 'Abd al-Raḥmān. *Kitāb al-Fiqh 'alā al-Madhāhib al-Arba'ah* [Book of Fiqh of the Four Schools of Jurisprudence]. Beirut: Dār Iḥyā' al-Turāth al-'Arabī, 1969.

Al-Jundī, 'Abd al-Ḥalīm. *Aḥmad bin Ḥanbal: Imām Ahl al-Sunnah* [Aḥmad bin Ḥanbal: Imām of the Sunnis]. Cairo: Dār al-Ma'ārif, n.d.

———. *Al-Imām al-Shāfi'ī*. Reprint. Cairo: Dār al-Ma'ārif, 1994.

Kahālah, 'Umar Riḍā. *A'lām al-Nisā' fī 'Ālamayy al-'Arab wa'l Islām* [Prominent Women in the Arab and Muslim Worlds]. Beirut: Mu'assasat al-Risālah, 1f977.

Kamali, Muhammad Hashim. *Principles of Islamic Jurisprudence*. Cambridge, UK: The Islamic Texts Society, 2003.

Khālid, Muḥammad. *Rijāl Ḥawl al-Rasūl* [Men around the Prophet]. Beirut: Dār al-Jīl, 1996.

Al-Khālidī, Maḥmūd. *Ma'ālim al-Khilāfah fi'l Fikr al-Siyāsī al-Islāmī* [Features of the Caliphate in Islamic Political Thought]. Beirut: Dār al-Jīl, 1984.

Al-Khamlīshī, Muḥammad. *Al-Ta'līq 'alā Qānūn al-Aḥwāl al-Shakhṣiyyah* [Commentary on Personal Status Code]. Rabat: Maktabat al-Ma'ārif, 1987.

Al-Kilbī, Muḥammad. *Kitāb al-Tashīl li 'Ulūm al-Tanzīl* [The Book of Facilitation of Revelation Studies]. Reprint. Beirut: Dār al-Kitāb al-'Arabī, 1973.

Lamrabet, Asma. *Women and Men in the Qur'an: Which Equality?* Paris: Al-Bouraq, 2011.

Maḥmaṣānī, Ṣubḥī. *Al-Awḍā' al-Tashrī'iyyah fi'l Duwal al-'Arabiyyah* [Legal Systems in the Arab World]. 3rd ed. Beirut: Dār al-'Ilm li'l Malāyīn, 1965.

———. *Falsafat al-Tashrī' fi'l Islām* [The Philosophy of Legislation in Islam]. 3rd ed. Beirut: Dār al-'Ilm li'l Malāyīn, 1961.

———. *Muqaddimah fī Iḥyā' 'Ulūm al-Sharī'ah* [Introduction to the Revival of *Sharī'ah* Studies]. Beirut: Dār al-'Ilm li'l Malāyīn, 1962.

Al-Mir'ashlī, Muḥammad. *Ikhtilāf al-Ijtihād wa Taghayyuruhu wa Athar dhālik fi'l-Futyā* [Differences and Change in *Ijtihād*, and Their Effect on Fatwa Rulings]. Beirut: Al-Mu'assasah al-Jāmi'iyyah li'l Dirāsāt wa'l Nashr wa'l Tawzī', 2003.

Mubayyiḍ, Muḥammad Sa'īd. *Mawsū'at Ḥayāt al-Ṣaḥābiyyāt* [The Encyclopedia of *Ṣaḥābī* Women]. Qatar: Dār al-Thaqāfah, 1990.

Muṭahharī, Murtaḍā. *Al-'Adl al-Ilāhī* [Divine Justice]. Qum: Al-Dār al-Islāmiyyah li'l Nashr, n.d.

Muslim, Ibn al-Ḥajjāj al-Nīsābūrī. *Ṣaḥīḥ Muslim* [The Authentic *Ḥadīths* (as compiled by) Muslim]. In Muḥyī al-Dīn Abū Zakariyyā al-Nawawī's *Ṣaḥīḥ Muslim bi Sharḥ al-Nawawī*. See *al-Nawawī* below.

Mutawallī, 'Abd al-Ḥamīd. *Al-Islām wa Mabādi' al-Ḥukm fi'l Māriksiyyah wa'l Dīmuqrāṭiyyah al-Gharbiyyah* [Islam and the Principles of Governance in Marxism and Western Democracy]. Alexandria: Al-Ma'ārif, 1990.

Al-Nadawī, Abū al-Ḥasan. *Al-Sīrah al-Nabawiyyah* [Biography of the Prophet]. Jeddah: Dār al-Shurūq, 1977.

Naṣīf, Fāṭimah. *Ḥuqūq al-Mar'ah wa Wājibātuhā fī Ḍaw' al-Kitāb wa'l Sunnah* [Women's Rights and Duties in Light of the Book and Sunnah]. Jeddah: Tahāmah, 1992.

Nasr, Seyyed Hossein. *Islam: Religion, History, and Civilization*. HarperOne, 2002.

———. *The Heart of Islam: Enduring Values for Humanity*. HarperOne, 2004.

———. *Science and Civilization in Islam*. New York: Barnes & Noble, 1968.

Al-Nawawī, Muḥyī al-Dīn Abū Zakariyyā. *Ṣaḥīḥ Muslim bi Sharḥ al-Nawawī* [The Authentic *Ḥadīths* of (i.e., compiled by) Muslim, with Exegesis by al-Nawawī]. Reprint. Beirut: Dār Iḥyā' al-Turāth al-'Arabī, n.d.

———. *Riyāḍ al-Ṣāliḥīn* [The Meadows of the Righteous]. Reprint. Beirut: Mu'assasat al-Risālah, 1992.

Al-Nīsābūrī, Niẓām al-Dīn al-Ḥasan bin Muḥammad bin Ḥusayn. *Tafsīr Gharā'ib al-Qur'ān* [Explaining the Unusual in the Qur'an], published in the margin of Abū Ja'far al-Ṭabarī's *Jāmi' al-Bayān fī Tafsīr al-Qur'ān* (see below for al-Ṭabarī).

Nyang, Sulayman. *Islam in the United States of America*. Chicago: ABC International Group, 1999.

Qabalān, Hishām. *Ādāb al-Zawāj fi'l Islām* [The Etiquette of Marriage in Islam]. Beirut: Manshūrāt 'Uwaydāt, 1983.

Al-Qāsimī, Muḥammad Jamāl al-Dīn. *Qawā'id al-Taḥdīth* [Rules (the Discipline) of Narration of *Ḥadīth*]. Beirut: Dār al-Nafā'is, 1987.

Quick, Abdullah Hakim. *Deeper Roots: Muslims in the Americas before Columbus*. 2nd ed. London: Ta-Ha Publishers, 1996.

Al-Qurṭubī, Abū 'Abdillāh. *Al-Jāmi' li Aḥkām al-Qur'ān* [Compilation of Qur'anic Rulings]. Reprint. Beirut: Dār Iḥyā' al-Turāth al-'Arabī, 1985.

Rahman, Fazlur. *Islam*. 2nd ed. University of Chicago Press, 1979.

Al-Raysūnī, Aḥmad. *Naẓariyyat al-Maqāṣid 'ind al-Imām al-Shāṭibī* [The Theory of the Objectives of *Sharī'ah* (as viewed) by Imām al-Shāṭibī]. Herndon, VA: International Institute of Islamic Thought, 2007.

Al-Rāzī, Muḥammad Fakhr al-Dīn. *Tafsīr al-Fakhr al-Rāzī* [The Exegesis of al-Rāzī]. Reprint. Beirut: Dār al-Fikr, 1985.

———. *Tafsīr al-Qur'ān al-Ḥakīm* [Exegesis of the Noble Qur'an] (known as *Tafsīr al-Manār*). Reprint. Beirut: Dār al-Ma'rifah, n.d.

———. *Al-Maḥṣūl fī 'Ilm Uṣūl al-Fiqh* [The Harvest in the Study of the Foundations of Fiqh] Reprint. Beirut: Mu'assasat al-Risālah, 1992.

Riḍā, Muḥammad Rashīd. *Al-Khilāfah* [The Caliphate]. Reprint. Cairo: Al-Zahrā', reprint, 1988.

Ṣadr al-Dīn, Muḥammad bin 'Abd al-Raḥmān Abū 'Abdillāh. *Raḥmat al-Ummah fī Ikhtilāf al-A'immah* [Mercy to the Ummah Lies in the Disagreement of the Imāms]. Reprint. Beirut: Mu'assasat al-Risālah, 1994.

Said, Edward. *Orientalism*. New York: Pantheon Books, 1978.

Said, Jawdat. "Law, Religion and the Prophetic Method of Social Change," *Journal of Law and Religion* 15 (2000–2001), 83–150.

Sale, George. *The Koran: Commonly Called the Alcoran of Mohammed*. 2nd ed. London: for L. Hawes, W. Clarke, & R. Collins, and T. Wilcox, 1764.

Al-Ṣāliḥ, Ṣubḥī. *Mabāḥith fī 'Ulūm al-Qur'ān* [Research in Qur'anic Studies]. Beirut: Dār al-'Ilm li'l Malāyīn, 13th print, 1981.

———. *'Ulūm al-Ḥadīth* [Ḥadīth Studies]. Beirut: Dār al-'Ilm li'l Malāyīn, 1959.

Al-Ṣallābī, 'Alī. *Sīrat Amīr al-Mu'minīn 'Umar Ibn al-Khaṭṭāb* [The Biography of the Commander of the Faithful 'Umar Ibn al-Khaṭṭāb]. Beirut: Dār al-Ma'rifah, 2004.

Al-Sanhūrī, 'Abd al-Razzāq. *Fiqh al-Khilāfah wa Taṭawwuruhā* [Jurisprudence of the Caliphate and Its Development]. Cairo: Al-Hay'ah al-'Āmmah al-Miṣriyyah li'l Kitāb, 1989.

Al-Shāfi'ī, Muḥammad Idrīs. *Al-Umm* [The Mother (of Knowledge)]. Reprint. n.p.: Dār al-Wafā', n.d.

Shaḥrūr, Muḥammad. *Naḥwa Uṣūl Jadīdah li'l Fiqh al-Islāmī* [Towards New Foundations of Islamic Jurisprudence]. Damascus: al-Ahālī, 2000.

Shalabī, Muḥammad. *Uṣūl al-Fiqh al-Islāmī* [Foundations of Islamic Jurisprudence]. Beirut: al-Dār al-Jāmi'iyyah, n.d.

Al-Shangīṭī, Muḥammad. *Aḍwā' al-Bayān fī Iḍāḥ al-Qur'ān bi'l Qur'ān* [Explanatory Lights in Clarifying the Qur'an by the Qur'an]. Reprint. Beirut: Dār al-Kutub al-'Ilmiyyah, 2006.

Al-Sharbāṣī, Aḥmad. *Al-A'immah al-Arba'ah* [The Four Imāms]. Beirut: Dār al-Jīl, n.d.

Al-Shāṭibī, Abū Isḥāq. *Al-Muwāfaqāt fī Uṣūl al-Sharī'ah* [Concordances in the Fundamentals of *Sharī'ah*]. Reprint. Beirut: Dār al-Ma'rifah, n.d.

Al-Shāwī, Tawfīq. *Fiqh al-Shūrā wa'l Istishārah* [The Jurisprudence of Consultation and Seeking Advice]. Manṣūrah, Egypt: Dār al-Wafā' 1992.

Al-Suyūṭī, Jalāl al-Dīn. *Al-Durr al-Manthūr fī Tafsīr al-Ma'thūr* [Scattered Gems in Transmitted Exegesis]. Reprint. Beirut: Dār al-Kutub al-'Ilmiyyah, 2000.

———. *Al-Itqān fī 'Ulūm al-Qur'ān* [Mastery of Qur'anic Studies]. Reprint. Beirut: Dār al-Nadwah al-Jadīdah, 1951.

Al-Ṭabarī, Abū Ja'far. *Jāmi' al-Bayān fī Tafsīr al-Qur'ān* [Comprehensive Exegesis of Qur'anic Interpretation]. Includes in the margin, Niẓām al-Dīn al-Ḥasan bin Muḥammad bin Ḥusayn al-Nīsābūrī. *Tafsīr Gharā'ib al-Qur'ān* [Explaining the Unusual in the Qur'an]. Reprint: Beirut: Dār al-Ma'rifah, 1978.

———. *Tārīkh al-Ṭabarī: Tārīkh al-Umam wa'l Mulūk* [History of Nations and Kings]. Reprint. Beirut: Dār al-Kutub al-'Ilmiyyah, 1991.

Al-Tha'ālibī, 'Abd al-Raḥmān. *Tafsīr* [Exegesis]. Reprint. Beirut: Dār Iḥyā' al-Turāth al-'Arabī, 1997.

Al-Tirmidhī, Muḥammad Ibn 'Isā. *Al-Jāmi' al-Ṣaḥīḥ: wa Huwa Sunan al-Tirmidhī* [Comprehensive Compilation of the *Ṣaḥīḥ* (*ḥadīths*), and it is Sunnahs of al-Tirmidhī]. Beirut: Dār al-Kutub al-'Ilmiyyah, 2000.

Al-'Umarī, Akram Ḍiyā'. *Al-Sīrah al-Nabawiyyah al-Ṣaḥīḥah* [The Authentic Biography of the Prophet]. Riyadh: Maktabat al-'Ubaykān, 1995.

———. *Buḥūth fī Tārīkh al-Sunnah al-Nabawiyyah* [Research in the History of Prophetic Sunnah]. 4th print. n.p.: 1984.

Al-Wāḥidī al-Nīsābūrī, Abū al-Ḥasan. *Asbāb al-Nuzūl* [Occasions of the Revelation]. Damascus: Dār Ibn Kathīr, 1988.

Al-Wazīr, Zayd bin 'Alī. *Al-Fardiyyah: Baḥth fī Azmat al-Fiqh al-Fardī al-Siyāsī 'ind al-Muslimīn* [Individualism: A Study of the Crisis of Political Jurisprudence of Muslims]. Virginia: Yemen Heritage and Research Center, 2000.

Wizārat al-Awqāf wa'l Shu'ūn al-Islāmiyyah. *Al-Mawsū'ah al-Fiqhiyyah* [The Jurisprudential Encyclopedia]. Egypt: Dār al-Ṣafwah, 1993.

Wright, W. *A Grammar of the Arabic Language*. 3rd ed. Cambridge University Press, 1933.

Al-Zabīdī, Muḥammad Murtaḍā. *Tāj al-'Arūs min Jawāhir al-Qāmūs* [The Bride's Crown of the Lexicon's Jewels]. Reprint. Beirut: Manshūrāt Dār Maktabat al-Ḥayāt, n.d. [18th century].

Al-Zamakhsharī, Abū al-Qāsim. *Al-Kashshāf* [The Revealer]. Reprint. Cairo: Maṭba'at al-Bābī al-Ḥalabī, n.d.

Al-Zarkashī, Badr al-Dīn. *Al-Burhān fī 'Ulūm al-Qur'ān* [Proof in Qur'anic Studies]. Reprint. Beirut: Dār al-Jīl, 1988.

Al-Zuḥaylī, Wahbah. *Al-Fiqh al-Islāmī wa Adillatuhu* [Islamic Jurisprudence and Its Evidence]. Damascus: Dār al-Fikr, 1984.

About the Author

Dr. Azizah Y. al-Hibri is Professor Emerita of law at the T. C. Williams School of Law, University of Richmond, where she taught for twenty years. Born in Beirut, Lebanon, Dr. al-Hibri received her college education at the American University of Beirut, and later at the University of Pennsylvania where she received her Ph. D. in philosophy and a J.D. in law. Dr. al-Hibri became the first Muslim woman tenured in an American law school.

Dr. al-Hibri is a former professor of philosophy and the founding editor of the first feminist philosophy journal in the country: *Hypatia: a Journal of Feminist Philosophy*. She is also founder and chair of KARAMAH: Muslim Women Lawyers for Human Rights, a nonprofit organization (see http://www.karamah.org).

Dr. al-Hibri has lectured extensively in the U.S., around the Muslim World and in Europe about her Islamic worldview. She has published widely in law journals on important constitutional and Islamic law issues, with special focus on women's rights and religious freedom. Dr. al-Hibri has also published Op Eds in various newspapers on similar issues, and has appeared on many television programs in support of these rights. She has received many awards in recognition of her contributions. Dr. al-Hibri was a presidential appointee to the United States Commission on International Religious Freedom (2011-13), and a Fulbright scholar (2001).

Index

N

O

P

Q

R

S